Konstantin Sheiko, Stephen Brown

HISTORY AS THERAPY

Alternative History and Nationalist Imaginings in Russia, 1991-2014

ibidem-Verlag
Stuttgart

Bibliografische Information der Deutschen Nationalbibliothek
Die Deutsche Nationalbibliothek verzeichnet diese Publikation in der Deutschen Nationalbibliografie; detaillierte bibliografische Daten sind im Internet über http://dnb.d-nb.de abrufbar.

Bibliographic information published by the Deutsche Nationalbibliothek
Die Deutsche Nationalbibliothek lists this publication in the Deutsche Nationalbibliografie; detailed bibliographic data are available in the Internet at http://dnb.d-nb.de.

Coverpicture: Viktor Vasnetsov's famous painting 'Sirin and Alkonost: the Birds of Joy and Sorrow'. Sirin and Alkonost are sirens whose songs enchant the listener so that he or she forgets the dreary reality of their everyday life. Alternative History is the modern siren that has seduced millions of Russian readers with its song of long-lost Russian greatness.
Source: http://www.wikipaintings.org/en/viktor-vasnetsov/sirin-and-alkonost-the-birds-of-joy-and-sorrow-1896. Public Domain.

∞

Gedruckt auf alterungsbeständigem, säurefreien Papier
Printed on acid-free paper

ISSN: 1614-3515

ISBN-13: 978-3-8382-0665-3

© *ibidem*-Verlag
Stuttgart 2014

Alle Rechte vorbehalten

Das Werk einschließlich aller seiner Teile ist urheberrechtlich geschützt. Jede Verwertung außerhalb der engen Grenzen des Urheberrechtsgesetzes ist ohne Zustimmung des Verlages unzulässig und strafbar. Dies gilt insbesondere für Vervielfältigungen, Übersetzungen, Mikroverfilmungen und elektronische Speicherformen sowie die Einspeicherung und Verarbeitung in elektronischen Systemen.

All rights reserved. No part of this publication may be reproduced, stored in or introduced into a retrieval system, or transmitted, in any form, or by any means (electronic, mechanical, photocopying, recording or otherwise) without the prior written permission of the publisher. Any person who does any unauthorized act in relation to this publication may be liable to criminal prosecution and civil claims for damages.

Printed in Germany

Soviet and Post-Soviet Politics and Society (SPPS)
ISSN 1614-3515

General Editor: Andreas Umland,
Kyiv-Mohyla Academy, umland@stanfordalumni.org

Commissioning Editor: Max Jakob Horstmann,
London, mjh@ibidem.eu

EDITORIAL COMMITTEE*

DOMESTIC & COMPARATIVE POLITICS
Prof. **Ellen Bos**, *Andrássy University of Budapest*
Dr. **Ingmar Bredies**, *FH Bund, Brühl*
Dr. **Andrey Kazantsev**, *MGIMO (U) MID RF, Moscow*
Dr. **Heiko Pleines**, *University of Bremen*
Prof. **Richard Sakwa**, *University of Kent at Canterbury*
Dr. **Sarah Whitmore**, *Oxford Brookes University*
Dr. **Harald Wydra**, *University of Cambridge*
SOCIETY, CLASS & ETHNICITY
Col. **David Glantz**, *"Journal of Slavic Military Studies"*
Dr. **Marlène Laruelle**, *George Washington University*
Dr. **Stephen Shulman**, *Southern Illinois University*
Prof. **Stefan Troebst**, *University of Leipzig*
POLITICAL ECONOMY & PUBLIC POLICY
Prof. em. **Marshall Goldman**, *Wellesley College, Mass.*
Dr. **Andreas Goldthau**, *Central European University*
Dr. **Robert Kravchuk**, *University of North Carolina*
Dr. **David Lane**, *University of Cambridge*
Dr. **Carol Leonard**, *University of Oxford*
Dr. **Maria Popova**, *McGill University, Montreal*

FOREIGN POLICY & INTERNATIONAL AFFAIRS
Dr. **Peter Duncan**, *University College London*
Dr. **Taras Kuzio**, *Johns Hopkins University*
Prof. **Gerhard Mangott**, *University of Innsbruck*
Dr. **Diana Schmidt-Pfister**, *University of Konstanz*
Dr. **Lisbeth Tarlow**, *Harvard University, Cambridge*
Dr. **Christian Wipperfürth**, *N-Ost Network, Berlin*
Dr. **William Zimmerman**, *University of Michigan*
HISTORY, CULTURE & THOUGHT
Dr. **Catherine Andreyev**, *University of Oxford*
Prof. **Mark Bassin**, *Södertörn University*
Prof. **Karsten Brüggemann**, *Tallinn University*
Dr. **Alexander Etkind**, *University of Cambridge*
Dr. **Gasan Gusejnov**, *Moscow State University*
Prof. em. **Walter Laqueur**, *Georgetown University*
Prof. **Leonid Luks**, *Catholic University of Eichstaett*
Dr. **Olga Malinova**, *Russian Academy of Sciences*
Prof. **Andrei Rogatchevski**, *University of Tromsø*
Dr. **Mark Tauger**, *West Virginia University*
Dr. **Stefan Wiederkehr**, *BBAW, Berlin*

ADVISORY BOARD*

Prof. **Dominique Arel**, *University of Ottawa*
Prof. **Jörg Baberowski**, *Humboldt University of Berlin*
Prof. **Margarita Balmaceda**, *Seton Hall University*
Dr. **John Barber**, *University of Cambridge*
Prof. **Timm Beichelt**, *European University Viadrina*
Dr. **Katrin Boeckh**, *University of Munich*
Prof. em. **Archie Brown**, *University of Oxford*
Dr. **Vyacheslav Bryukhovetsky**, *Kyiv-Mohyla Academy*
Prof. **Timothy Colton**, *Harvard University, Cambridge*
Prof. **Paul D'Anieri**, *University of Florida*
Dr. **Heike Dörrenbächer**, *DGO, Berlin*
Dr. **John Dunlop**, *Hoover Institution, Stanford, California*
Dr. **Sabine Fischer**, *SWP, Berlin*
Dr. **Geir Flikke**, *NUPI, Oslo*
Prof. **David Galbreath**, *University of Aberdeen*
Prof. **Alexander Galkin**, *Russian Academy of Sciences*
Prof. **Frank Golczewski**, *University of Hamburg*
Dr. **Nikolas Gvosdev**, *Naval War College, Newport, RI*
Prof. **Mark von Hagen**, *Arizona State University*
Dr. **Guido Hausmann**, *University of Freiburg i.Br.*
Prof. **Dale Herspring**, *Kansas State University*
Dr. **Stefani Hoffman**, *Hebrew University of Jerusalem*
Prof. **Mikhail Ilyin**, *MGIMO (U) MID RF, Moscow*
Prof. **Vladimir Kantor**, *Higher School of Economics*
Dr. **Ivan Katchanovski**, *University of Ottawa*
Prof. em. **Andrzej Korbonski**, *University of California*
Dr. **Iris Kempe**, *"Caucasus Analytical Digest"*
Prof. **Herbert Küpper**, *Institut für Ostrecht Regensburg*
Dr. **Rainer Lindner**, *CEEER, Berlin*
Dr. **Vladimir Malakhov**, *Russian Academy of Sciences*

Dr. **Luke March**, *University of Edinburgh*
Prof. **Michael McFaul**, *US Embassy at Moscow*
Prof. **Birgit Menzel**, *University of Mainz-Germersheim*
Prof. **Valery Mikhailenko**, *The Urals State University*
Prof. **Emil Pain**, *Higher School of Economics, Moscow*
Dr. **Oleg Podvintsev**, *Russian Academy of Sciences*
Prof. **Olga Popova**, *St. Petersburg State University*
Dr. **Alex Pravda**, *University of Oxford*
Dr. **Erik van Ree**, *University of Amsterdam*
Dr. **Joachim Rogall**, *Robert Bosch Foundation Stuttgart*
Prof. **Peter Rutland**, *Wesleyan University, Middletown*
Prof. **Marat Salikov**, *The Urals State Law Academy*
Dr. **Gwendolyn Sasse**, *University of Oxford*
Prof. **Jutta Scherrer**, *EHESS, Paris*
Prof. **Robert Service**, *University of Oxford*
Mr. **James Sherr**, *RIIA Chatham House London*
Dr. **Oxana Shevel**, *Tufts University, Medford*
Prof. **Eberhard Schneider**, *University of Siegen*
Prof. **Olexander Shnyrkov**, *Shevchenko University, Kyiv*
Prof. **Hans-Henning Schröder**, *SWP, Berlin*
Prof. **Yuri Shapoval**, *Ukrainian Academy of Sciences*
Prof. **Viktor Shnirelman**, *Russian Academy of Sciences*
Dr. **Lisa Sundstrom**, *University of British Columbia*
Dr. **Philip Walters**, *"Religion, State and Society"*, *Oxford*
Prof. **Zenon Wasylw**, *Ithaca College, New York State*
Dr. **Lucan Way**, *University of Toronto*
Dr. **Markus Wehner**, *"Frankfurter Allgemeine Zeitung"*
Dr. **Andrew Wilson**, *University College London*
Prof. **Jan Zielonka**, *University of Oxford*
Prof. **Andrei Zorin**, *University of Oxford*

* While the Editorial Committee and Advisory Board support the General Editor in the choice and improvement of manuscripts for publication, responsibility for remaining errors and misinterpretations in the series' volumes lies with the books' authors.

Soviet and Post-Soviet Politics and Society (SPPS)
ISSN 1614-3515

Founded in 2004 and refereed since 2007, SPPS makes available affordable English-, German-, and Russian-language studies on the history of the countries of the former Soviet bloc from the late Tsarist period to today. It publishes between 5 and 20 volumes per year and focuses on issues in transitions to and from democracy such as economic crisis, identity formation, civil society development, and constitutional reform in CEE and the NIS. SPPS also aims to highlight so far understudied themes in East European studies such as right-wing radicalism, religious life, higher education, or human rights protection. The authors and titles of all previously published volumes are listed at the end of this book. For a full description of the series and reviews of its books, see
www.ibidem-verlag.de/red/spps.

Editorial correspondence & manuscripts should be sent to: Dr. Andreas Umland, DAAD, German Embassy, vul. Bohdana Khmelnitskoho 25, UA-01901 Kyiv, Ukraine. e-mail: umland@stanfordalumni.org

Business correspondence & review copy requests should be sent to: *ibidem* Press, Leuschnerstr. 40, 30457 Hannover, Germany; tel.: +49 511 2622200; fax: +49 511 2622201; spps@ibidem.eu.

Authors, reviewers, referees, and editors for (as well as all other persons sympathetic to) SPPS are invited to join its networks at
www.facebook.com/group.php?gid=52638198614
www.linkedin.com/groups?about=&gid=103012
www.xing.com/net/spps-ibidem-verlag/

Recent Volumes

122 Michael Moser
Language Policy and the Discourse on Languages in Ukraine under President Viktor Yanukovych (25 February 2010–28 October 2012)
ISBN 978-3-8382-0497-0 (Paperback edition)
ISBN 978-3-8382-0507-6 (Hardcover edition)

123 Nicole Krome
Russischer Netzwerkkapitalismus
Restrukturierungsprozesse in der Russischen Föderation am Beispiel des Luftfahrtunternehmens "Aviastar"
Mit einem Vorwort von Petra Stykow
ISBN 978-3-8382-0534-2

124 David R. Marples
'Our Glorious Past'
Lukashenka's Belarus and the Great Patriotic War
ISBN 978-3-8382-0574-8 (Paperback edition)
ISBN 978-3-8382-0675-2 (Hardcover edition)

125 Ulf Walther
Russlands "neuer Adel"
Die Macht des Geheimdienstes von Gorbatschow bis Putin
Mit einem Vorwort von Hans-Georg Wieck
ISBN 978-3-8382-0584-7

126 Simon Geissbühler (Hrsg.)
Kiew – Revolution 3.0
Der Euromaidan 2013/14 und die Zukunftsperspektiven der Ukraine
ISBN 978-3-8382-0581-6 (Paperback edition)
ISBN 978-3-8382-0681-3 (Hardcover edition)

127 Andrey Makarychev
Russia and the EU in a Multipolar World
Discourses, Identities, Norms
With a foreword by Klaus Segbers
ISBN 978-3-8382-0629-5

128 Roland Scharff
Kasachstan als postsowjetischer Wohlfahrtsstaat
Die Transformation des sozialen Schutzsystems
Mit einem Vorwort von Joachim Ahrens
ISBN 978-3-8382-0622-6

129 Katja Grupp
Bild Lücke Deutschland
Kaliningrader Studierende sprechen über Deutschland
Mit einem Vorwort von Martin Schulz
ISBN 978-3-8382-0552-6

130 Konstantin Sheiko, Stephen Brown
History as Therapy: Alternative History and Nationalist Imaginings in Russia, 1991-2014
ISBN 978-3-8382-0665-3

Table of Contents

Foreword	7
Introduction: The End of History	9
Chapter One: Imperial Dilemmas and Historical Therapy	27
Chapter Two: 'Porridge in the Head': Why a New Future needs a New Past	37
Chapter Three: Empire, nation, nationalism	45
Part One: Russia's Multiple Identities	45
Part Two: Civic or Imperial Nationalism	55
Part Three: Eurasianism	58
Chapter Four: Empires of the Mind: Russia's Ancient History	65
Part One: Scholarly Ruminations	65
Part Two: The Patriotic Tradition	69
Part Three: Fomenko, the Terminator	74
Part Four: The Hyperborean Exodus	80
Part Five: History as Hoax	83
Part Six: Civilizations East and West	85
Part Seven: The Russian Tower of Babel	91
Part Eight: Good versus Evil	92
Part Nine: Local Heroes and Family Feuds	95
Conclusion	96

Chapter Five: Vikings and Slavs — 99

    Part One: Nestor the Normanist and Russophobe — 99
    Part Two: Slavs as State Builders — 106
    Part Three: Western Plot (1) — 120
    Part Four: Western Plot (2) — 122

Chapter Six: Farewell to the Mongols: Fomenko and his 'Horde' — 135

    Part One: Mongols—Demons or Phantoms? — 135
    Part Two: Interpretations — 139
    Part Three: Fomenko Russifies the Mongols — 142
    Part Four: Gumilev and the steppe — 145
    Part Five: Western Fantasies — 148
    Part Six: Selecting the Evidence — 151
    Part Seven: How could the Mongols have succeeded when Napoleon and Hitler failed? — 155
    Part Eight: Benevolent Invaders — 160
    Part Nine: Russian Eurasia? — 166
    Part Ten: Russia's Medieval Civil War — 172
    Part Eleven: The Russian Columbus — 176

Chapter Seven: Terrible History: the Four Ivans — 183

    Part One: Good and Bad Ivans — 183
    Part Two: 'How it really was' according to Fomenko — 195
    Part Three: The True Boris Godunov and the False Dmitrii — 197
    Part Four: Traces of the Horde: the Cossacks — 201

Chapter Eight: Icebreakers — 205

Conclusion — 213

Bibliography — 215

Foreword

In 2009, we wrote a book entitled *Nationalist Imaginings of the Russian Past. Anatolii Fomenko and the Rise of Alternative History*. Its focus was the explosion of 'alternative' history, a publishing phenomenon that emerged in Russia after the collapse of the Soviet Union in 1991. The leading light in this movement was, and remains, Anatolii Fomenko, a Soviet-era mathematician who claimed that the standard historical chronology was hopelessly inaccurate and that conventional history had failed to notice the existence of a remarkable Slav-Turk empire that dominated much of the world before modern times. Ridiculed by the academic establishment, Fomenko had his revenge when his books outsold the conventional historians many times over. Fomenko's books inspired countless imitators and critics writing within the field of 'alternative history'. The common themes of these writers are the greatness of Russia and the Western plot against Russian history. For Russians disillusioned with their initial experience of capitalism and democracy, alternative history offered a therapy in which the problems of today gave way to new images of past glory.

We are grateful for this opportunity to update and substantially revise the earlier book. Pseudo-history has continued to flourish not just in Russia, but throughout the former Soviet space. Alternative historians aim to show that the greatness of Russia extended far back in time and that its power and influence reverberated from Eurasia to the New World. In recent years, the geopolitical strategy of the Putin regime and the imperial dreams of alternative history have synchronized. This book explains the rise of alternative history within an older historical pattern. In each period of Russian history, a new regime has insisted upon the rewriting of the past to suit the needs of the present. Long before it was fashionable to do so, alternative historians wrote the ideological script for a new Russian Empire. Alternative history serves as a warning not just to the degree to which nationalism is gathering strength in the former Soviet space, but also how difficult it will be to contain this force in the future.

Konstantin Sheiko and Stephen Brown

Introduction: The End of History

'The farther backward you can look the farther forward you are likely to see.'

Winston Churchill

'Alternative history' is a term often used in present-day Russia to describe a disparate group of popular writers and amateur historians who are actively reimagining Russia's past. The vast majority of these writers have no professional training in the academic discipline of History. They are often scientists or popular writers from the Soviet era with a passion for history and story telling. In the West, this type of writing is often described as 'pseudo history'. These writers have become popular at a time when Russia's identity is up for grabs, and when it is by no means clear whether Russia's present rulers will succeed either in building a Western-style nation state or in reestablishing Russia as the powerful international actor it was in centuries past.

The shared premise of alternative historians is that Russian History, as we know it, contains countless errors, misinterpretations, and willful neglect of the evidence. Just as importantly, these inaccuracies did not come about by accident. According to alternative history, conventional historians have acted, wittingly or unwittingly, as the accomplices of Russia's external and internal enemies. These enemies aim to disempower Russia by depriving it of its true past. Alternative historians often accuse the pre-revolutionary Russian academy of working hand-in-glove with the Romanovs, the 'Prussian' dynasty that ruled Russia for three hundred years for the benefit of the West.[1] The Romanovs and their retinue of corrupt courtiers, foreign historians, and a pro-Western intelligentsia constituted a 'fifth column' working against Russia.

Conversations about history that were previously taboo or even punishable by imprisonment or death are now flourishing in Russia, even though the

---

1 See, for example, LI Bocharov et al., *Zagovor protiv russkoi istorii (fakty, zagadki, versii)* (Moscow: Kuchkovo Pole, 1998), p. 4. Andrei Kobyla, the earliest-known Romanov, was allegedly of Prussian origins, although virtually nothing is known about him. In 1761, Peter the Third, whose mother was a German princess, ascended the throne, only to be murdered and replaced by his German wife who became Catherine the Great.

content of these discussions causes professional historians to cringe. Alternative history has become a clearing house for all manner of competing ideas about Russia and Russian history; Communists, anti-Communists, Eurasianists, neo-Nazis, Slavophiles and neo-Pagans all write alternative history and they compete for the attention of the book-buying and Internet-viewing public.[2] 'Alternative history' is just one of the descriptors used for these writers. They are also described as pseudo-historians, pseudo-scientists, alternate historians, conspiracy theorists, and, more imaginatively, as historians of a 'non-traditional orientation'.[3]

In the West, we usually describe such writers as 'Russian nationalists', 'ultra-nationalists', or advocates of 'ethno nationalism'. In Russia, the term 'nationalist' is usually reserved for individuals and groups that wish to separate themselves from Russia.[4] Those Russians, whom Western writers would label as nationalists, describe themselves as patriots.[5] This book refers to the writers under discussion here as 'nationalists' even though the writers themselves would strongly object to this term. This study expands upon our earlier account of the 'New Chronology' movement whose prodigious publishing efforts and fantastic claims about Russia and its history first established the popularity of alternative history.[6]

The context for the rise of alternative history in Russia was the painful birth of post-Communist Russia. In 1991, for the first time in its modern history, Russians became the majority ethnic group within the borders of a clearly defined Russian state. But for Russian nationalists, this was no cause for celebration. The territorial settlements that accompanied the collapse of the Soviet Union meant that Russia was cut off from Ukraine, Belarus, the Crimean peninsula and large parts of the southern steppe, lands that for long periods in the last five hundred years belonged to Moscow. More than

---

2 For a summary of these various tendencies, see Marlene Laruelle, 'Conspiracy and Alternate History in Russia: A Nationalist Equation for Success?' *The Russian Review*, 71 (2012): 565–580.
3 Vladimir Lapenkov, *Istoriia Netraditsionnoi Orientatsii, Legendy i Mify Vsemirnoi Istorii* (Moscow: Bystrov, 2006).
4 Alexander Yanov, 'Russian nationalism in Western studies: misadventures of a moribund paradigm', *Demokratizatsiia* 9:4 (Fall 2001): 552–562, p. 562.
5 Tishkov, *Ethnicity, Nationalism and Conflict in and after the Soviet Union. The Mind Aflame* (London: Sage, 1997), p. 230.
6 See Konstantin Sheiko in collaboration with Stephen Brown, *Nationalist Imaginings of the Russian Past. Anatolii Fomenko and the Rise of Alternative History in Post-Communist Russia* (Stuttgart: Ibidem-Verlag, 2009).

twenty million ethnic Russians now lived in the 'near abroad', the fourteen former Soviet republics that became independent countries in the post-Soviet space. There was a danger that the Russian Federation itself would implode as new nationalist discourses made their presence felt from the Caucasus to Siberia.

Territorial integrity was not the only issue. The birth of a Russian nation-state revived questions about whether Russia was part of the West or the East, whether its government was instinctively autocratic or a fledgling democracy, and whether Russia should aim to be a super power or simply a middle-ranking regional power. These issues arose at a time of plummeting living standards and economic collapse when ordinary citizens rapidly lost faith in the new democratic institutions, and when the suspicions of many Soviet citizens that they had been systematically lied to for the best part of a century were confirmed as censorship broke down. Having been assured for decades that the Soviet Union was a beacon of humanity, that the Communist state was fast overtaking the United States, that there was no crime, and that their living standards were constantly improving, Soviet citizens learned in the Gorbachev and Yeltsin eras that the reverse was true. Meanwhile, economic and social problems of unemployment, crime, corruption and collapsing life expectancy seemingly spiraled out of control.[7]

As ever more challenges arose to its power, the administration of President Boris Yeltsin (1991–1999) became more authoritarian and at the same time all the more weak as powerful oligarchs divided up Russia's economic resources between them. The perception grew that the new financial elites were interested only in personal gain and had no interest in the public's welfare.[8] Commentators suggested that the Russian state had become in effect the largest of Russia's criminal gangs.[9] The new market economy lacked both private capitalists and the impartial rule of law.[10] This 'crony

---

7 See, for example, Stefan Hedlund, *Russia's 'Market' Economy: A Bad Case of Predatory Capitalism* (London: LCL Press, 1999).
8 See, for example S. Rosefelde, 'Russia: An Abnormal Country', *The East European Journal of Comparative Economics*, 2:1 (2005), pp. 3–16.
9 See for example, David Satter, *Darkness at Dawn: The Rise of the Russian Criminal State* (New Haven: Yale University Press, 2003).
10 Stefan Hedlund, 'Vladimir the Great, Grand Prince of Muscovy: Resurrecting the Russian Service State', *Europe-Asia Studies*, p. 797.

capitalism' left Russian voters and many critics of the old Soviet system unimpressed.[11]

In the late 1980s and early 1990s, the momentum behind Russia's movement into the realm of the Western liberal democracies appeared unstoppable. Since the mid 1990s, the trend in voting patterns in Russia has moved away from pro-Western reformers, usually described as the political 'right' or 'liberals' in Russia. In Presidential and Duma elections, politicians described as patriots, conservatives, and 'state-builders' dominate. Embodying this new modified version of Russian autocracy is Russia's most successful politician of the post-Communist era, Vladimir Putin. President from 2000 to 2008, Prime Minister from 2008 to 2012, and President once more from 2012, Putin's political longevity and personal power over the resources of the state allow for meaningful comparisons with previous tsars and Communist Party leaders.[12] The four political parties represented in the Duma that survived the Putin era—United Russia, Just Russia, the Communist Party, and the Liberal Democratic Paty—have all promoted a version of authoritarian patriotism.[13]

From 2003, the main liberal political parties did not receive enough votes even to enter the State Duma. As one account put it, by 2012, 'the liberals' views have been so marginalized that they are associated with strictly opposition politicians who have no significant influence'.[14] Russian television has essentially been renationalized and promotes the official version of the new patriotism.[15] Dissident oligarchs and investigative journalists alike faced severe repression.[16] Developments such as these caused some Western commentators to fear that its long history of autocracy left Russia

---

11 Ellen Carnaghan, 'The Difficulty of Measuring support for democracy in a changing society: evidence from Russia', *Democratisation*, 18:3, 682–706, p. 689.
12 For a discussion of parallels between Putin and his Communist and Tsarist predecessors, see, for example, J. Arch Getty, *Practicing Stalinism: Bolsheviks, Boyars, and the Persistence of Tradition* (New Haven: Yale University Press, 2013), pp. 13–18.
13 Timm Beichelt, 'Two variants of the Russian radical right: Imperialism and social nationalism', *Communist and Post-Communist Studies* 42 (2009) 505–526, pp. 514–15.
14 Andrew C Kuchins and Igor A. Zevelev, 'Russian Foreign Policy: Continuity in Change', *The Washington Quarterly* (Winter 2012), pp. 147–161, 149.
15 Miguel Vazquez Linan, 'History as a Propaganda Tool in Putin's Russia', *Communist and Post-Communist Studies*, 2010, Volume 43, Issue 2, pp. 167–178.
16 The Committee to Protect Journalists listed fifty-six journalists murdered in Russia between 1992 and 2013.

unprepared for life as a liberal nation-state. There were predictions that Russia would follow the example of the Weimar Republic, the depressing path travelled by Germany in the 1920s and 30s from infant democracy to an aggressive, nationalistic and racist dictatorship under the leadership of Adolf Hitler.[17] For some, Putin's presidency fulfilled this unhappy forecast. In the West, Putin is often presented as a charismatic and autocratic nationalist, reminiscent of Hitler and his Nazi regime.[18] For others, the Putin era represents a return 'to the tactic tested in the past by Stalin and Mao, who maintained society in a state of constant tension and used the "besieged fortress" idea to justify violence'.[19]

Putin's assertive foreign policy and his strongman image are often mistaken for evidence that ethnic nationalism is already victorious in Russia. Yet, for Russians inclined to embrace a radical nationalism, the Putin/Medvedev administrations have proved much too moderate and pro-Western. While Western media tended to view the government-orchestrated imprisonment of Mikhail Khodorkovsky, the oligarch and political rival of Putin, as evidence of Russia's slide into dictatorship, Russian nationalists complain that, on the whole, oligarchs continue to thrive at the expense of ordinary people. Nationalists accuse Putin's government of unwarranted tolerance, even favoritism, towards ethnic minorities instead of discriminating positively in favour of ethnic Russians.[20] In other words, for many Russians, Russia's post-Communist identity is far from settled.

It should be remembered too that there remains significant opposition both to Putin and his government, even if this opposition is seriously divided. During the parliamentary elections of 2011 and presidential elections of 2012, there were anti-government demonstrations in Moscow. In the mass protests in Moscow in October 2011, television footage showed how the

---

17 See, for example, Rogers Brubaker, *Nationalism Reframed. Nationhood and the National Question in the New Europe* (Cambridge: Cambridge University Press, 1996), and Judith Devlin, *Slavophiles and Commissars* (Basingstoke: Macmillan, 1999), p. 204.
18 Dmitrii Shlapentokh, 'Russian Nationalists as Georgian Allies', *Iran & The Caucasus* [serial online] 16:3 (October 2012): 337–353.
19 Lilia Shevtsova, 'The Next Russian Revolution', *Current History*, 111.747 (Oct 2012) 251–257, p. 252.
20 For an account of this discourse, see Shlapentokh, 'Russian Nationalists' and Aleksandr Verkhovskii and Emil Pain, 'Civilizational Nationalism. The Russian Version of the "Special Path",' *Russian Politics and Law*, 50:5, (September–October 2012), pp. 52–80, 53–54.

protesters marched in three columns. The first column comprised left-leaning 'patriots', including young and old Communists, some wearing their medals from the victory over the Nazis in World War Two and waving Red flags adorned with the hammer and sickle. The second column, waving the current Russian flag of white, red and blue, comprised those advocating a more liberal Russia oriented towards the West. The third column comprised right-wing nationalists, many wearing the black shirts of the neo-Nazis, who marched under the old imperial, black, yellow, and white standard. Each column represented a potential political future for Russia. One scholar, semi seriously, has described modern Russia as suffering collectively from Borderline Personality Disorder.[21]

Amid the bewildering political and economic change that began in the 1990s, there were, unsurprisingly, new calls for Russia to reevaluate its past in order to chart a course into the future. Many luminaries of present-day alternative history were already working on their projects in the Soviet period, but it was the transition from the monotonous certainties of Soviet 'historical science' to the intellectual free-for-all that obtained in Russia during the Yeltsin era that provided an opportunity to connect with a wider audience.

In the immediate aftermath of the collapse of Communism, Russian universities were in an especially parlous economic position. In the 1990s, history writing, like the Russian state itself, entered a state of flux. The erstwhile conformism of Soviet academia collapsed from within as some historians defended the Communist past, others became trenchant critics of the former regime, and the majority looked anxiously to see which way the political wind was blowing.[22] Their Western counterparts were keen to investigate and publish materials relating to the more sensational aspects of the Soviet period such as the Stalinist purges. But in Russia and the West, there was only a limited market for scholarly ruminations on arcane controversies connected to Russia's ancient and medieval past.

It was into this virtually empty space that alternative historians, led by the likes of the New Chronology movement of Anatolii Fomenko and Gleb Nosovskii, ventured. Fomenko (1945–) is a renowned mathematician who has

---

[21] Arias-King, Fredo, Arlene King De Arias, and Fredo Arias De La Canal, 'Russia's Borderline Personality', *Demokratizatsiya* 16.2 (2008): pp. 117–129.
[22] Nina Tumarkin, 'The Great Patriotic War as myth and memory', *European Review*, 11:4 (2003) 595–611, pp. 605.

belonged to the academic staff of Moscow State University since the Soviet era. He is a member of Russia's Academy of Sciences, a professor with a doctorate in applied physics and mathematics, head of the Mechanical-Mathematical Department of Moscow State University, and author of more than one hundred and eighty scientific works. He has written dozens of well-respected monographs and textbooks in his specialist field of mathematics. Fomenko was awarded Russia's State Award in 1996 for his scientific achievements.[23] The qualifications of Nosovskii (1958–) include a PhD in physics and mathematics. More notoriously, they are the authors and co-authors of more than one hundred publications dealing with Russian and world history. The volume of their output is astonishing and reflects both their enthusiasm and their mass-production methods as different members of their team specialize in different periods and locations.[24]

Since the collapse of Communism, New Chronology has thrived as a publishing phenomenon, despite and partly because of the hefty criticisms directed at it from conventional scholars. It has become better known in the West too, attracting the attention of scholars who are concerned about its

23 Anatolii Fomenko and Gleb Nosovskii, *Novaia khronologiia i kontseptsia drevnei Rusi, Anglii, Rima. Fakty, statistikia, gipotesy* II volumes (Moscow: Moscow State University press MGU, 1995, 1996); Anatolii Fomenko, *Novaia khronologiia Gretsii. Antichnost' i srednevekov'e* II volumes (Moscow: MGU, 1996); Anatolii Fomenko and Gleb Nosovskii, *Imperiia: Rus', Turtsia, Kitai, Evropa, Egipet. Novaia matematicheskaia khronologiia drevnosti* (Moscow: Faktorial press, 1996, 1997, 1998, 1999); Anatolii Fomenko and Gleb Nosovskii, *Rus' i Rim. Pravil'no li my poinimaem istoriiu Evropy i Azii?* II volumes (Moscow: Olimp, AST print house, 1997); Anatolii Fomenko and Gleb Nosovskii, *Novaia khronologiia Rusi*, (Moscow: Faktorial press, 1997); Anatolii Fomenko and Gleb Nosovskii, *Matematicheskaia khronologiia bibleiskikh sobytii*, (Moscow: Nauka, 1997); Anatolii Fomenko, "Smysl russkogo dela v sokhranenii Imperii," *Nezavisimaia Gazeta*, 21 November 1996; Anatolii Fomenko and Gleb Nosovskii, *Rekonstruktsia vseobshchei istorii* (Moscow: Delovoi Ekpress, 1999); Anatolii Fomenko and Gleb Nosovskii, *Bibleiskaia Rus'* II volumes (Moscow: Faktorial press, 1998, 2000); Anatolii Fomenko and Gleb Nosovskii, *Rus'-Orda na stranitsakh bibleiskikh knig* (Moscow: Anvik, 1998); Anatolii Fomenko and Gleb Nosovskii, *Vvedenie v novuiu khronologiiu, kakoi seichas vek?* (Moscow: Kraft+Lean, 1999); Anatolii Fomenko, *New Methods of Statistical Analysis of Historical Texts. Applications to Chronology* III volumes (New York: Edwin Mellen Press); Anatolii Fomenko and Gleb Nosovskii, *Rekonstruktsia vseobschei istorii. Issledovania 1999–2000* (Moscow: Delovoi ekspress, 1999); Anatolii Fomenko and Gleb Nosovskii, *Kakoi seichas vek?* (Moscow: Aif-Print, 2002).

24 For a complete list of their publications, a summary of New Chronology's rewriting of history, and even a sample of Fomenko's art-work, the interested reader should consult the official New Chronology website.

impact upon ordinary Russians' understanding of history and Russia's place in the world.[25] The English language title of Fomenko's magnum opus is *History. Fiction or Science*.[26] Fomenko's ambition is to replace the existing 'fiction' with the 'science' of alternative history. Fomenko and New Chronology represent a popular rebellion against the version of history preferred by Russia's scholarly elite.[27] Or, as one scholar has put it, New Chronology is a prime example of 'the conjunction between conspiracy theory and the rewriting of history [that] makes up one of the main instruments for disseminating nationalist theories in today's Russia, theories based on a kind of post-modern, paranoid cultural imaginary'.[28]

The number of critics of Fomenko and his fellow alternative historians has certainly grown in recent years, and there have been premature announcements of New Chronology's imminent demise.[29] Yet alternative history has shown a remarkable capacity to absorb the blows inflicted by its critics and move forward, its momentum enhanced rather than deflated. So far, alternative history has not succeeded in winning over the academic departments of major universities, nor has it replaced the existing school textbooks. The alternative strategy is not to outscore the professional historians in a debate over a particular controversy or time period. Rather, the plan is to render conventional scholarship irrelevant by winning over the book-buying public and Russia's growing army of Internet users. Their passion is expressed in their apocalyptic version of patriotism for, in the words of one alternative historian:

> When a nation maintains her historical memory, she will fight not only for material values, but also for the honour of the state (*derzhava*). ... But if this nation is forced to abandon traditional national values and substitute instead a set of alien principles, then this nation is like a giant that was defeated not by the sword, but poisoned with a substance that darkens the mind and paralyses the will.[30]

---

25 See, for example, James Billington, *Russia in Search of Itself* (Washington: Woodrow Wilson Research Center, 2004).
26 Anatolii Fomenko, Gleb Nosovskii, History: *Fiction or Science* VII vol. (Paris, London, New York: Delamere, 2003).
27 See 'Introduction' to Fomenko *History: Fiction or Science*.
28 Laruelle, 'Conspiracy and Alternate History in Russia', p. 566.
29 See, for example, S. Shmidt, *Fenomen Fomenko* (Moscow: Nauka, 2005).
30 Alexey Kungurov, *Kievskoi Rusi ne bylo, ili chto skryvaiut istoriki* (Moscow: Eksmo, Algoritm: 2011), p. 31.

Fomenko's intellectual heroes include Mikhail Lomonosov, the eighteenth century polymath, scientist, and Russian patriot, who famously accused the Romanov dynasty of supporting a history profession that praised the West, while diminishing Russia's own historical achievements. Fomenko's writing is inspired too by the work of the Eurasianists of the early twentieth century who argued that Russia was neither European nor Asian but a distinctive society. The academic leader of this group, Nikolai Trubetskoi, claimed that Asia was the natural home of Russia in much the same way that Europe was a traditional enemy.[31] Another influential figure in preparing the ground for alternative history was Lev Gumilev, a maverick Soviet-era dissident who argued that there was no neat division of Eurasia into its Asian and European halves.[32]

Russian public opinion remains deeply divided, but the trends are not encouraging for Russia's 'Westernizers'. Immediately after the Communist collapse, opinion polls suggested that more than two-thirds of Russians expected 'positive change and a return to the "family of civilized nations" and the beaten track of world development—modernization, democracy, and liberalism'. By the late 1990s, public opinion had changed dramatically to the point where two-thirds were of the view that 'Russia has its own special path'.[33] Divisions over Russia's eastern and western orientations remain. By the end of the first decade of the twenty-first century, Russian public opinion had undergone what one researcher described as 'a deep transformation of Russian identity, in the course of which its Eurasian component is becoming stronger'. The view that Russia was a 'part of Europe, and it will be associated with Europe most closely in the future just as it was in the past' enjoys about the same level of popularity as the view that 'Russia is not a purely European country but is a special, Eurasian civilization, and the center of gravity in Russian policy will be shifting to the East'. The momentum, however, is shifting in the direction of the Eurasian view.[34]

---

31 Nikolai Trubetskoi, *The Legacy of Chengiz Khan and other Essays on Russia's identity* (Michigan Slavic Publications, 1991), pp. 161–67.
32 See, for example, Lev Gumilev, *Drevniaia Rus i velikaia step'* (Moscow: Mysl', 1992), Lev Gumilev, *Poiski vymyshlennogo tsarstva* (Moscow: Tanais, 1994), and Lev Gumilev, *Chernaia legenda* (Moscow: Ekopros, 1994).
33 Verkhovskii and Pain, 'Civilizational Nationalism', pp. 53–54.
34 A.L. Andreev, 'Europe or Asia', *Herald of the Russian Academy of Sciences*, 2010, Vol. 80, No. 5: 461–465, p. 463.

Just as importantly, the outlook of the Russian intelligentsia, its educated elite, has clearly changed. Educated Russian opinion was firmly in the camp of the Westernizers in the early 1990s. The claims of Frances Fukuyama that history had come to an end because humanity's ideological wars were over and of Samuel Huntington about the link between the growth of the middle class and increased support for political and economic freedom appeared triumphant. Just about every poltical commentator recognizes that the mood in Russia is very different now. In the words of one observer, twenty years after the collapse of Communism, not a shred of the liberal optimism of the early 1990s remains.[35]

It seems likely that the relative dynamism of the Asian economies in comparison to the stagnation of the European and American economies in the wake of the Great Financial Crisis—which began in earnest in 2008 and was still impacting the world economy in 2013—contributed to this shift in perspective. On the other hand, it seems clear that an increasing proportion of Russians are embracing the notion of a Russian special path or *sonderweg*. This is a pleasing development for most writers of alternative history. It is also an outcome for which alternative history can take some credit.

Fomenko began to puzzle over the issues of conventional chronology as far back as the 1970s. Fomenko's original claim was that the accepted dating system was bedeviled with errors and deliberate falsifications. Conventional dating amounted to little more than the ill-informed guesses of early modern scholars, who, Fomenko alleged, added thousands of years to the story of civilization and filled in the gaps with the mythology that we know today as ancient and medieval history.[36] For Fomenko, recorded history was nowhere near as old as previously thought, ancient history was a duplicate of medieval history, Egyptians, Greeks and Romans deserved far less atten-

---

[35] For a summary of the difficulties, see Lilia Shevtsova, 'What's the Matter with Russia?', *Journal of Democracy* 21.1 (2010): 152–159.

[36] Fomenko, Nosovskii, *Bibleiskaia Rus'*, I, 21–24; for a mathematical-statistical critique of Skaliger/Petvius see also Anatolii Fomenko, *Metody statisticheskogo analiza narrativnykh tekstov i prilozhenie k khronologii* (Moscow: MGU, 1990, 1996); Anatolii Fomenko, *Globalnaia khronologiia* (Moscow: MGU, 1993); Anatolii Fomenko and Gleb Nosovskii, *Geometrical and statistical methods of analysis of star configurations. Dating of Ptolemy's Almagest* (USA: CRC-Press, 1993); Anatolii Fomenko, *Empirical-statistical analysis of narrative material and its application to historical dating* II volumes (the Netherlands: Kluwer Academic publications, 1994); Fomenko and Nosovskii, *Kakoi seichas vek?* pp.16–33.

tion than was usually accorded them, and the Bible's Old Testament was written after the New Testament. According to Fomenko, confusion has arisen because many historical figures are duplicates and triplicates, that is, copies of the one historical personage known in different contexts and eras by different names. Roman history is mostly the history of the Holy Roman Empire, which turns out to be the story of Russia projected westwards and backwards in time. Jesus Christ was also known to history as Pope Gregory the Seventh and lived in Rome in the eleventh century. Only in the seventeenth century did the dating of conventional history and Fomenko's dates achieve unison.

Fomenko's initial challenge to the Soviet historical academy invoked only ridicule from historians trained to think in terms of party thinking (*partiinost'*), class war, and Soviet patriotism. His speculations, based on arguments from astronomical data, were often opaque to the non-specialist reader, although they excited at least some interest among fellow mathematicians.[37] Fomenko's new version of Biblical history, however, drew fire from the Russian Orthodox Church. Having been labelled an anti-Christ in the early 1990s, Fomenko soon became a celebrity academic of interest to popular newspapers and the makers of television documentaries. Fomenko began to trawl through the history of Eurasia, Byzantium, and Rome to show that historians all around the world appropriated the achievements of Russians to boost the prestige of their own national history. Arguably, Fomenko's greatest achievement is the invention of a Slav-Turk empire that allegedly dominated the first half of world history, that is, the period we know as the ninth to the seventeenth centuries. This 'Russian Horde' as Fomenko named it, was based in the area that we normally associate with the Golden Horde founded by the Mongol khans in the thirteenth century.[38]

Fomenko's vision is an inspiring one for those who measure Russia's greatness by the amount of space it occupies on a map. He offers an account of the Russian state as if it were the history of all of Eurasia. One of Fomenko's claims, often repeated in the works of popular writers, is that the Mongols or Tatars, as the Russians called them, did not come from far off

---

37 For an account of Fomenko's mathematical reasoning and its reception in Russia, see Florin Diacu, *The Lost Millennium: History's Timetables under Siege* (Baltimore: Johns Hopkins University Press, 2011).

38 The 'Golden Horde' is the latter-day name that Russians applied to the Kipchak Khanate.

Central Asia but had always lived within the lands of European Russia along the Volga River and adjacent steppes. Genghis Khan had European features, spoke Slav and Turkic languages, and never invaded Russia. One of Fomenko's goals is to achieve what his thirteenth-century ancestors could not, the expulsion of the Mongols from the historical record. According to Fomenko, the myth of the Mongol invasion was an invention of Church chroniclers and the Romanov dynasty, designed to glorify their own contributions to Russian history.

Fomenko and alternative history are a recent example of one of the oldest stories in Russian history. This is the constant reimagining of Russia, or, as one historian has put it, the 'agony of the Russian idea'.[39] There have been several obvious breaks with the past in Russia's history—the coming of Christianity, Peter the Great, the Communist revolution, Stalin's revolution from above, the collapse of the Soviet Union. At each point, those who came to power obliterated the past from the historical record and invented a new history.

According to the early Russian chronicles, Vladimir the First converted Kiev Rus *en masse* to Christianity in 988 and literally destroyed all traces of the pagan gods. Peter the Great attacked almost everything old from the existing church hierarchy to the beards of his subjects and then set up an Academy of Sciences in St. Petersburg in 1725 whose mission included the writing of Russian history. After 1917, Lenin and Stalin destroyed the pillars of the former establishment, tsar, nobility, church and peasantry and then destroyed any information that could be viewed as positive concerning their imperial predecessors. The pattern continued after the fall of Communism in 1991 when Russian reformers declared an end to the Communist period as if Russia was a land with a future but no past.

Fomenko reads this pattern of history as suggesting that at every crisis in Russia's history, a new idea is needed to account for the crisis and to enable Russia to move forward. Because there is a point to history, it is too important to be left to purely academic research. The Marxist historian Pokrovsky put this idea most cynically when he described history as politics projected into the past. When pseudo-historians like Fomenko are told that the past they have invented is full of lies and distortion, they invariably reply that the history written by conventional historians suffers from the same de-

---

[39] Tim McDaniel, *The Agony of the Russian Idea* (Princeton: Princeton University Press, 1996), pp. 16–17.

fects. Their aim is to unsettle the consensus built upon the lies and distortions of a previous rewriting of history that in their view has paralyzed not just Russia's historians but the revival of Russia as a state. Fomenko and his allies consider that history determines the future, that the sudden collapses to which Russia has been prone in the twentieth century are evidence of how far Russia has strayed from its true historical roots.

One of the many criticisms that can be directed at alternative historians is their failure to think historically. For alternative history, the past is not a 'foreign country', but rather a country that closely resembles the Russian Empire of recent times. The political and demographic realities of the modern Russian Empire and Soviet Union most likely obtained for thousands, if not tens of thousands, of years. In other words, they are very imaginative in their use of historical evidence, but lack an historical imagination. They find it difficult to accept that there might have been a world without a powerful and remarkable Russia.

Edward Said has pointed out that historians, like explorers or missionaries, have, whether they are conscious of it or not, promoted the colonial enterprise by creating an image of the 'other' preparatory with or simultaneous to its conquest.[40] This is literally true in the case of Fomenko. For his critics, Fomenko's ideas are providing fuel for those who would reconstitute a Russian Empire. It is not just modern-day Mongols who are deprived of part of their heritage. In Fomenko's history, Ukraine, Belarus, and central Asia too have no identity outside of their connection to Russia. Fomenko and his allies are unrepentant, noting that the Mongolian, Turkic, and Ukrainian peoples are sadly mistaken in the delusion that they were ever anything other than elements of the Russian Horde.

For his scholarly critics in Russia, Fomenko quickly became both an embarrassment and a potent symbol of the depths to which the Russian academy and society generally had sunk amid the economic disasters and political and military humiliations heaped upon Russia since the fall of Communism. Yet even his staunchest critics admit that Fomenko's writings are popular. One of Fomenko's critics noted that alternative h stories occupy the best shelves in Moscow's bookshops, while the more scholarly works evade the eyes of the customer.[41] Another critic complained that Fomenko's writings

---

40 Edward Said, *Orientalism* (London: Penguin, 1995).
41 See Alexei Laushkin, *Lozh' novoi khronologii. Kak voiuet s khristianstvom A.T. Fomenko i ego edinomyshlenniki* (Moscow: Palomnik, 2002).

gave rise to a new publishing phenomenon – whole sections of bookstores dedicated to the topic of 'conspirology (conspiratology)'.[42] From 2006, New Chronology introduced its readers to a new series of books under the title of the 'Golden Row' (*Zolotoi Riad*). These books contain only new material and are printed with an attractive gold cover; neophytes are warned that they are expected to familiarize themselves with the basics of New Chronology before proceeding to the Golden Row. In the first decade of 2000s, Internet sites such as 'YouTube' were saturated with Fomenko's view of world history, while popular television programs, newspapers and radio stations have dedicated lengthy discussions to the 'revelations' of these 'modern' historians. One scholarly exposition of the 'anti-history' of Fomenko ran to three large volumes and more than thirty articles.[43] Just as importantly, New Chronology continues to inspire and embolden an army of like-minded amateur historians and imitators.[44]

---

42 Stefanie Ortmann and John Heathershaw, 'Conspiracy Theories in the Post-Soviet Space', *The Russian Review* 71 (October 2012): 551–64.
43 See Igor Nastenko et al., eds., *Istoriia i antiIstoriia: Kritika "novoi khronologii" akademika A. Fomenko* (Moscow: Iazyki russkoi kultury, 2000); Igor Nastenko et al., eds., *Antifomenkovskaia mozaika* 5 books (Moscow: Russkaia panorama, 2000, 2001, 2002, 2003); Dmitrii Volodikhin and Dmitrii Oleinikov in collaboration with Olga Eliseeva, *Istoriia Rossii v melkii goroshek* (Moscow: ManufASTura-Edinstvo, 1998); Laushkin, *Lozh' novoi khronologii; Astronomiia protiv 'Novoi Khronologii'* (Moscow: 2001); *Russkaia Istoriia protiv 'Novoi Khronologii'* (Moscow: 2001); *Sbornik Russkogo istoricheskogo obshchestva* 3:151 (Moscow: 2000); also see Sergey Fatiushkin's impressive collection of web materials critical of Fomenko, Bushkov and Co: http://fatus.chat.ru/foma.htm (as of November 17, 2008).
44 Among the many popular historians who corroborate Fomenko or criticise conventional historical accounts of Russian and world history are Anatolii Abrashkin, *Predki russkikh v drevnem mire* (Moscow: Veche, 2001); Anatolii Abrashkin, *Drevnie Rossy: Mifologicheskie paralleli i puti migratsii* (Nizhnii Novgorod: NNGU print house, 1999); Anatolii Abrashkin, *Chudo-Uydo: Istoriia odnogo perevoplashchenia* (Nizhnii Novgorod: NNGU print house, 1999); Anatolii Abrashkin, *Rus' sredizemnomorskaia i zagadki Biblii* (Moscow: Veche, 2003); Anatolii Abrashkin, *Tainy Troianskoi voiny i sredizemnomorskaia Rus'* (Moscow: Veche, 2006); Anatolii Abrashkin, *Sredizemnomorskaia Rus': velikaia derzhava drevnosti* (Moscow: Veche, 2006); Anatolii Abrashkin, *Skifskaia Rus'. Ot Troi do Kieva* (Moscow: Veche, 2008); Alexander Bushkov, *Rossiia kotori ne bylo* (Moscow: 'OLMA-Press', 1997); Alexander Bushkov and Andrey Burovskii, *Rossiia kotoroi ne bylo II, Russkaia Atlantida* (Moscow: 'OLMA-Press', 2001); Alexander Bushkov, *Rossiia kotori ne bylo III, mirazhi i prizraki* (Moscow: "OLMA-press', 2004); Alexander Bushkov, *Rossiia kotori ne bylo IV. Blesk i krov' gvardeiskogo stoletia* (Moscow: 'OLMA-press', 2005); Alexander Bushkov, *Zemlia. Planeta prizrakov* (Moscow: "OLMA-press', 2007); Alexander Bushkov, *Ivan*

Fomenko is now an ageing giant of alternative history, but his influence remains important. It is often noted that Fomenko received a major boost in the late 1990s when Garry Kasparov, Russia's greatest Chess champion, endorsed New Chronology in an impassioned piece written for the journal *Ogoniek*. Kasparov's boast that 'I can spread any historian against the wall

---

Groznyi. Krovavyi poet (Moscow: 'OLMA-press', 2007); Alexander Bushkov, *Chingizkhan. Neizvestnaia Azia* (Moscow: 'OLMA-Press', 2008); Alexander Bushkov, *Rasputin. Vystrely iz proshlogo* (Moscow: 'OLMA-press', 2008); Alexander Bushkov, *Stalin. Krasnyi monarkh* (Moscow: 'OLMA-press, 2008); Alexander Bushkov, *Stalin. Ledianoi tron* (Moscow: 'OLMA-press', 2008); Andrey Burovskii, *Nesbyvshaiasia Rossiia* (Moscow: Eksmo, 2007); Andrey Burovskii, *Ariiskaia Rus': lozh' i pravda o vyshei rase* (Moscow: Eksmo, 2007); Leonid Bocharov, Nikolai Efimov, Igor Chachukh and Igor Chernyshev, *Zagovor protiv russkoi istorii* (Moscow: ANVIK, 2001);; Alexander Guts, "Mif o vosstanovlenii istoricheskoi pravdy," *Matematicheskie struktury i modelirovanie* 1 (1998); Alexander Guts, *Podlinnaia Istoriia Rossii* (Omsk: OMGU, 1999); Alexander Guts, 'Modeli mnogovariantnoi istorii', *Matematicheskie struktiru i modelirovanie* 4 (1999); Viktor Kandyba, *Istoriia russkogo naroda* (St-Petersburg: Lan', 1996); Viktor Kandyba and Peter Zolin, *Real'naia istoriia Rossii* (St-Petersburg: Lan', 1997); Viktor Kandyba and Peter Zolin, *Istoriia i ideologia ruskkogo naroda* II volumes (St-Petersburg: Lan', 1997); Viktor Kandyba, *Zaorechshennaia Istoriia* (St-Petersburg: Lan', 1998); Iaroslav Kesler, *Russkaia tsivilizatsia* (Moscow: Eko-press, 2000, 2002); Iaroslav Kesler and Igor Davidenko, *Kniga tsivilazatsii* (Moscow: Eko-press, 2001); Iaroslav Kesler, *Azbuka i Russko-Evropeiskii slovar'* (Moscow: Kraft+, 2001); Iaroslav Kesler and Dmitrii Kaliuzhnyi, *Zabytaia Istoriia Moskovii. Ot stroitel'stva Moskvy do raskola* (Moscow: Veche, 2003); Iaroslav Kesler and Dmitrii Kaliuzhnyi, *Zabytaia Istoriia Rossiiskoi imperii* (Moscow: Veche, 2004); Igor Davidenko, *Lozhye maiaki istorii* (Moscow: Eko-press, 2002); Vladislav Poliakovskii, *Tataro-Mongoly, Evrazia, Mnogovariantnost'* (Kaluga: GUP Oblizdat, 2002); Anatolii Storozhev and Vladimir Storozhev, *Rossiia vo vremeni*, book I, (Moscow: Veche, 1997); Sergey Valianskii and Dmitrii Kaliuzhnyi, *Put' na vostok ili bez vesti propavshie vo vremeni* (Moscow: Kraft+Lean, 1997); Sergey Valianskii and Dmitrii Kaliuzhnyi, *Drugaia Istoria nauki* (Moscow: Veche, 2002); Sergey Valianskii and Dmitrii Kaliuzhnyi, *Drugaia Istoriia Rusi* (Moscow: Veche, 2002); Dmitrii Kaliuzhnyi and Alexander Zhabinskii, *Drugaia Istoriia voin* (Moscow: Veche, 2003); Sergey Valianskii, *Uslovia Vyzhivania Rossii* (Moscow: Kraft+, 2005); Murad Adzhi, *My—iz roda Polovetskogo* (Rybinsk: 1992); Murad Adzhi, *Polyn' polovetskogo polia* (Moscow: Pik-Kontekst, 1994); Murad Adzhi, *Taina Sviatogo Georgia, ili podarennoe Tengri* (Moscow: 1997); Murad Adzhi, *Evropa, Turki, velikaia step'* (Moscow: Mysl', 1998); Murad Adzhi, *Kipchaki* (Moscow: Novosti, 1999); Murad Adzhi, *Tiurki i mir: sokrovennaia Istoriia* (Moscow: AST, 2004); Murad Adzhi, *Aziatskaia Evropa* (Moscow: AST, 2006); Murad Adzhi, *Dykhanie Armagedonna* (Moscow: AST, 2006); Vladimir Shcherbakov, *Gde zhili geroi eddicheskikh mifof* (Moscow: 1989); Vladimir Scherbakov, *Gde iskat' Atlantidu* (Moscow: 1990); Vladimir Shcherbakov, *Asgard—gorod Bogov* (Moscow: 1991); Valerii Khamtsiev and Alexander Balaev, *David Soslan, Friedrich Barbarosse, Alania ot Palestiny to Britanii* (Vladikavkaz: IR, 1992).

in a debate about Russian history' was typical of the pugnacious confidence of Fomenko's acolytes.[45] Since taking a more prominent place in Russian politics as part of the anti-Putin movement, Kasparov has distanced himself from Fomenko. But his parting of the ways with Kasparov has not harmed Fomenko's cause in the slightest. It is Kasparov, and not Fomenko, who is fast becoming irrelevant. If anything, there is a case to be made that the reach of alternative history has dramatically increased because alternative historians have colonized YouTube much more effectively than their professional rivals. In the words of one historian, pseudo-history has become 'the main source of the general public's knowledge both of the remote past and the origins of the Slavs'.[46] Or, as another commentator has put it, Fomenko and his ilk have become 'an aspect of social consciousness' in Russia.[47]

In the 1990s, alternative historians relied upon books whose print and illustrations were of variable quality, but, in more recent times, they have proved expert in producing seemingly credible and professional historical 'documentaries' aimed at a younger and post-Soviet audience. It helps that many alternative historians are consummate performers in front of a camera. However dubious their claims, alternative historians have come to represent a significant part of what R.W. Davies described as the 'mental revolution' that has taken place after the collapse of Communism.[48]

But what does all this mean? How is the phenomenon of Fomenko or alternative history more broadly, to be understood and explained? Just as importantly, what is its significance for Russian politics and history? The aim of this book is to place the success of Fomenko and alternative history more generally, in its political and historical context. It is often pointed out that Fomenko's personal popularity reflects the reverence for science, and especially mathematics, cultivated in the former Soviet Union.[49] While this is

---

45 For Kasparov's endorsement, see Gary Kasparov, 'Chernye dyry istorii', *Ogoniek* 1, 2, 3 (January 1999). Fomenko's endorsement of Kasparov's contribution is to be found in the foreword to Fomenko, Nosovskii, *Novaia khronologiia i kontseptsia drevnei Rusi, Anglii, Rima. Fakty, statistikia, gipotesy*.
46 Victor Shnirelman, 'Russian Response. Archaeology, Russian Nationalism, and the "Arctic Homeland"' in Philip L. Kohl et al, *Selective Remembrances: Archaeology in the Construction, Commemoration, and Consecration of National Pasts*, (Chicago: University of Chicago Press, 2007), p. 32.
47 Khlebnikov, *Teoriia zagovora*, p. 411.
48 See Robert William Davies, *Soviet history in the Yeltsin era* (Basingstoke: Macmillan, 1997), pp. 49–75.
49 Diacu, *The Lost Millenium*, p 199.

undoubtedly true, it does not explain the success of literally thousands of popular books devoted to alternative history written over the last two decades.

Of course, it was not just history, but science and medicine that were subjected to the challenge of less orthodox, self-proclaimed scientific experts in the 1990s. In 1998, the Russian Academy of Sciences even established a 'Commission for the Struggle against Pseudo Science' to fight against the proponents of telepathy, 'torsion fields', and other wonders. The Commission commenced its work, but the production of pseudo science continued apace. Fifteen years later, the heads of the Commission against Pseudo-Science in effect acknowledged their failure when they urged President Putin to fund a more serious effort to combat this anti-scientific scourge.

Science, history and politics all seem under threat in modern-day Russia. That this is a world turned upside down was perhaps most vividly reflected in a campaign launched in 2008 by Communist Party leaders to have the Orthodox Church recognize Stalin as a saint. For outsiders reading this seemingly endless stream of strange science, fabulous pseudo-history, conspiracy theory, and ultra-nationalist discourse, it might seem that Russia is on the brink of losing its collective mind. The argument here is that, while the individual texts offered by alternative history may be fanciful, alternative history as a whole can be located and understood in the context of more mundane political considerations concerning the future of Russia. We focus here upon Fomenko and New Chronology, but place his work in the wider context of alternative history and modern Russian politics.

Outside of the former Soviet space, alternative history appears as an outrageous perversion of what is normally considered good historical practice. On the other hand, alternative history feeds into the broader rewriting of Russian history along more patriotic lines that is now taking place in Russia. The foundational principles common to nearly all alternative historians—that the Russian Empire was a great civilizational achievement, that there is evidence throughout history of a 'plot (*zagovor*)' aimed at destroying Russia, and that there needs to be a fundamental rewriting of Russian history—are routinely embraced now by more conventional historians and politicians, including those presently charged with writing an authoritative and new post-Communist version of Russia's past.[50]

---

[50] See, for example, Vladimir Medinskii, *O russkom pianstve, leni i zhestokosti. Mify o Rossii* (Moscow: OLMA, 2010) and Vladimir Medinskii, *Voina. 1939–1945* (Moscow: OLMA, 2011).

Chapter One: Imperial Dilemmas and Historical Therapy

'A nation is a society united by a delusion about its ancestry and a common fear of its neighbours'.

W. R. Inge

> In the 1990s there had been a high demand for the books of Fomenko. This newly baked guru, academic-mathematician, proclaimed a revolution in historical science. Professionals do not have the time or patience to answer this gibberish, while the general public has been fooled and confused.[51]

Pseudo history, of course, is not just a Russian phenomenon. Amateur historians all around the world are cherry-picking the historical record to uncover a secret past, concoct or unravel a conspiracy, and compile evidence that enhances the achievements of their country, ethnic group or religion. They tend to find what they want to find and discard all evidence to the contrary.[52] In countries like the United States or the United Kingdom where national borders and political traditions are relatively well established, pseudo-history has focused upon a vast array of conspiracies that allegedly lie behind, for example, the Kennedy assassination, the 9/11 Al Qaeda attack, the government concealing information about UFOs, or the mysterious internal workings of the Catholic Church. In the states that once made up the Soviet Union, where borders and politics are less certain, alternative historians have displayed a much sharper patriotic focus. Throughout Eastern Europe and Central Asia, the new freedom to publish has resulted in an explosion of literature purporting to uncover the real, stolen, and unacknowledged history of the new states' ethnic groups.

The fantastic tales of the ancient past that have emerged in every corner of the lands of the former Soviet Union are part of a zero-sum 'competition for ancestors' in which glorious antecedents are claimed at the expense of a

---

51 Igor Nastenko, a leading figure in the publishing house *Russkaia Panorama*, wrote this in a forward to a collection of critiques of Fomenko. See Igor Nastenko et al., eds., *Istoriia i antilstoriia: Kritika "novoi khronologii" akademika A. Fomenko* (Moscow: Iazyki russkoi kultury, 2000); Igor Nastenko et al., eds., *Antifomenkovskaia mozaika* 5 books (Moscow: Russkaia panorama, 2000, 2001, 2002, 2003).

52 See, for example, David Aaronovich, *Voodoo histories. The Role of Conspiracy in Shaping Modern History* (London: Johnathan Cape, 2009).

neighboring ethnic group or state.[53] Russia now finds itself in a serious competition with Ukraine for the Scythian and Sarmatian inheritance, and with the newly independent states of Central Asia over the legacy of the steppe peoples and the civilizations of Eurasia. These disputes over history continue to multiply. They are not simply a case of Russians versus the rest, but of the rest versus each other.[54] Uzbeks position themselves at the center of a great Turkic empire, which once dominated central Asia, while Lithuanians and Belarusians both claim ownership of the medieval Jagiellonian dynasty.

It is alternative history that has often acted as the flag-bearer of Russia in this seemingly endless competition for illustrious antecedents. To do so, it has had to tailor its narrative to three important aspects of Russian identity. The first of these is the importance of 'empire' to the Russian historical imagination. While this term is seriously out-of-fashion in most parts of the world, it resonates positively in Russia. Vera Tolz has pointed out that, for Russia, the process of nation building has been complicated because:

> Russia has traditionally been the centre of an empire, and therefore confusion over the 'just borders' of the new state is greater among politicians, intellectuals and even ordinary people than is the case in the non-Russian newly independent states...what is important to note is that the early creation of an empire (well before the process of Russian nation building began), the empire's land-based character and the resulting high level of mutual cultural influences and assimilation between conquerors and conquered to some extent blurred the feeling of difference between the imperial people and other subjects of the empire.[55]

While non-Russian nationalists opposed to the Russian or Soviet states were able to identify Russia as the enemy against which they had to struggle, Russian nationalists have to contend with the fact that non-Russian nationalities have long been part of the Russian state. Thus, Russian nationalists 'do not have clear options of identifying the 'other' which deprives them of an important instrument of self-identifiction'.[56]

---

53 Victor A. Shnirelman, *Who Gets the Past? Competition for Ancestors among Non-Russian Intellectuals in Russia* (Washington: The Woodrow Wilson Center Press, 1996), pp. 1–7.
54 For examples of both types of conflict, see J. Heathershaw (2012), 'Of National Fathers and Russian Elder Brothers: Conspiracy Theories and Political Ideas in Post-Soviet Central Asia', *The Russian Review*, 71: 610–629.
55 Vera Tolz, *Russia* (London: Arnold, 2001), pp. 70–73.
56 Beichelt, 'Two variants of the Russian radical right', p. 514.

It is not just extreme Russian chauvinists, but mainstream public opinion in Russia that views the concept of 'empire' positively. The qualification is usually attached that, unlike the British or American Empires, Russia enriched, rather than exploited, the imperial periphery. The villain in this story of empire, ironically, is 'nationalism', which in modern-day Russia is a pejorative term attached to separatists such as those in the Caucasus who are seeking to leave the Russian Federation. Nor is there much sympathy for the countries of the 'near abroad' when their leaders criticize Russia or accusations are made of discrimination against their Russian minorities.[57] While much historical revisionism outside of Russia is focused upon telling the story of Russian oppression of others, alternative history highlights the virtues of the Russian Empire and its repression by others.

For advocates of national independence in the former republics of the Soviet Union, the disintegration of the Soviet Union was an inevitable outcome for Europe's last empire. According to the critics, the 'official nationality' of the nineteenth century and Soviet 'internationalism' of the twentieth century were masks that hid the chauvinism of the Great Russians. Russia was, according to the early Communists, a 'prison of the peoples' and its demise was inevitable. Richard Pipes has described 'the so-called 'nationality question' in the Soviet Union as a euphemism for what is elsewhere known as imperialism and colonialism'.[58] According to Szporluk, the Soviet Union was simply the Russian Empire.[59] Elite and popular opinion in Russia mostly disagrees with this equation of Russia and imperial oppression.

A second distinguishing feature of Russian identity is that the majority of intellectuals in Russia see the 'West', rather than non-Russians of the former Soviet Union, as 'the constituting other' in opposition to which Russia seeks to understand itself. According to the historian Alexander Yanov, Russians have always been divided into those who viewed Russia as part of the European tradition and those who favour a special path or *sonderweg* for Russia. For many of the latter, there was a clash of civilisations, a war between individualistic Romano-German Europe and the more spiritual and collectiv-

---

57 Richard Sakwa, 'Conspiracy Narratives as a Mode of Engagement in International Politics: The Case of the 2008 Russo-Georgian War', *The Russian Review*, 71 (2012), pp. 581–609.
58 Richard Pipes, 'Russia's shuddering empire: the prospects for Soviet disunion', *The New Republic* 201:19 (November 6, 1989): p. 52.
59 Roman Szporluk, 'After Empire: What?', *Daedalus* 123:3 (Summer 1994): p. 1.

ist world of Orthodox Russia.[60] Russian nationalists are uniformly alienated from and hostile to the West.[61] On the other hand, the West is Russia's measuring stick in terms of civilizational achievement.

In the writings of the alternative historians, the external enemies of Russia are invariably Westerners along with their lackeys inside Russia. It is never claimed, for example, that the Chinese, Japanese or Persians purloined and misrepresented Russian history. It was because all of the world's most important civilizations contained a Russian kernel at their core that a jealous and ungrateful West conspired to hide and destroy the truth about Russian history. The heroes of alternative history are invariably European in appearance. The message is that Russia was always the good and noble version of Europe as opposed to the rapacious and decadent West. German propagandists from the Nazi era would have been disappointed to learn that, according to Russia's alternative historians, the mysterious Aryans responsible for the Indo-European family of languages were proto-Slavs and not ancient Germans.

While xenophobia has been a distinctive feature of Russian discourse over the centuries, in the 1990s it seemed possible that this hostility towards the West was dying away along with other ideological hangovers of the Communist era. In 1999, Putin as Russian Prime Minister even floated the idea of Russia joining NATO. During the 2000s, however, Russia mostly found itself in disagreement with the West on foreign policy issues like the 'color revolutions' in Ukraine and Georgia or regime change in Iraq and Syria. The Russian government, nationalist writers, and popular opinion have tended to view anti-Russian protests in Ukraine as a Western-inspired plot aimed at transforming the geopolitics of the former Soviet space.[62] The 2008 war between Russia and Georgia over Georgia's separatist province of South Ossetia represented a low point in Russia's post-Communist relationship with the West.[63] Meanwhile, the government used its virtual control of the media tirelessly to alert the public to the danger of Western interference in Russian

---

60 Alexander Yanov, 'Russian nationalism in Western studies: Misadventures of a Moribund paradigm', *Demokratizatsiia* 9:4 (Fall 2001): p. 552.
61 Beichelt, 'Two variants of the Russian radical right', p. 512.
62 Evgeny Finkel & Yitzhak M. Brudny, 'Russia and the colour revolutions', *Democratization*, 19:1 (2012), pp. 15–36 and Andreas Umland, 'Russia's New "Special Path" After the Orange Revolution', *Russian Politics & Law*, 50.6 (2012): 19–40.
63 See Sakwa, 'Conspiracy Narratives as a Mode of Engagement in International Politics'.

affairs. Putin has warned against foreigners meddling in the writing of Russian history, claiming that these historians receive grants from foreign institutions and then write history that suits their benefactors.[64] This theme also resonates strongly in the ranks of the alternative historians.

A third element of Russian identity of relevance to this study is what Vladimir Shlapentokh has described as the 'greatness syndrome'. Historically, Russians have compared the status of their state to the greatest power of the day—France in the eighteenth century, Britain in the nineteenth century and Germany and the United States in the twentieth century. Shlapentokh noted opinion polls in the mid 1990s that suggested 75% of Russians were nostalgic for the Soviet Union and its superpower status. About the same number looked forward to the reappearance of Russian greatness in the future.[65] Putin famously declared the collapse of the Soviet Union as the greatest catastrophe of the twentieth century.

In preparation for the 2014 Winter Olympic Games to be held in the southern Russian city of Sochi, the organizers arranged for the Olympic torch to sail on an icebreaker to the North Pole, to travel in a submarine to the bottom of the world's largest and deepest body of fresh water, Lake Baikal, in Siberia, to scale Europe's highest peak, Mount Elbrus in the Caucasus, and even to fly to the International Space Station as it orbited the earth. The longest torch relay in the history of the Olympic Games was designed to showcase the size, importance, and civilizational achievement of Russia. This is the 'greatness syndrome' in action.

Underpinning this book is an argument that alternative history should be viewed, at least in part, as an act of therapy or emotional management. Understandably, most academics take a patronizing tone when dealing with the fantastic claims made by nationalistic pseudo-historians. Eric Hobsbawm has described this type of history as the intellectual equivalent of poppy-growers supplying a gullible public with dangerous drugs.[66] Karl Marx, Hobsbawm's intellectual forebear, also deployed narcotic imagery to explain the effects of a powerful ideology or discourse. Marx described religion as the 'opium of the people', although he seems to have had in mind

---

64 David Brandenberger, 'A new Short Course? A. V. Filippov and the Russian state's search for a 'usable past' ' *Kritika* 10.4 (2009): 825–833.
65 Dmitrii Shlapentokh, 'Is the greatness Syndrome Eroding?', *The Washington Quarterly* 25:1 (January 1, 2002): p. 132.
66 Eric Hobsbawm, Introduction in Eric Hobsbawm and Terence Ranger (eds), *The Invention of Tradition* (Cambridge: Cambridge University Press, 1983), p. 13.

religion's capacity to offer comfort to a damaged world rather than its potential for numbing the mind.

There is no shortage of evidence that post-Communist Russian society has undergone major convulsions since 1991, and that many Russians have experienced the loss of empire and the ensuing decline of Russia as a great power as a 'psychological injury'.[67] Putin spoke for many when he complained in 2007 of the distress and confusion, the 'porridge in the head' (*kasha v golove*), that the endless debates and competing interpretations of history that emerged after the collapse of the Soviet Union had caused the Russian people.[68] Alternative history is an attempt to rescue Russia from this intellectual and psychological morass.

The psychological injury felt by many Russians in the wake of the collapse of the Soviet state has deep cultural roots. In her study of the rituals of socialist realism, Katerina Clark has noted that one of the favorite plots of Soviet novels of the 1930s was that of orphans in search of parents. The message was that 'the child without a father is…a child without an identity'.[69] The historian, Yuri Slezkine, who grew up in Russia, has recalled:

> Children often fantasize about discovering an enviable set of 'real parents'; nations can do something about it. One popular strategy is simply to lay claim to more prestigious progenitors (Noah's sons and Herodotus's distant tribes, e.g., have proven their usefulness on numerous occasions); another is to boost the status of existing ones (my own Russian ancestors, I learned in grade (sic) school, had invented the radio, airplane, steam locomotive, and light bulb, while also defending their neighbors from barbarian invasions).[70]

Russia has often been described as the quintessential 'patrimonial state', that is a state that resembles a family with an all-powerful father at its head. With the sudden and simultaneous disintegration of the Soviet fatherland (*otechestvo*) and motherland (*rodina*), these old certainties disappeared in

---

67 Victor Shnirelman, 'Russian Response. Archaeology, Russian Nationalism, and the "Arctic Homeland"' in Philip L. Kohl et al, *Selective Remembrances: Archaeology in the Construction, Commemoration, and Consecration of National Pasts* (Chicago: University of Chicago Press, 2007), p. 34.
68 See Leon Aron, 'The Problematic Pages', *New Republic*, 239 (5) 2008, pp. 35–41.
69 Katerina Clark, *The Soviet novel: history as ritual* (Bloomington: Indiana University Press, 2000), p. 135.
70 Yuri Slezkine, 'Who Gets the Past: Competition for Ancestors Among Non-Russian Intellectuals in Russia (book review)', *The Journal of Modern History* 70: 3 (September 1998): p. 754.

the 1990s and a frantic search for new parents in the shape of prestigious and ancient ancestors began.

Therapy involves talking through issues and problems, often with the aim of raising a fragile individual's self-esteem. Rather than typecasting themselves as powerless victims, patients undergoing therapy are advised to re-assert their identity and to take control of their destiny. Something similar appears to be occurring at a societal level in Russia since the collapse of Communism. The anthropologist Sergei Oushakine has described how Russians responded to the rapid and often bewildering changes in their lives not by disengaging from politics and history, but by developing new conversations about these hitherto tightly controlled areas of discourse. For Oushakine, ordinary people sought new narratives to make sense of their lives by attempting 'to rediscover real national values, uncontaminated by the logic of the market   .to overcome the corrupt and false present'.[71] These narratives sought out the 'missing links' and 'hidden structures' that state authorities had long suppressed. This was the perfect psychological environment for alternative history.

At least part of the appeal of alternative historians lies in their broad, 'fresh', perspectives and their self-proclaimed patriotic motives. Alternative history rejects the conventional historian's cautious world with its shades of grey, hair-splitting and multiple interpretations. The Russia described in the pages of alternative history was feared and envied. Brutally effective on the battlefield, this fantastical Russia was also sophisticated, benevolent and humane, a beacon to humanity. For those nostalgic for the powerful and multinational Russian Empire and Soviet Union, convinced of Russia's civilizational mission as a 'Third Rome' or Communist utopia, or seeking answers to present-day problems in the myths and legends of the ancient past, alternative history has the capacity both to comfort and to inspire. The message of alternative history is clear: Russia in the past was great, the greatest of the civilizational entities that have appeared on the pages of world history.

It should also be noted that Russians are used to viewing politics through the prism of a conspiracy. Conspiracy theories often revolve around the mythologization of state power and the idea that a small group of actors are

---

71 Sergei Ooushakine, '"Stop the Invasion!": Money, Patriotism, and Conspiracy in Russia', *Social Research*, 76.1 (Spring 2009), pp. 71–116.

able to use that power to achieve their desires.[72] Many scholars would argue that in Russia the concept of powerful actors working in secret is not just a mythology about state power, but also a well-established 'deep structure' of Russian history. Long before Communism, Russian rulers habitually 'personalized' power by building tight-knit patronage groups in place of the rule of law, tightly controlled information, and conducted their business in secret.

Conspiracy narratives have long dominated political discourse in Russia. Tsarist authorities encouraged the publication of *the Protocols of the Elders of Zion*, the most influential forgery of the twentieth century, with its 'revelation' of a dark, sinister and global plot. The Soviet state constantly warned its citizens that various Western powers were plotting against Russia. In 1937–38, Stalin ordered the execution of nearly seven hundred thousand 'enemies of the people' whose crimes included their alleged connection to foreign governments and their security services.

Russian nationalists continue to stress the existential threat posed by the plot against Russia. The claim is often made, for example, that successive Russian governments have never truly ruled in the interests of ethnic Russians. Pro-German Romanovs, 'Jewish' Bolsheviks and the transition to Western-style capitalism under Yeltsin and Putin are cited as evidence that the 'true' Russian government is yet to come. Only when the plot against Russia has been uncovered and revealed for what it is can Russia proceed on the road to recovery and regain both its former glory and its lost empire. This is the 'closure' that alternative history offers.

Critics claim that building a Russian identity by means of an imaginary history will simply inflame ethno-nationalism and territorial disputes in ways that harm Russia's long-term interests. It is certainly true that the readers of alternative history are bombarded with the claim that Russia is the victim of a fiendish international plot. They are likely to gain a sense that their history, and therefore their identity, has been stolen from them. Frank Furedi has described the attractiveness and the danger of modern 'therapy culture' in the Western world in the following terms:

> In a fatalistic fashion, we are increasingly advised to interpret all of our current problems as the inevitable outcomes of past events. History is used as a form of

---

[72] For a discussion of these and many other aspects of conspiratorial thinking, see Ortmann and Heathershaw, 'Conspiracy Theories in the Post-Soviet Space', pp. 552–559.

therapy. Sadly, for some people what really matters is not what they accomplish today, but what happened to them a long time ago. The construction of identity through the therapeutic management of history is talked about as a brave effort to correct past wrongs and to express oneself in a new, dramatic fashion.[73]

It is a warning that has relevance to the post-Soviet space, and not just to Russia. There is a danger that history as therapy encourages a sense of victimhood; it is a call to change the past, rather than confront present challenges. On the other hand, the writers of alternative history hope to galvanize their readers to such a degree that they will indeed confront present challenges armed with the knowledge of a (mythological) past. The intensification of their efforts at the present time is no accident. It is precisely now, two decades after the collapse of Communism, that the Putin administration has become serious about the need for a new and official version of history.

---

[73] Frank Furedi, *Therapy Culture: Cultivating Vulnerability in an Uncertain Age* (London: Routledge, 2003).

Chapter Two: 'Porridge in the Head': Why a New Future needs a New Past

'Blind patriotism has been kept intact by rewriting history to provide people with moral consolation and a psychological basis for denial.'

William H. Boyer

In Russia, the future always begins with rewriting the past, and the current situation is no exception. At the moment, different concepts of Russia's past are competing with attempts to define Russian national identity and the country's future. Inasmuch as history is open to different interpretations, it continues to be ideologized and remains a battlefied where different political forces and social groups are contending for victory or revenge. Historical facts, myths, and symbols in this contest are reinterpreted and invented to control collective memory and to justify contemporary politics.[74]

In their seemingly quixotic battle with the academic establishment, alternative historians continue to research tirelessly and publish at a furious pace. For more than two decades, new historical 'evidence', as sensational as it is dubious, has been served up to curious and confused Russian readers on a daily basis. The overarching theme in the production of this new information remains the crisis of Russian identity. Who are the Russians, after all? The related sub themes of a long lost Russian historical greatness and a timeless conspiracy against Russia are aimed at constructing, or reconstructing, a Russian national identity firmly rooted in the past. But why should anybody outside of Russia care about this bizarre, albeit colorful, rewriting of Russian and world history? The answer is that the Russian state itself is in a state of transition and debates about history are a crucial part of this transition.

Russia is arguably the most enduring and successful imperial project of the last four hundred years.[75] The myth that Russians successfully managed such an empire without the exploitation or racism typical, for example, of the British Empire, is a matter of pride among patriotic Russians. Of course,

---

[74] Khazanov, A, 'Ethnic nationalism in the Russian Federation', *Daedalus*, summer 1997, v126, i3.

[75] William Wohlforth, 'The Russian-Soviet Empire: a test of neo-realism', *Review of International Studies*, 27.5, 2001, p. 27.

non-Russian subjects of the Russian Empire and its Soviet successor often took a different view. What is clear is that the legacy of hundreds of years of empire has exerted a strong influence upon the Russian historical imagination. It is arguably the most serious stumbling block to Russia's transition from the last of the polyglot empires to a modern nation-state.

The empire created by Moscow after the expulsion of the Mongols in the fifteenth century was strikingly autocratic with seemingly limitless power placed in the hands of the tsar. Early European travellers to the Muscovite court assumed that this distinctive Russian polity reflected a character flaw, that is, an unnatural slave mentality characteristic of the Russians.[76] Scholars have tended to view the distinctiveness of Russian politics through a different lens. Systemic factors or 'path-dependency' largely determined the massive expansion of Russia after 1480. The nature of Russia's politics tended to reflect the exigencies of maintaining the world's largest land empire rather than the slavish character of the Russians.

Russia's geography and history conspired to favour a highly militarized state organized around service to the tsar. The Eurasian plain stretches from the North Sea to the Pacific Ocean; there are no natural barriers to prevent migration or invasion. The Ural Mountains supposedly represented a dividing line between Europe and Asia but this mountain range nowhere exceeds two thousand meters in height. Navigable rivers crisscross European Russia, Ukraine, and Siberia. Existential threats to Russia appeared in each and every century. At various points in its history, Russia was in danger of becoming an appendage of neighboring powers including Sweden, the Ottoman Empire, and Poland-Lithuania. Russia's rulers neutralized potential threats using a strategy of continuously expanding, co-opting local elites, garrisoning conquered lands, and brutally suppressing rebellions.[77]

It was not just the absence of natural frontiers, but also the fact that its peasant population produced barely enough food for its own subsistence that challenged Russia's rulers. The soil north of the steppe is much poorer than that of Western Europe and the winters are much longer and colder. To extract the necessary resources to sustain an enormous garrison state, Russia's rulers preferred an autocratic style of government that invested

---

[76] Marshall Poe, *A People Born to Slavery, Russia in early modern European ethnography, 1476–1748* (Ithaca: Cornell University Press, 2000).

[77] Stefan Hedlund, 'Vladimir the Great, Grand Prince of Muscovy: Resurrecting the Russian Service State', *Europe-Asia Studies*, 58.5 (July 2006), pp. 775–801.

enormous power in the tsar.[78] The obligation of nobles and peasants alike was to serve the tsar in their different ways. The nobles became soldiers and tax collectors, while the peasants were enserfed. Official propaganda sang the praises of empire and its unaccountable ruler.[79]

While power changed hands from the Rurikid to the Romanov dynasty in 1613, and from the Romanovs to the Communists in 1917, the Russian service state proved enduring. This explains why useful comparisons can be made connecting Putin's image to that of the tsars or Stalin's collectivization to the serfdom of the tsarist era. The only thing that changed was how the service state chose to represent itself to its people and rival states. The question that arose in 1991 was whether Russia would finally escape its past or reconstitute another version of the service state. So far Russia has not followed the liberal script of an inevitable transition to capitalism and democracy. The other side of the coin to nationalism was liberalism, at least in Europe. As one observer has put it, Russia's 'middle class has preferred to integrate itself into the regime's service class'.[80]

If writers such as Hellie and Eklund are correct, the decision has been made and the service state is being recreated in the opening decades of the twenty-first century. At the same time, the prospect of Russia positioning itself as a political and military ally of the West appears to be receding. While in the early 1990s, Russian foreign policy was supposedly aimed at a new non-ideological, 'normal' pursuit of Russia's national interests, discourses of Russia's *sonderweg* and Eurasian destiny dominated in the late 1990s. Evgenii Primakov, Russia's Prime Minister in 1998–1999, was the leading advocate of Russia becoming a Eurasian global power. While the goal remains elusive, the Russian government appears more and more determined to move in this direction. Putin has proposed the creation of a Eurasian Union, an obvious attempt to offer an alternative to the European Union. Taken together with Russia's strong support for the Collective Security Treaty Organisation (CSTO), it seems clear that Putin has in mind a much more integrated and effective political and military partnership for the

---

78 Richard Hellie, 'The Structure of Russian Imperial History. Toward a Dynamic Model', *History and Theory*, 44 (December 2005), 88–112, p. 39.
79 See Stefan Hedlund, 'Vladimir the Great'.
80 See Shevtsova, 'The Next Russian Revolution'.

post-Soviet space.[81] Putin often speaks of the need to balance against the unipolar power of the United States; Russia's attempts to build strategic partnerships with central Asia, China, India, Turkey, Iran and the Arab world are part of the plan to restore a multi polar world.

Putin may well imagine that the strategic hub of this geopolitical and civilizational alternative to the West will be Moscow. If a Eurasian Union becomes a reality, it will inevitably lead to a loss of sovereignty for those states that join Russia. Meanwhile, Putin has used Russia's oil and gas revenues to improve and reform the armed forces. Although still plagued by chronic problems, Russia's armed forces are undergoing an expensive modernisation. More importantly, the strategic defense component has been renewed with the rockets and materiel that at least make it appear that Russia is ready and, if necessary, willing, to fight a global war. Putin has cultivated partnerships and clients everywhere, from Ukraine and Armenia to Kazakhstan, China, and India.

The Shanghai Co-operation Organisation (SCO) founded in 2001 comprises China, Russia, Kazakhstan, Kirgizia, Tadzhikistan, and Uzbekistan. The Collective Security Treaty Organisation established in 2002 and including Russia along with eight other former Soviet republics, established a rapid reaction corps in 2008 so that they could cooperate more effectively in a war against drug traders, terrorists, separatists, and other political extremists. In the manner of Peter the Great, it is possible that Russia will learn from the West. Sending tanks to Budapest and Prague as Khrushchev and Brezhnev did in 1956 and 1968, did not work in the long term. Putin appears to hope that the 'new oil road led by Russia' will lead to 'a new order in the Eurasian continent'.[82] Just as France and Germany have been able to exert power while still working within the rules of the political and economic framework established by the European Union, Russia might achieve something similar by drawing the economies of the states that once constituted the Soviet Union into closer cooperation. Those who dream of a renewal of Russian greatness hope that Russian oil and gas and the relative

---

81 Mark Katz, 'Primakov Redux? Putin's Pursuit of "Multipolarism" in Asia', *Democratizatsiya*, 14.1 (Winter 2006), 144–152, Teemu Naarajarvi, 'China, Russia and Shanghai Cooperation Organisation: blessing or curse for new regionalism in Central Asia?', *Asia Europe Journal* 10 (2012) 113–126, p. 114.

82 Yeongmi Yun and Kicheol Park, 'An Analysis of the Multilateral Cooperation and Competitin between Russia and China in the Shanghaii Cooperation Organization: Issues and Prospects', *Pacific Focus*, XXVII: 1 (April 2012) 62–85, p. 62.

wealth of Moscow may yet prove seductive to the Soviet Union's 'lost' republics.

What has been missing so far in Putin's efforts to fashion a post-Communist Russian empire is a political narrative. The social anthropologists Lottman and Uspenskii have described how even though the basic system—the service state—remained in place, the image and discourse of the new regime were invariably presented as radically different to the outgoing regime. Thus, 'the deep structure of the preceding regime is preserved but completely renamed, while all the fundamental structural contours of the old are preserved'.[83] This then is the trick for those in power. They aim to preserve the service state while advertising their regime as something new and positive. So far, Russia's post-Communist leaders have proved singularly unsuccessful in 'renaming' their new order.

When Communism collapsed and the new Russian state was established in 1991, there were half-hearted attempts at galvanizing popular opinion around a new sense of what it meant to be Russian. President Yeltsin appointed an expert committee 'to establish the true nature of Russia', and newspapers offered prizes for 'the best definition of Russianness'.[84] Nonetheless, the 1990s came and went without any clear answer from the state as to who the Russians were and what Russia stood for. Even Putin when he emerged as Yeltsin's protégé and likely successor in 1999 portrayed himself as a technocrat rather than as an ideologue.

What Putin and his administration failed to develop was some sort of overarching narrative to inspire popular support. As Graham Gill has put it, the presidential administrations of Yeltsin and Putin failed 'to articulate a consistent narrative embodying a vision of either Russia's future or of how it was to be constituted .... No presidential vision has become embedded in the public lore of the society'.[85] Instead of a widely accepted national idea' that described Russia's new circumstances and inspired enthusiasm among ordinary people, an ideological void emerged, which was soon filled by a cacophony of competing voices that ranged from Communists to ultra-nationalists, from the Orthodox Church to neo-Pagan occultists, and from

---

[83] Quoted in J. Arch Getty, *Practicing Stalinism : Bolsheviks, Boyars, and the Persistence of Tradition*, p. 10.
[84] Riasonovsky, *Russian identities*, p. 231.
[85] Graham Gill, *Symbolism and Regime Change in Russia* (Cambridge: Cambridge University Press, 2012), p. 212.

Eurasianist empire builders to national separatists. Russia's rulers soon came to fear that they might have built their new state upon the ideological equivalent of quicksand.

It is this fear of having no firm historical foundation in place that lies behind the increasingly desperate efforts of Putin and his allies, from the mid 2000s, to write a 'usable history' that explains and justifies the new post-Communist Russia. We get a sense of how important the post-Communist elites view the writing of history from the reflections of Putin himself. From Putin downwards, there is little patience with the multiplicity of views and competing interpretations that are the stock-in-trade of conventional history writing. In 2007, Putin told a gathering of schoolteachers that there was a need for a new primer in Russian History to overcome the confusion and errors contained in the dozens of school texts then in use.

The result was a text credited to Fillipov that became notorious among its liberal critics for reinventing Stalin as an effective state builder who made occasional mistakes. The logic of this text implied that authoritarian rather than liberal rule worked best for Russia. Leon Aron has argued that Putin and his administration's understanding of history can be summarized in two axioms:

> The first axiom appears to be this: although there were 'mistakes' and 'dark spots', what mattered was the survival and strengthening of the state—by whatever means necessary. And by that standard, the Soviet Union was a glittering success, and the costs were justified...the second axiom of modern Russian history according to Putin is that the Soviet Union was a 'besieged fortress', forever under the threat of attack by the West, and that the machinations of the West were responsible not only for Soviet foreign policy but also for a great deal of domestic misfortune. The overarching aim of this and all future historical narratives is the 'normalisation' of the monstrosity of Soviet totalitarianism, the manufacture of justifications and excuses for its crimes.[86]

As Brandenberger has put it, Fillipov's textbook did not explicitly rehabilitate Stalin, but rather established the justification for authoritarian rule. Russia's survival depended upon a '500-year political tradition which demanded that power be concentrated in the hands of a single, autocratic ruler and his centralized administrative system'.[87] Thus, Russian unity and strength from

---

[86] Aron, 'The Problematic Pages', p. 38.
[87] Brandenberger, 'A New Short Course?,' p. 826.

above will better safeguard Russian national interests than grassroots political parties, social movements, or civic organizations.[88]
In 2009, President Medvedev declared that Russia's history had undergone a process of falsification during the 2000s, and that in recent times the attacks from abroad had become more angry and aggressive.[89] His answer to this problem was to establish the Presidential Commission of the Russian Federation to Counter Attempts to Falsify History to the Detriment of Russia's Interests, which would operate from 15 May 2009 to 14 February 2012. Putin and Medvedev entrusted staunch allies from their political retinue with the task of fashioning this history. Key figures in these efforts are the Speaker of the Duma and Chairman of the Russian Historical Society, Sergei Naryshkin, and the Minister of Culture and Chairman of the Russian Military-Historical Society, Vladimir Medinskii. The president of the Commission charged with protecting Russian history was Naryshkin. No doubt conscious of the accusations of Orwellian thought control that the Commission would attract, Naryshkin assured his listeners that his organization never intended to make historians speak with one voice. Instead, the Commission's aim was to rebut the harmful propaganda that had been directed at Russia as a result of the rewriting of history in other countries.
Like Fillipov's textbook, Naryshkin's commission signalled the regime's intentions but did not immediately solve the problem. Obviously dissatisfied with the results of previous attempts to end the 'porridge in the head', the re-elected President Putin in 2013 outlined yet another attempt to establish a new historical regime. He ordered the Ministry of Education, the Russian Academy of Sciences, and the Historical Society to collaborate in producing textbooks without 'contradictions and ambiguities'.[90] The textbooks are expected to emphasise patriotism, Russian Orthodoxy, civic mindedness (*grazhdanstvennost*), the multi ethnic nature of Russia, and its mighty civilisational and martial achievements.
Happily, some of this work was already being undertaken at a popular level. Alternative history is much too radical to be embraced in full by government officials, let alone Putin. Yet, as we shall see, there is good reason for think-

---

88 Brandenberger, 'A New Short Course?,' p. 826.
89 Laruelle, 'Conspiracy and Alternate History in Russia,' p. 566.
90 See, for example, Oleg Sukhov, 'Putin Says State History Texts Will Not Impose Ideology', *Moscow Times*, 17 January 2014 and Leon Aron, 'The Kremlin's Propaganda Campaign and Russia's Regression', *The American*, 24 October 2013.

ing that Putin and his ideologues are borrowing ideas from alternative history to populate their own hitherto dreary, unimaginative, and, often, absent narrative about what post-Communist Russia stands for. It is not too much to suggest that alternative history and regime propaganda are moving in the same direction, just at different speeds.

Putin's propagandists have recently discovered what has been well described in the scholarly literature as 'civilizational nationalism'.[91] Russia's imperial restoration will need ideas and enthusiasm, and not just oil and gas. Thus:

> The Kremlin's canonization of the idea of a special thousand-year-old civilization that predetermines a "special path" for Russia is gradually elevating to the rank of an official "one true doctrine" to replace Marxism–Leninism. An army of paid and unpaid propagandists are mining this vein of gold, turning a theory into a political technology.[92]

This 'army of paid and unpaid propagandists' contains a good many regiments of alternative historians and the readers with whom they are in conversation. Precisely because of its unabashed nationalism, alternative history has foreshadowed the type of 'political technology' that Putin and his administration is likely to deploy in order to resolve the complicated issue of Russian identity. A radicalized ethno-nationalism might yet shape public opinion in unpredictable ways, enhancing the potential for a new Russian Revolution. Tamed and harnessed, however, 'civilizational nationalism' may provide the glue that the present administration needs to maintain its grip on power.

---

91 Verkhovskii and Pain, 'Civilizational Nationalism'.
92 Verkhovskii and Pain, 'Civilizational Nationalism', p. 56.

Chapter Three: Empire, nation, nationalism

'The most effective way to destroy people is to deny and obliterate their own understanding of their history.'

George Orwell

Part One: Russia's Multiple Identities

To make sense of alternative history, we first need to explore in more detail Russia's identity crisis. Fomenko entitled his major work *Imperiia* or Empire, a word that has much more positive connotations in Russia than it does in the West. Empire, for Fomenko and for many Russians, means the repository of political and economic power projected across a huge geographic era. This meaning is very different to Lenin's concept of exploited and subjugated colonial peoples. This positive view of the imperial past is reflected in the fact that the overwhelming majority of Russians have found it impossible to distinguish between Russia as nation-state and Russia as empire. Thus the term 'nationalism', in the context of Russia, is a problematic one.

The growing vitality of nationalism has been one of the most remarked upon aspects of the post-Communist history of Eastern Europe and the former Soviet Union.[93] The context for Fomenko is the collapse in 1991 of the Soviet Union, the Communist state that more or less occupied the territory inherited from the Tsarist Empire. The Soviet Union's principal successor state, the Russian Federation, is the world's largest state even if it is only half the size of its Communist and Tsarist predecessors. Politically and geographically, modern Russia occupies the same space today as it did approximately three hundred years ago in the era of Peter the Great. Since the collapse of Communism, Russian intellectuals and political commentators have sought out solid ground in order to make sense of Russia's new geography and its diminished place in the hierarchy of the world's great powers.

---

93 See Charles Kupchan, 'Introduction. Nationalism Resurgent' in C Kupchan (ed.), *Nationalism and Nationalities in the New Europe* (Ithaca: Cornell University Press, 1995), pp. 1–15.

Soviet ethnographers counted 194 nationalities in 1926, 97 in 1939, 126 in 1959 and 92 in 1979.[94] For its supporters, the Russian Empire and its Soviet successor represented an alternative to the nation-state of Western Europe and to the exploitative and individualistic Western model of society.[95] To the dismay of those who saw the Soviet Union and the Russian Empire in positive terms, not one of the former Soviet republics, or former Tsarist provinces, chose unity or federation with Russia after 1991. Of the 104 named nationalities in the former Soviet Union, fifteen obtained statehood in 1991. The largest of the new states, the Russian Federation, is a patchwork of at least fifty-three ethnic groups.

For those who desire that Russia make the transition from empire to nation-state, this shrinking was a positive development. The Russian Federation is much more Russian than its Tsarist and Soviet predecessors. In the Tsarist and Soviet periods, Russians constituted only about half the population of the state whereas about 80% of the post-Communist Russian Federation is ethnically Russian. At the same time, Russia is more firmly placed in the Asian part of the Eurasian land mass than it ever was during Tsarist or Soviet times. With the breakup of the Soviet Union, Russia lost its recently acquired borderlands and its Slavic heartland of Ukraine and Belarus. It is by no means clear that the shrinking of the territory under the control of Moscow has come to an end. Secessionist movements in the Caucasus are the most obvious example of the potential for further disintegration.

As for why alternative historians have made such fantastic claims about Russia, it must be remembered that Russian alternative history is in competition with the alternative history of other national groups. The writers under consideration in this book have found themselves in a contest with their counterparts in Ukraine, Central Asia, and the Turkic peoples within the Russian Federation. Popular, as distinct from state-inspired, chauvinism was frowned upon both in Tsarist and Soviet times. Only in the last two decades has nationalism become part of a public conversation about the merits of rival ethnic histories.[96] As Shnirelman has put it:

> For people who believe they have been deprived of their cultural legacy, invention of the past becomes a powerful instrument—first, for the raising of self-esteem and the re-evaluation of their position among other peoples, and second,

---

94 Basile Kerblay, *Modern Soviet Society* (London: Methuen, 1983), p. 39.
95 McDaniel, *The Agony of the Russian Idea*, pp. 22–23.
96 Shnirelman, 'Russian Response'.

for demanding special rights and privileges with respect to others who lack their glorious past...[97]

Since the 1980s, a huge literature has developed around terms such as patriotism, nations, and nationalism. Patriotism seems less problematic and can be defined as strongly positive feelings towards one's homeland.[98] As for the term 'nation', Hobsbawm distinguishes between the nation as citizenship, 'in which the nation consists of collective sovereignty based in common political participation', and the nation as ethnicity, 'in which the nation comprises all those of supposedly common language, history, or broader cultural identity'.[99] Gellner came up with the most enduring definition of nationalism itself when he wrote that 'Nationalism is primarily a political principle which holds that the political and the national unit should be congruent'.[100] While definitions are important, assigning ethnic groups to a particular homeland has proved more challenging.

Russian identity is a distinctive puzzle within the wider debate. It is so puzzling that Tolz has recommended a close reading of the three main approaches to the study of nationalism.[101] The first approach is the primordialism common among practitioners of nationalism. They claim that Russians have always been as enthusiastically loyal to their country as they are today. They point to the classics of medieval Russian literature to make their point. A much-quoted example is *The Lay of Igor's Host*, an appeal to a sense of collectivity among the peoples of Kiev Rus in connection to a military campaign against the neighboring Polovtsi in 1186. The unknown author of *The Lay of Igor's Host* lamented the defeat of Prince Igor, and summoned princes from beyond Kiev to come forward to fight for the land of Rus as if it were their land too.[102] These same patriots claim that anti-German feelings among the Slavs can be traced back at least to the famous plea made in 1659 by Krizanic, a Croat and Roman Catholic priest, who appealed to Tsar

---

97 Shnirelman, *Who Gets the Past*, p. 2.
98 See, for example, David Brandenberger, *National Bolshevism: Stalinist Mass Culture and the formation of modern Russian national identity, 1931–1956* (Cambridge: Harvard University press, MA, 2002), pp. 12–13.
99 Verdery, 'Whither "nation" and "nationalism"?' pp. 37–38.
100 For a discussion, see David Rowley, 'Imperial versus nationalist Discourse: the case of Russia,' *Nations and Nationalism* 6:1 (2000) p. 24.
101 Tolz, *Russia*, p. 4.
102 'Slovo o pogibeli Russkoi zemli' in *Drevnerusskaia literatura* (Moscow: Shkola, 1993), p. 135.

Alexis 'to succor the Trans-Danubians, Poles and Czechs, to begin to know their oppressed and shameful state and to think about the enlightenment of the people that they might take the German yoke from their necks'.[103] Primordialists tend to favour an ethnic model of nationalist political practice.

The second approach to nationalism is the 'nation as a modern phenomenon' idea advocated by most scholars. Gellner traced nationalism to the need for an emerging industrial society in the nineteenth century to find a means of connecting individuals who had abandoned the collectivist principles of the village. Benedict Anderson's 'imagined communities' arose from the coming of print culture, which made it possible for utter strangers to think of themselves as kin. Anthony D. Smith and Adrian Hastings make a concession to primordialism when they argue that the roots of nationalism, proto-nationalism, extend deep into history.[104] The pre-modern attachment to an *ethnie*, in Smith's view, resembled and to an extent gave rise to the modern sense of national identity. Still, Smith insists that nations are different to *ethnie* because they are more complex and rely upon citizenship, economic integration, and a collective's consciousness of being part of a particular nation. This second approach to nationalism is more amenable to the notion that nationalism can be joined to a civic, rather than an ethnic model of political practice.

The third, post-modernist, approach stresses the importance of discourses of nationalism and not simply the list of objective criteria modernists usually apply to test the presence of nationalism. This issue is especially relevant to Russia where nationalism is the ideology that refuses to speak its name. Very few Russians to this day have ever described themselves as nationalists. As Yanov has put it, 'even the most reactionary nationalist forces... never call themselves nationalists, only 'patriots'.[105] Tishkov has pointed out that 'In Russia, nationalism is understood exclusively as ethnic nationalism—and that with a strongly negative connotation'.[106]

What is called Russian nationalism is often better described as Russian imperialism.[107] Hosking notes that the most important fact about Russian his-

---

103 See Michael Boro Petrovich, *The Emergence of Russian Panslavism, 1856–1870* (New York: Columbia University Press, 1956), p. 7.
104 Adrian Hastings, *The construction of nationhood: ethnicity, religion, and nationalism* (Cambridge: Cambridge University Press, 1997).
105 Yanov, 'Russian nationalism in Western studies', p. 562.
106 Tishkov, *Ethnicity, Nationalism and Conflict in and after the Soviet Union*, p. 230.
107 Rowley, 'Imperial versus Nationalist Discourse', p. 25.

tory was that in Russia 'the empire has always oppressed the nation. State building has impeded nation building'.[108] Nationalism was triumphant in Europe in 1918 everywhere except Russia. Before World War One, ethnic minorities comprised approximately half of most European states. After World War One, this figure was reduced to a quarter.[109] The Russian Empire, by contrast, more or less became the Soviet Union minus Finland, Poland, the Baltic States and Bessarabia. Thus, the Russians remained part of an imperial world, forming only half the population of the land they dominated.

The longevity of the Russian Empire was no accident. Peter the Great is widely credited with having been the creator of the modern Russian state, the revolutionary who waged war against an out-dated medieval system of government, church and customs. The service state that emerged was aimed at ensuring Russia's competitiveness in the struggle for mastery of northern Europe. Part of Peter the Great's legacy was a Westernized elite divorced from a mainly traditionalist and rural population.[110] Neither this elite nor Peter's successors could envisage Russia as anything other than an empire.

After Peter, it took another century for Russian rulers to formulate an official vision of what Russia was. Under Tsar Nicholas the First and his Minister for Education, Uvarov, the trinity of 'Autocracy, Orthodoxy and Narodnost' was coined. *Narodnost'* is deliberately vague in the way it evokes a bond between the peoples of Russia and the land they occupy. It was in effect an antidote to nations within the Russian empire seeking their own states. Its aim was to bind the people of Russia together by suggesting that they were special and morally superior to the West.[111]

The earliest Russian historians, Tatishchev, Lomonosov and Karamzin, were all fervent monarchists whose histories were directed towards explaining and justifying the emergence of imperial power in Russia. Tatishchev thought that Russia would develop into a single community rallied around

---

108 Geoffrey Hosking, 'The Russian Myth; Empire and People', in Duncan and Rady (eds), *Towards a New Community: Culture and Politics in Post-Totalitarian Europe* (Hamburg and Munster: LIT Verlag), p. 37.
109 Khazanov, 'Ethnic nationalism in the Russian Federation', p. 121.
110 McDaniel, *The Agony of the Russian Idea*, p. 10.
111 Nicholas Riasanovsky, *Nicholas I and official nationality in Russia, 1825–1855* (Berkeley: University of California Press, 1959), pp. 266–72.

the rule of law and monarchy.[112] Tatishchev's aim was to offer an image of empire to the newly acquired lands as the only way to consolidate Russia's restive frontier.[113] Karamzin, Russia's most popular nineteenth–century historian, praised the Romanovs who well knew that 'our ancestors, while assimilating many advantages which were to be found in foreign customs, never lost the conviction that an Orthodox Russian was the most perfect citizen and Holy Rus' the foremost state in the world'.[114]

Nor did history writing fall under the influence of Western-style nationalism in the remainder of the nineteenth century. Black's study of the state school historians of the nineteenth century concluded that Karamzin, Soloviev, Kavelin and Kliuchevskii were united in their Great Russian patriotism.[115] Soloviev famously denounced the Mongol invaders as an unmitigated evil, a plague that devastated Russia economically and spiritually. Fiercely patriotic, Soloviev was a believer in empire as the best defence against another catastrophe like the Mongol invasion.[116] Kliuchevskii is arguably the most popular and the most liberal of the nineteenth-century Russian historians in both Russia and the West, but he wrote about Russians, Belorusians and Ukrainians as if there were no differences between them, all part of a single Russia tied to the Russian land.[117] Russians who read history would have come to the conclusion that Russia needed an empire.

Meanwhile, the tsars rejected any form of nationalism among their subjects as potentially dangerous to the regime. The resistance of Tatars and Bashkirs was put down with much severity and labeled as the rebellion of bandits and thieves. The Tsar was the steward of the peoples of this land, an image that tapped into the oldest form of customary practice or group instinct. This approach profited also from the belief that foreigners, whether from east or west, were evil. The iron curtain of medieval Russia that West European

---

112 Rudolph Daniels, *V N Tatishchev, Guardian of the Petrine Revolution* (Philadelphia: Franklin Publishing Company), p. 95.
113 Daniels, *Tatishchev*, p. 65.
114 Edward C Thaden, *The Rise of Historicism in Russia* (New York: Peter Land, 1999), p. 17.
115 Joseph Lawrence Black, 'The State School Interpretation of Russian History: A reappraisal of its genetic origins,' *Jahrbucher for Geschichte Osteuropas* 21 (1973): p. 521.
116 Soloviev, *Istoriia Rossii s drevneishikh vremen*, volume II, p. 489; volume IV, p. 179.
117 Robert Byrnes, *V. O. Kliuchevskii. Historian of Russia* (Bloomington: Indiana University Press, 1995), pp. 225–229; See also Vasilii Kliuchevsky, *Kurs russkoi istorii*, volume V (Moscow: 1989).

travelers wrote so much about encouraged the growth of xenophobia in Russia, which has remained a key element of Russian identity to this day.[118]

Even in the late tsarist period, Russian attempts to consolidate their state in ideological terms revolved around the strengthening of an imperial rather than a national idea. Rowley argues that what is usually regarded as Russification under Alexander the Third and Nicholas the Second from 1881 to 1905 was so half-hearted that it amounted to little more than an attempt to modernize the Russian Empire to ensure its loyalty and fitness for the next war.[119] Thus Russification was mainly directed at Ukrainians and Poles, not the peoples of the Caucasus or Central Asia. Tuminez has pointed out that 'Russification did not elicit great enthusiasm among Russians—even those who were ethnic nationalists'.[120]

The Russian tsars ended up with the worst of both worlds because Russification, however half-hearted, still provoked nationalist sentiment at the edges of empire in 1905 and 1917. As Seton Watson put it, 1905 was 'as much a revolution of the non-Russian against Russification as it was a revolution of workers, peasants and radical intellectuals against autocracy. The two revolts were, of course, connected: the social revolution was in fact most bitter in non-Russian regions, with Polish workers, Latvian peasants and Georgian peasants as protagonists'.[121] On the other hand, Russia was not sufficiently Russified to provide the necessary glue to hold Russia together in World War One. When the Tsarist regime collapsed in 1917, it disappeared almost overnight as if it were a hollow shell. The historian Vasilii Rozanov wrote in 1917: 'Russia has collapsed in two or three days ... there is no Tsardom, no Church, no army ... what is left behind? Absolutely nothing'.[122]

The Westernizers within Russia's elite have themselves routinely harboured imperial ambitions. Before 1991, the Provisional Government that replaced the tsar in March 1917 could claim to have been the only liberal government in Russia's history. Yet this government risked everything by aggressively committing itself to a new offensive in July 1917, inspired by the territorial

---

118 Marshall Poe, *A People Born to Slavery: Russia in early modern European ethnography, 1476–1748* (Ithaca: Cornell University Press, 2000).
119 Rowley, 'Imperial versus Nationalist Discourse', pp. 25–27.
120 Tuminez, *Russian Nationalism Since 1856*, p. 40.
121 Hugh Seton-Watson, *Nations and States* (London: Methuen, 1982), p. 87.
122 Vasilii Rozanov, *O Sebe i Zhizni Svoei* (Moscow: Respublika, 1990), p. 79.

rewards promised Russia after the defeat of the German, Austro-Hungarian and Ottoman Empires.[123] Leading Westernizers of this era, such as Pavel Miliukov, were as keen on Russia's imperial expansion as the tsars were. This pattern was repeated when, in the 1990s, the post-communist governments of Yeltsin and Putin went to war twice over Chechnya to prevent what they perceived to be the dismemberment of Russia at the hands of nationalist separatists. To achieve this goal of state unity by cracking down on nationalism at the periphery, Yeltsin and Putin were prepared to jettison their credentials as post-Communist liberal reformers.

Russia did produce its own conservative romantics of the type that helped to create modern nationalism in Western Europe. These were the Slavophiles who railed against Western influence in Russia and the repressions carried out under the government of Nicholas the First. From its origins in the 1830s and 40s, Slavophilism became a way of life and a moral conviction. Slavophiles derived their inspiration from the image of a golden age of pre-Petrine Russia when there were few Western influences in Russia, the bureaucracy was relatively small, and the Tsar lived, at least in theory, as a demigod in harmony with his people. Yet while critical of Peter the Great's reforms, the Slavophiles did not represent a nationalist alternative as they were firmly committed to the ideal of the Tsar and Orthodoxy as the foundations on which Russia was based as opposed to the political liberalism emanating from the West.[124] Slavophiles insisted upon the spiritual superiority of Russia and that Moscow was a Third Rome. Russia was home to all eastern Slavs, who were united by common origin and culture.[125] Dostoevsky thought the Russian soul more capable than any other of achieving 'the idea of universal union and brotherhood'.[126] This is not nationalism in the Western sense of the term.

The Bolsheviks, by contrast, described themselves as 'internationalists' who were opposed both to the old empires and to nationalism. Lenin was shrewd enough to appreciate the appeal of nationalism, declaring in 1917

---

123 Rowley, 'Imperial versus Nationalist Discourse', p. 26.
124 Rowley, 'Imperial versus Nationalist Discourse', p. 27.
125 On the Slavophiles see N. L. Brodsky (ed.), *Rannie slavianofily* (Moscow, 1910), XXX–XXXVIII; on Pan Slavists see Mark Bassin, 'Russia between Europe and Asia: The Ideological Construction of Geographical Space,' *Slavic Review* 50:1 (1991): Vladimir Soloviev, *Natsional'nyi vopros v Rossii* (St Petersburg, 1888; Nikolai Berdiaev, *Sud'ba Rossii* (St Petersburg: 1918).
126 Quoted in Rowley, 'Imperial versus Nationalist Discourse', p. 34.

that 'all nations have the right to self-determination'.[127] Of course, there was a cynical side to these appeals given that Lenin looked upon nationalism as a transitory phase in history's movement towards Communism. Yet, Lenin and Stalin were, surprisingly for Marxists, prepared to accept nations as the basic building blocks in the world in which they lived. The Soviet government went out of its way to divide its territory into nationally based regions with their own language and, where possible, ethnic bureaucracy.

Lenin was fortunate that while Ukrainian or Georgian states emerged briefly after 1917, they proved unstable and were easily toppled. Yet, as Suny has pointed out, nationalism would eventually have its revenge.[128] The Bolsheviks' decision in the early 1920s to link territoriality and ethnicity in the form of union republics helped to ensure that nationality eventually gained a new importance in a 'state of all the people'.[129] Under Stalin, the Soviet state reconfigured the nationalities policy of Nicholas the First's trinity, where autocracy was preserved in the form of Communist dictatorship, Orthodoxy was replaced with communist ideology, and narodnost' found expression in a multi-ethnic 'new Soviet man'. Brandenberger has pointed out that Soviet internationalism was transformed into Russo-centric patriotism from the mid 1930s when Stalin launched a propaganda barrage aimed at exposing the evil deeds of the German and Polish governments.[130] Stalin, however, was still extolling the virtues of a Russia-centred empire and was certainly no advocate of nationalism as it was understood in the West. Sarah Davies in her study of letters written in the 1930s noted that ordinary Russians did not seem to have a clear idea of who they were except in terms of who they were not, that is Jews, Armenians and so on.[131] Meanwhile, Stalin himself took every opportunity to be photographed posing with representatives of the Soviet borderlands as if all of Eurasia were united with him in resistance to the evil of the West.

---

127 Quoted in Nigel Harris, *National Liberation* (London: Tauris, 1990), p. 88.
128 Yuri Slezkine, 'The USSR as a Communal Apartment, or How a Socialist State promoted Ethnic Particularism,' in Geoff Eley and Ronald Grigor Suny (eds), *Becoming National: a Reader* (London: Oxford University Press, 1996), pp. 204–206.
129 Ronald Suny, *The Revenge of the Past* (Stanford: Stanford University Press, 1993), pp. 84–126.
130 Brandenberger, *National Bolshevism*, p. 109.
131 Sarah Davies, *Popular Opinion in Stalin's Russia: terror, propaganda, and dissent, 1934–1941* (Cambridge: Cambridge University Press, 1997), pp. 88–89.

If Stalin hedged his bets in the 1930s by encouraging a symbolic Russocentrism while building a revitalized garrison state that included nearly all the peoples of the former Russian Empire, much the same was true of representations of the victory over the Nazis after 1945. Stalin would single out the Russian people for their exceptional contribution to the victory, but at the same time the concept of the 'Great Patriotic War' was designed to recognize all Soviet nationalities, with the partial exception of those that the dictator had deemed disloyal and had repressed during the war. It was difficult for those growing up in the Soviet Union after the war—a category that includes many present-day writers of alternative history—to escape the impression that the strength of the Soviet Union was its authoritarian leadership presiding over a Russocentric multi-ethnic alliance.

No republic seceded from the Soviet Union until its collapse. Nonetheless, the very act of allowing Ukrainians or Georgians a homeland and the opportunity to use their native language contributed to the collapse of 1991 by creating obvious successor states. Whether the economic collapse of the Soviet Union called forth or greatly accelerated a sense of nationalism or whether long-suppressed nationalism was itself the cause of the Soviet Union's collapse is difficult to know. As his experiment with a mixed market economy collapsed around him, Gorbachev found that political elites in the non-Russian republics of the Soviet Union resorted to ethnic nationalism as a first port of call once it was clear that Communism was nearing the end of its life. According to Khazanov 'loyalty to one's nationality was stronger than loyalty to the Soviet state'.[132] On the other hand, nationalism was a convenient ideological justification for the republican elites of the old Soviet Union as they positioned themselves for independence after the collapse of Communism.

As for Russia itself, its status was always complicated by the fact that the Russian Socialist Federal Republic within the Soviet Union, unlike the national republics, did not have its own Communist Party or academic institutions. Many Russians identified themselves with the Soviet Union as if it were their nation-state.[133] Rowley has argued that the events of 1991 broke the pattern of Russian history and that Yeltsin was the first Russian politi-

---

[132] Khazanov, 'Ethnic nationalism in the Russian Federation', p. 122.
[133] Brudny, *Reinventing Russia: Russian Nationalism and the Soviet State, 1953–1991*, p. 7.

cian to successfully deploy the discourse of nationalism.[134] Historians are clearly split on this issue. Brudny has argued that Yeltsin was not a nationalist at all and his discourse of 'Russia for the Russians' was simply a manoeuvre against his rival, Gorbachev.[135] For some commentators, nationalism was the lion that did not roar in the 1990s. They compare the relatively peaceful territorial realignments in the former Soviet space compared to the violent ethno-nationalism of former Yugoslavia.[136]

Scholars are in general agreement that nationalism in Russia was less prominent as an ideology than elsewhere because of the preference of successive regimes and their educated elites for an 'imperial' identity. The establishment of new national borders after 1991 based upon the principles of civic nationalism immediately raised the question of Russia's self-identity. Would the old 'imperial' identity give way to the 'normal' civic nationalism of other nation-states? Or would Russia seek its own *sonderweg*, maintaining an imperial identity in preparation for the eventual rebuilding of some form of Russian Empire? For more than a decade, the Russian government evaded the issue, but in more recent times, a much clearer answer is beginning to emerge. The empire will be recreated, albeit on an economic and ideological basis rather than a reliance on military force. Alternative history has helped with the imagining of this new empire and why it was, as it were, foreordained to reappear.

Part Two: Civic or Imperial Nationalism

According to Geoffrey Hosking, there were four options facing the new post-Communist Russia in the 1990s. The first was to restore the Tsarist and Soviet empire. The second was to reunite with Ukrainians and Belarusians as a nation of eastern Slavs. The third was to reconstitute Russia on the basis of Russian speakers, incorporating Russian- speaking areas like northern Kazakhstan and eastern Ukraine in the process. The fourth was to

---

134 Rowley, 'Imperial versus Nationalist Discourse', pp. 35–36.
135 Brudny, *Reinventing Russia*, p. 262. See Malia, Martin, *The Soviet Tragedy. A History of Socialism in Russia, 1917–1991* (New York: The Free Press, 1994), or Astrid Tuminez, 'Nationalism, Ethnic Pressures, and the Break-up of the Soviet Union', pp. 81–136.
136 Anatol Lieven, 'The Weakness of Russian Nationalism', *Survival*, vol 41, no 2, Summer 1999, pp. 53–70.

build a Western-style nation state dedicated to the principles of civic and not ethnic nationalism.[137]

Only the Western-style nation state is a new idea in Russian history. Since 1991, the Russian Federation has defined itself in civic terms—its members are Russian citizens or *Rossiiane*, and not ethnic Russians or *Russkie*. Anyone living on the territory of the Russian Federation at the time of the law's adoption on 28 November 1991 automatically became a citizen of the Russian Federation. It was hoped that economic success and a genuinely federal structure would ensure that a murderous ethno-nationalism would not tear apart the former Soviet Union as it had done the former Yugoslavia.[138] Liberal optimism after the collapse of Communism was partly inspired by the hope of a civic nationalism that would quickly take root and that Russia would become a 'normal' nation-state in the post-Communist world.[139]

It is still not clear how successful this strategy will prove. Brudny concluded that Russia's liberal reformers squandered their opportunity when their popularity was at its height in the early 1990s to develop an inspiring ideology to legitimise democracy, market capitalism, and the pre-imperial borders of Russia.[140] Russia's ethnic minorities have used Russia's federal system to promote a suitably ethnic nationalism into their school curricula while Russian school textbooks ignore or belittle the contribution of ethnic minorities to the national history.[141] The dominating presence of Putin as President for much of the first decade of the twentieth-first century is often looked upon as proof that Russia had reverted to its autocratic and imperial roots. According to the liberal former Prime Minister Gaidar, the contest during the Putin period was over 'who will be most anti-Semitic, who will be blaming the non-Russians for Russian problems, who will be most anti-American'.[142] Critics of the 'shock therapy' approach taken by liberal economic reformers in the 1990s would respond that the reformers brought this development upon themselves.

---

137 Hosking, *Russia and the Russians*, pp. 56–7.
138 Tolz, *Russia*, p. 125.
139 Tolz, *Russia*, p. 207.
140 Brudny, *Reinventing Russia: Russian Nationalism and the Soviet State, 1953–1991*, pp. 259–65.
141 See Victor Shnirelman, 'Stigmatized by History or by Historians?: The Peoples of Russia in School History Textbooks', *History & Memory* 21.2 (2009): 110–149.
142 Quoted in 'Former PM decries Russian nationalism', *United Press International* (January 28, 2004): p. 1.

At the state level, Russia has remained steadfastly committed to building a civic version of national identity ever since the demise of Communism. The textbook that Putin has in mind for Russian schools will emphasise the multi-ethnic and multi-confessional nature of Russia and the importance of mutual respect and civility among its peoples. The strength of civic nationalism is that it offers an alternative to the endless turmoil and violence that a virulent ethno-nationalism promises to bring to Russia.

The other models of national identity listed by Hosking are hostile to the liberal/civic model. As Khazanov has put it: 'It was hard for Russia to free itself from the legacy of the empire, just as it was difficult for many Russians to free themselves from a certain empire-oriented psychology'.[143] The imperial model asserts that the Russians are, for reasons of geography and history, an imperial people whose nature is strongly shaped by their mission to create a supranational state. Imperial thinking is so pervasive that it overlaps with other categories. For Slavophiles, Russians are more spiritual than other peoples; Solzhenitsyn himself became a notable supporter of Putin's increasingly authoritarian rule.[144] For Tsarist bureaucrats and Communist Party activists, Russia was a source of enlightenment for backward neighbors. For Russian or Soviet generals, building an empire was the only guarantee of protection in a hostile environment.

Apart from the most liberal Westernizers, the only source of enthusiasm for a 'small' post-Imperial Russia comes, ironically, from the splintered neo-Nazi skinead movement. The proponents of a racial view of Russia include modern neo-Nazis, whose thuggery on the streets of the major cities and towns has achieved widespread publicity. Some commentators fear that neo-Nazism is a growing phenomenon in Russia, although overtly racist political parties remain divided and relatively unpopular. Racist groups target Central Asians and Muslim peoples of the North Caucasus as well as Jews. According to Shlapentokh, neo-Nazis are now much more interested in expelling 'alien' peoples from 'ethnically Russian' cities and territories than they are in restoring the multi-ethnic Soviet Union. Herein lies the problem for the Neo-Nazis who extol the virtues of the 'White Race' and seem to be arguing for a smaller Russia shorn of its non-Russians. The Neo-Nazis in that sense are increasingly in tune with modern definitions of nationalism

---

143 Khazanov, *After the USSR*, p. 38.
144 See R Horvath (2011) 'Apologist of Putinism? Solzhenitsyn, the Oligarchs, and the Specter of Orange Revolution', *The Russian Review* 70: pp. 300–318.

but may well suffer from further division and a loss of public support because of their hostility to empire.[145]

Part Three: Eurasianism

Rebuilding a Russian empire is not a straightforward task given that Russia itself is a predominantly Asian land with a predominantly European population. The influence of Eurasianism and the Turkic rejection of Russian imperialism need to be considered if we are to make sense of Russia's post-Communist imperial imagination. Eurasianism has attracted notoriety in the West. In 1993 when Duma elections were held, an alliance emerged between the rump of the Communist Party and a resurgent Russian nationalism.[146] After the Communists peaked in the 1996 presidential election and then receded, concern in the West focused upon Eurasianism. Eurasianism presupposes 'an organic unity of cultures born in this zone of symbiosis between Russian, Turkic, Muslim, and even Chinese worlds'.[147]

Eurasianists celebrate Russia as a multi-ethnic, multi-confessional state, an ancient entity that has always existed even if its form or name underwent superficial changes. It is an appropriate name because Eurasia suggests a people who are different to Europeans and to Asians. According to Eurasianist mythology, multi-ethnic Russia embraced Slavic, Finno-Ugric, Tatar-Turkic and even Mongolian and Iranian peoples yet in some intangible way evolved into the Russian nation after centuries of interaction between these peoples. For most Eurasianists, the measuring stick for Russian greatness was still Europe and not Asia. Russia needed Asia if it were to be a genuine competitor with the West.[148]

There were at least three phases of Eurasianism. The first was a cultural movement best represented in Alexander Blok's poetic homage to the Scyths, the people described by the ancient Greeks who occupied the area north of the Black Sea. As Blok's poem of 1918 put it, 'Just try to fight with

---

145 Dmitrii Shlapentokh, 'Russia on the Eve. The Illusions and Realities of Russian Nationalism', *The Washington Quarterly* 23:1 (2000): 173–186.
146 See, for example, Judith Devlin, *Slavophiles and commissars: enemies of democracy in modern Russia* (New York: St. Martin's Press, 1999), x–xvi.
147 Marlene Laruelle, 'The Two Faces of Contemporary Eurasianism: An Imperial Version of Russian Nationalism', *Nationalities Papers*, 32: 1, (March 2004): 115–136.
148 Mark Bassin, 'Asia', in Nicholas Rzhevsky, ed., *Modern Russian Culture* (Cambridge: Cambridge University Press, 1988), pp. 76–77.

us!/ Yes we are Scythians! Yes we are Asiatics!/ With slanting and greedy eyes'. It does not matter to Russian patriots that historians came to the conclusion that Scyths most likely spoke an Iranian and not a Slavic language. Everything else about them seemed Russian, including their passion for strong drink and bathhouses. Scyths had a reputation as fearsome warriors, the model of an Asian barbarian whose history could be traced back at least to the sixth century BCE when, Herocotus tells us, Scythian warlords having encountered the Persian army north of the Black Sea fought not to protect their riches but the burial mounds of their ancestors. Herodotus's account of Scythian martial valour and their willingness to fight to the death for their homeland became further proof that Scyths and Slavs were one and the same, at least in the patriotic imagination.

The second phase of Eurasianism was an academic movement formed mainly from émigré writers in the years following the Bolshevik conquest of power.[149] Trubetskoi and his followers mostly lived outside the Soviet Union but sympathized with the Soviet goal of uniting the peoples of Eurasia. In the west, George Vernadsky wrote a positive account of the Mongols and related Russian nationality to its Mongol past.[150] Petr Savitskii embodied the extreme when he described Eurasia as one people in a biological sense given the process of genetic mutation that had taken place during centuries of interaction.[151]

A third phase comprised scholars and political activists at the end of the Soviet period and in post-Communist Russia. The most famous of the scholars was Gumilev who argued that the Mongols were a proud addition to Russia's heroic history. For Gumilev, humanity is divided into various ethnoses whose fortunes depend upon the drive (*passionarnost*) of brilliant leaders.[152] One such leader was Genghis Khan, the great Mongol conqueror of the thirteenth century.

In the 1990s, Eurasianism once more constituted a political as well as an academic challenge to Russia's Westernizers. Shlapentokh considered the Eurasianists to be a totalitarian force in their worship of traditional Russian

---

149 See M. Laruelle, *Russian Eurasianism: An Ideology of Empire* (Washington, 2008).
150 See George Vernadsky, *The Mongols and Russia* (New Haven: Yale University Press, 1953).
151 See Tolz, *Russia*, p. 202.
152 Viktor Shnirelman and Sergei Panarin, 'Lev Gumilev His Pretensions as a Founder of Ethnology and his Eurasian Theories', *Inner Asia* 3 (2001): 1–18.

and eastern models of government.[153] Yanov has argued that a liberal and European Russia is a less likely outcome than an aggressive and Eurasianist one.[154] Like most Russian political movements, Eurasianism is a broad spectrum of views in contemporary Russia united by a preference for the spritiual and collective values of a mythologized East as opposed to the mechanistic and individualistic Euro-American world of the West. It is the right wing of the Eurasianist movement that is best known in the West because it is articulated by political firebrands like Vladimir Zhirinovsky and Alexander Dugin, the latter claiming that Russia's task consists in 'taking over the Tatar geopolitical mission' of confronting 'the Roman-German world whose pathological culture is a dead-end of degradation and decay'.[155] Dugin resembles the classical European fascism of the early twentieth century with his calls for a 'conservative revolution', his obsession with new geopolitical civilizational contests, and his recycling of the idea that Russia has its own special mission.[156] Dugin's extremism has done his career no harm; he is a prolific publisher, a senior academic at Moscow State Univeristy and one of twenty-five founding members of the newly-formed think tank and political lobby group, the Izborsk Club. Eurasianism, like Dugin, has moved from the fringe to the centre of Russian politics.

Russia's internal geopolitics certainly changed dramatically after the collapse of the Soviet Union. Without Ukraine, Belarus and central Asia, Russia is much more Russian today than it was under the tsars or Communists. It is also much more Turkic. The largest minorities of the Russian Federation are, for the most part, Turkic nationalities, even though Russians dwarf the proportions of their non-Russian neighbours. The nationalities within Russia comprise: Russian 81.5%, Tatar 3.8%, Ukrainian 3%, Chuvash 1.2%, Bashkir 0.9%, Belarusian 0.8%, Moldavian 0.7% and others 8.1%.

It is no real comfort for Russian patriots to know that most Tatars live outside of Tatarstan and that its leaders mostly deny that independence from the Russian Federation is an option. The fear is that on the basis of history, Tatars or Turks in general could lay claim to a historic homeland that

---

153 See, for example, Shlapentokh, 'Russia on the Eve'.
154 Yanov, 'Russian nationalism in Western studies', p. 52.
155 Nikolai Trubetskoi, *Nasledie Chingizkhana*, 'Predislovie Alexandra Dugina' (Moscow: 1999), p. 10.
156 Marlene Laruelle, 'The Two Faces of Contemporary Eurasianism', p. 126 and Natalia Morozova, 'Geopolitics, Eurasianism and Russian Foreign Policy Under Putin', *Geopolitics* 14 (2009), 667–686, pp. 681–682.

stretches from Kazan to Astrakhan, Crimea and beyond. The writing of this type of history is already under way and political demands may follow. From the perspective of many Russian patriots, the former imperial subjects are rewriting the past with a view to becoming the new elite.

In the 1930s, a group of Tatar historians attempted to link the history of their nation to the history of the Golden Horde, and thus, to the history of the Mongols. Their approach was doomed in Stalinist Russia, where the Golden Horde and the Mongols were demonized as much as the Vikings. Tatar historians were forced to trace their ancestry not from the Golden Horde, but from the ancient Bulgar state that was one of the first to fall victim to the Mongol onslaught. Just like the Russians, Turkic pseudo-historians now write much more fantastic tales about their ancestors.

In the 1990s, each Turkic nationality has produced its own 'pen and ink' warriors. Nationalistic historians emerging from among the Chuvash, Tatars and Bashkirs have tried to connect the history of their peoples to ancient ancestors such as the Sumerians, Scythians, Egyptians, and Etruscans.[157] According to these histories, the Turkic peoples were once the benevolent conquerors of the Russians and the latter owe the former a huge cultural debt. This debt not only includes the Russian words for paper, bathhouse, boots, money, and pencils, but the ancestors of Peter the Great, field-marshal Kutuzov, and the writer Dostoevskii.

For all the nationalist movements among the Turkic peoples of the Volga, Russia was and remains the enemy. Happily for the Russians, the Turkic revival of the middle Volga looks to the past for unity but has generated considerable intra-Turkic conflict. Tatars tend to believe that the Volga Bulgars spoke a Turkic language and lent their language to the Chuvash. Chuvash tend to the opposite conclusion, that Volga Bulgars spoke a specifically Chuvash language and not a generic Turkic language. For the Chuvash, Tatars had nothing to do with the Volga Bulgars and arrived only as part of the Mongol invasion of the thirteenth century. Non-Tatar nationalist historians of the Middle Volga tend to insist that the term Tatars was simply a generic name for many different Turkic peoples who found their way into the Golden Horde after the thirteenth century. The very term Tatar emerged first as a nickname for wandering nomads and not for a specific ethnic

---

157 Christian, *A History of Russia, Central Asia and Mongolia*, p. 5.

group. The tsars then used the term Tatar, with its negative connotations, to justify their war of aggression against the Bulgars.

In opposition to their Tatar and Chuvash counterparts, historians of the Bashkirs claim that their ancestors were the Bulgars. The Turkic-Iranian ancestors of the Bulgars lived in Bashkiria some 35,000 years ago, having created Idel-Ural, the world's first state. Bulgar migrations reached Central Asia, northern China, North and South Americas. Until the tenth century, Bulgars ruled much of Eastern Europe. It was brought to an end only in the thirteenth century under the dual pressures of the Golden Horde and then Russia.[158]

If Fomenko's has a Turkic counterpart it is probably Murad Adzhi (formerly Adzhiev), an ethnic Tatar, who considers the word 'Tatar' as a form of a racial slur perpetuated by Russians and other European peoples. Rather, as the titles of his books suggest, he identifies himself as a Kipchak - Polovets, a descendant of the ancient state of Desht-i-Kipchak.[159] Adzhi was a professional Soviet economist who wrote his dissertation on the subject of the Baikal-Amur railroad, before turning his hand to popular history.

Adzhi, like Fomenko, is xenophobic in outlook and despises the West. While Fomenko concentrates on evil Germans, Adzhi demonises the evil Greeks.[160] In contrast to Fomenko, Adzhi considers the Russians or Slavs to be a 'Western' outpost in Eurasia, and laments the fact that Russian propagandists changed, stole and twisted the otherwise great Turkic historical and cultural inheritance. According to Adzhi, Huns, Alans, Goths, Burgundians, Saxons, Alemans, Angles, Langobards and many of the Russians were ethnic Turks.[161] The list of non-Turks is relatively short and seems to comprise only Jews, Chinese, Armenians, Greeks, Persians, and Scandinavians. Adzhi is obsessed with the idea that, two hundred thousand years ago, an advanced people of Turkic blood lived in the Altai Mountains, the forefathers of the future Turks. Surprisingly, they were tall and blonde people. The Turks built the so-called ancient Russian cities and produced the first plough.[162] According to Adzhi, Saint George was also a Turk, buried in the Caucausian Mountains of Dagestan.

---

158 Shnirelman, *Who Gets the Past*, pp. 42–44.
159 M. Adzhi, M, *My – iz roda Polovetskogo* (Moscow: Rybinsk, 1992).
160 M. Adzhi, *Evropa, Turki, velikaia step'* (Moscow: Mysl', 1998) pp. 152, 191.
161 M. Adzhi, *Evropa*, p. 198.
162 M. Adzhi, *Evropa*, pp. 54–55.

Adzhi has maintained that Turks, through the barbarian invasions, liberated Europe from its slavish dependence on Rome, built temples, hundreds of cities and roads, brought monotheistic religion to the Europeans, and invented Christianity. Europe lavishly borrowed from the Turks. It was the Turks who built Russia's monasteries and even invented Christmas trees, forks and spoons. Turkic was the language Europe used up to sixteenth century. According to Adzhi, while the majority of the Turkic peoples of Russia were Kipchaks and Khazars, Turkic Cossacks became the eastern Slavs. Prior to the nineteenth century Slavs were called Caucasian Tartars and they spoke the same language as the Turks. Adzhi notes that there are millions of Slavs with typically Turkic facial features who believe they are Russian. Given his description of ancient Turk features, their confusion seems unsurprising.

While Fomenko feigns inclusiveness by invoking a once mighty Slav-Turk Empire and by inviting the Turks to rule this imaginary kingdom together with the Slavs, there is no place for the Slavs in Adzhi's Turkic Empire. Even the light cavalry that defeated the German knights in the famous confrontation on the ice in 1242 were obviously Turkic Cossacks.[163] Adzhi's logic resembles Fomenko's but his conclusions necessarily contradict. The plot against Turkic civilization was hatched by an alliance of sedentary nations, including the evil Greeks, barbaric Romans and mean-spirited Slavs.

---

163 M. Adzhi, *Evropa, Turki, velikaia step'*, pp. 152, 237.

Chapter Four: Empires of the Mind: Russia's Ancient History

'Today, anyone can do anything they want with history. They can turn over facts to suit their ethnic leanings. They can lean on dubious sources as if they were absolute proof. They can cite no facts at all. They can invent evidence where it does not exist, and even create whole chronicles on behalf of their ancestors, as if it were miraculously discovered in their granddad's shed.'[164]

Part One: Scholarly Ruminations

It has always been a matter of great disappointment to Russian patriots that the predecessors of the Russian and Soviet empires made so little impression upon what the West refers to as the classical civilisations of Greece and Rome. Russia, as the conventional histories tell the story, appears to be a very recent phenomenon. The first Russian state, Kiev Rus, is usually dated to the ninth century, thousands of years after the emergence of Sumer and Egypt, and much later than Greece and Rome. Just as irksome is the fact that the West usually looks upon Kiev Rus as an outpost of the Viking world and not as a creation of the Slavs. The earliest Slavs would appear to have created no great civilizations, contributed no early inventions or philosophy, and failed to gain the attention of the great writers of the ancient world.

Only after 500CE did writers refer to a specific barbarian tribe variously referred to as Veneti, Sclaveni, and Antes living north of the Danube River.[165] They were based around the Pripiat marshes, one of the least attractive locations on the East European plain. Some Slavs, it would seem, migrated eastwards and displaced the scattered Finno-Uralic peoples of central Russia in the sixth to the ninth centuries. These eastern Slavs, lacking both writing and a stable state, soon came under pressure from Vikings in the north and steppe peoples, notably the Khazar kaganate, from the East. Historians are mostly of the view that the Slavs had a common language, but no writing until Byzantine missionaries crafted an alphabet in the ninth century. Birch bark writing has been uncovered at Novgorod and other places

---

[164] Shnirelman and Panarin, 'Lev Gumilev', p. 16.
[165] Poe, *The Russian Moment in World History*, p. 12.

since the 1950s, but the earliest of these manuscripts also seem to date only to the ninth century.

For the writers of alternative history, the modest beginnings of the Slavs described in conventional history seem an improbable starting point for what would become the world's largest empire. Alternative historians have compensated for the apparent modesty of the standard accounts of Russian history by finding a Russian ancestor for almost all of the world's major civilisations. The argument from the critics of conventional history mostly runs along the following lines. Conventional history cannot be so because it is illogical. The vast southern steppe that connects modern-day Ukraine, south Russia and central Asia could not have been as thinly populated in ancient times as conventional history suggests.

For the patriotic tradition, it is simply inconceivable that a major historical entity such as the Slavs—350 million people and more than half of Europe's population at the beginning of the twenty-first century—had no past and seemingly emerged from the inhospitable swamps of the Pripiat' in the sixth century CE. Did the Slavs migrate to Europe from Asia as some scholars suggested, or did they emerge from Eastern Europe as others opined? If they are from Asia, then what part of Asia generated the exodus of so many people into Europe, when did it happen, and why is there no trace of these 'Asiatic' Slavs? Are the standard histories suggesting that what is now European Russia was mostly devoid of major populations apart from the relatively small Finnish, Magyar and Baltic tribes before the Slavs migrated there in the sixth century? Why would such valuable farmland, replete with all manner of natural resources, have remained virtually empty for centuries? Why are there so many physical and cultural resemblances between steppe peoples such as the Scyths and the Slavs that supposedly replaced them? These puzzles are resolved, alternative historians insist, if we accept that Slavs, proto-Slavs or proto-Russians were present in the population that occupied the steppe since time immemorial.

Of course, it has long been accepted by conventional scholars that important moments in the history of world civilization did indeed take place in ancient times in the territory that would later become the Russian Empire and the Soviet Union. The most popular of the theories about the ancient homeland of the tribe or tribes that gave us the Indo-European family of languages locates these peoples on the steppe north of the Black Sea. According to this theory, the 'kurgan' (burial mound) culture, in reality a succession of cultures that interacted with and replaced one another between

6000 and 3000BCE, constituted the most likely original speakers of proto-Indo-European. This kurgan culture was truly remarkable. The settlements constructed by the Tripol'e culture in what is now northern Romania and western Ukraine were the largest in Europe in 4800–3000 BCE. Srednyi Stog on the Dnieper River offers the first evidence for the domestication of the horse. The Yamnaia culture from 2800–2000BCE evidenced wheeled carts and kurgans. Further east along the steppe, the Sintashta culture of the southern Urals most likely invented the chariot.[166] There is at the very least a plausible case that these related peoples whose horses, chariots and metallurgy enhanced both their mobility and their war-making capacity, spread their power and their Indo-European language far and wide to Anatolia, Europe, Persia, and India.[167]

There have been a great many archaeological discoveries in the lands of the erstwhile Russian Empire, but Arkaim is arguably the most spectacular discovery. Unearthed in 1987, Arkaim in the southern Urals dates from 3000BCE. It housed between fifteen hundred and two thousand people, and boasted a temple and an observatory. The Sintashta culture that produced Arkaim was once dismissed as comprising 'primitive' steppe nomads, but it is now clear that the Sintashta were expert in metallurgy and the manufacture of chariots. As old as ancient Egypt and Babylon, Arkaim is striking evidence that the Eurasian steppe was for thousands of years a world of permanent settlements and industry, and not just a nomadic economy. As one scholar has put it, there are good reasons for thinking that the Sintashta culture produced 'the offspring who would later emerge into history as the Iranian and Vedic Aryans who created the earliest Indo-European writing we have—the Sanskrit Rig Veda and the Iranian Avesta'.[168] Conventional scholars date the oldest Indian writing to about 1500 BCE and its common Indian-Iranian predecessor to about 1700BCE.[169]

It should be noted that the term 'Aryan' is still used by scholars even though the Nazi obsession with the Aryan origins of the German 'race' has cast a large shadow over the search to find the original speakers of proto-Indo-European. In the case of Arkaim, Russians, Tatars and Bashkirs all claim it

---

166 Anthony, *The Horse, the Wheel and Language*, pp. 376–77.
167 Anthony, *The Horse, the Wheel and Language*, pp. 18–19.
168 Anthony, *The Horse, the Wheel, and Language*, p. 411.
169 Edwin Bryant, *Quest for the Origins of Vedic Culture: The Indo-Aryan Migration* (Oxford: Oxford University Press, 2004), p. 238.

as evidence of their ancient achievements. At the same time, Arkaim became a magnet for neo-Nazis and neo-pagans when reports emerged that its building plan resembled the shape of a swastika. Countless alternative histories claim to have found evidence across the length and breadth of the lands of the Soviet Union of the earliest 'Aryans'. It turns out that the Nazis were mistaken about their Aryan forefathers; the Aryans described in the pages of alternative history invariably turn out to be Slavs, and, increasingly, Russians.

There are good reasons for thinking that 'kurgan culture' was a remarkable period in human history and that the Black Sea steppe was the starting point for a culture and language that spread to Asia and Europe. But in what sense, if any, could these ancient steppe people be described as Russians? Conventional scholars for the most part saw no reason to connect 'kurgan culture' with the ancient Slavs. Conventional history accepts that Slavs were present long before there are written records of them, but does not view them as the direct descendants of the Tripol'e, Sintashta or Scythian cultures. The latter are thought to have spoken an Indo-Iranian language, quite different to the Slavic branch of the Indo-European tree. The Indo-Iranian homeland may well have been located between the southern Urals, northern Kazakhstan and southern Siberia. The Slavic language is thought to have emerged along with other 'northern' Indo-European languages from the Corded Ware culture whose home was in the forested area well to the north of the steppe.[170]

To be fair, serious scholars are often divided over what a change from one named culture to another really meant in this early period. Were changes the result of wars and migrations or did the culture evolve and the language change for other reasons?[171] As one scholar has put it, the 'period of Slavic migrations and the great and rather sudden expansion of the Slavic zone does raise serious problems'.[172] We know little about the physical appearance of the steppe peoples. At least one study of the DNA of the peoples who inhabited the southern Urals in the era of Arkaim suggests that they had 'European characteristics' such as blue and green eyes and blonde

---

[170] Victor Shnirelman, 'Russian Response', p. 39. Anthony, *The Horse, the Wheel, and Language*, p. 367.
[171] Anthony, *The Horse, the Wheel, and Language*, pp. 17–19.
[172] For a discussion, see Riasonovsky, *Russian Identities*, p. 10.

hair.¹⁷³ The artist charged with reconstructing the face of the celebrated 'Ice Maiden', the mummified remains found on the Altai steppe, claimed that her subject was 'an example of the Caucasian race with no typically Mongolian features'. Other experts disagreed. Alternative history has long believed that it has the answer to these thorny issues and it turns out to be much simpler than professional historians could ever have imagined.

In the imagination of Russia's alternative historians, all things are possible. Their answer to Russia's seemingly insoluble quest for a post-Soviet Russian identity is to imagine a new empire in the distant past. If Russians were able to comprehend their greatness in the past, their greatness in the future would become a more achievable goal. It would be a first step towards the recreation of a post-Communist version of the Soviet Union. In imagining Russia in this way, alternative historians are themselves part of a 'greatness' tradition that stretches back into history.

Part Two: The Patriotic Tradition

The original amateur patriotic historians of Russia were Vasilii Tatishchev (1686–1750) and Mikhail Lomonosov (1711–1765). In 1741–1745 Tatishchev was Astrakhan's governor and had access to the archive there. The sources available to Tatishchev amounted to native church chronicles as well as Greek, Roman and Byzantine writers, including Strabo, Ptolemey, Herodotus and Pliny.¹⁷⁴ As the historian Rogger has put it, Tatishchev posed enduring questions: the ethnic origins of the Russian people; the foundation of the Russian state; the degree of enlightenment among the ancient Slavs; and the problem of whether there was, historically speaking, an ideal form of government for Russia, prescribed for her by history.¹⁷⁵ He set an agenda for speculating about ancient Russian history that resonates to this day.

Lomonosov was, like Tatishchev, a polymath who studied chemistry and metallurgy in Germany before turning his hand to poetry and history. Lomonosov was moved to write history when he reviewed the draft of the oration prepared by the German-born historian Mueller for Empress Elizabeth

---

173 See C. Keyser et al, 2009, 'Ancient DNA provides new insights into the history of south Siberian Kurgan people', *Human Genetics*, 126:3: 395–410.
174 Rudolph Daniels, *V. N. Tatishchev: Guardian of the Petrine Revolution* (Philadelphia: Franklin Publishing Company, 1973), p. 92.
175 Rogger, *National Consciusness in Eighteenth Century Russia*, p. 197.

in 1749.[176] Lomonosov argued that Vikings or Byzantines did not found the Russian state or give birth to Russian culture as Mueller and other foreign historians claimed. Lomonosov insisted that the Vikings, or Varangians as the Primary Chronicle, the earliest of the available church chronicles, described them, were actually people of Slavic ancestry.[177] Ancient Slavs, Lomonosov claimed, participated in such great historic events as the defense of ancient Troy, and the destruction of Rome by the eastern hordes.

Like Tatishchev, Lomonosov's method was to compare the account of the *Primary Chronicle* with the ancient sources available to him. The ancient Greeks described many seemingly inter-related steppe peoples such as the Scyths, Sarmatians, and Roxolani who lived north of the Black Sea. Lomonosov conjectured that the term Rus derived from the Roxolani.[178] Not only were the Scyths and Sarmatians Slavs according to Lomonosov but so too were the Germanic barbarians. According to Lomonosov, in ancient times, Sarmatians migrated to the Baltic and mixed with Prussians and the Scandinavians there. Riurik, the Varangian who founded Kiev Rus according to the Primary Chronicle, was in fact a Baltic Slav, a contention that finds its share of supporters among modern anti-Normanists.[179] The Prussians derive their name from their connection to Russia; they were *po-russy* or *prussy*.[180] As Lomonosov would describe his goal in 1753, there was a need to write Russian history that 'would reveal to society the long and glorious history of the Russian people'. Lomonosov used descriptors such as 'awesome', 'the most noble', 'magnificent', 'splendid', 'brave', 'freedom-loving', and, above all, 'glorious' when describing the achievements of these early Slavs. The term 'Slav' itself came from the Slavic word *slava* meaning 'glorious'.

The tradition of Tatishchev and Lomonosov inspired a long line of popular and patriotic histories. A bestseller of the late tsarist period emerged from the pen of Alexander Dmitrievich Nechvolodov (1864–1924), a tsarist gen-

---

176 Gleason, 'The Course of Russian History According to an Eighteenth Century Layman', pp. 17–18.
177 Mikhail Lomonosov, *Polnoe sobranie sochinenii*, S. I. Vavilov et al., eds., 10 volumes (Moscow, Leningrad: 1950–59), 6, pp. 168–72.
178 Mikhail Lomonosov, *Trudy po russkoi istorii* 6, pp. 198–199.
179 See, for example, VV Fomin (ed), *Varyago-Russkii vopros v istoriografii* (Moscow: Russkaia panorama, 2010).
180 Joseph Black, *G.F. Mueller and the Imperial Russian Academy,* (Kingston and Montreal: McGill, 1986), p. 141.

eral and active member of the Imperial Russian Military-Historical Society. His four-volume history of Russia earned the praise of Nicholas II and is still being reprinted to this day.[181] Nechvolodov was struck by the similarities between the Scyths and the Cossacks. Conventional history describes the Cossacks as originating with Tatar renegades and runaway serfs who formed warrior communities in the southern borderlands at the end of the Mongol era. Later, the tsars transformed the Cossacks into a martial estate with military duties, compensated for by political and economic privileges. None of this made sense either to Nechvolodov or to modern-day alternative historians. From their perspectives, Cossacks, warrior-farmers who specialized in cavalry, were obviously the direct descendants of the Scyths and other ancient steppe peoples, and not peasant refugees fleeing central Russia in relatively modern times. The idea that the Cossacks were the 'real' Mongols of the steppe is now a staple of alternative history.[182]

A less reputable, but nonetheless important, source from the nineteenth century is Alexander Sulakadzev (1771–1830), a veteran of the prestigious Semenovskii Guards Regiment and later a titular advisor in the Ministry of Finances. Upon his retirement, Sulakadzev started to look for archaeological evidence from the Russian past. Sulakedzev conducted excavations in Novgorod and Sarai, the ancient Mongol capital, collected coins and boasted that he had in his possession priceless, albeit unlikely, artifacts such as the walking stick of Ivan the Terrible, a special stone where Dmitrii Donskoi had rested on the eve of his famous battle with the Mongols in 1380, and evidence that a Russian clergyman first flew in a hot air balloon in 1731, half a century before the Montgolfier brothers. Sulakadzev also claimed that he had a copy of a text written in proto-Slavic runes that predated all other Slavic writing.[183]

---

181 Nechvolodov, *Skazaniia o Russkoi Zemle* (Moscow: Belyi Gorod, 2007).
182 See Alexander Guts, *Mnogovariantnaia Istoriia Rossii* (Moscow: AST, 2000, 'Poligon', 2001).
183 See L. Revzin, *Bessmertnyi Sulakadzev*, (Moscow: Russkaia Literatura, 1979), 3 and Lapenkov, *Istoriia Netraditsionnoi Orientatsii, Legendy i Mify Vsemirnoi Istorii*, (Moskow: Bystrov, 2006), pp. 36–37.

Sulakadzev is one of many links that connects modern-day alternative historians, the Soviet era, and the early patriotic efforts to acquire a glorious past.[184] In the Soviet era, a stamp was produced to celebrate Russia's invention of manned flight. Just as remarkably, the name of the mysterious clergyman—who originally bore the German name Furtsel—was transformed into the Russian-sounding Kriakutnoi. All of the alternative historians mentioned in this chapter grew up during the Soviet era and imbibed this type of official patriotic imagining. For Fomenko, Sulakadzev is a hero who stubbornly fought for the truth despite the persecution of the Romanovs whose minions denounced this courageous truth-seeker as a charlatan and fraud.

Figure 1: The Soviet-era stamp depicting the first manned flight.
Source: Wikipedia

Soviet historians added to this patriotic version of Russian history, especially in the period after World War Two. In an attempt to breathe life into the Soviet historical meta-narrative, Stalin from the mid 1930s rehabilitated selected aspects of the tsarist past. His propagandists developed a Russo-centric history of the multi-ethnic Soviet Union, and tirelessly propagated the notion that the West was the enemy both of Russia and its history. Stalin-era historians disparaged the 'Normanist' arguments about the Viking or-

---

[184] See L. Revzin, *Bessmertnyi Sulakadzev, Russkaia Literatura*, 1979, 3. and Lapenkov, *Istoriia Netraditsionnoi Orientatsii*, pp. 36–37.

igins of Kiev Rus and offered support to the idea of continuity between Slavs/Russians and steppe peoples such as the Scyths. According to Soviet-era archaeology, the Scyths built an amazing ancient civilization in and around the Crimean peninsula. Their capital, Scythian Naples, located near modern-day Simferopol, boasted gigantic defensive towers and walls, monuments and sculptures, and a Mausoleum. The character of their buildings, their funeral rites and even their clothing anticipated the Slavic/Cossack culture of more recent times. Soviet readers of these publications were left in no doubt that Scyths and Sarmatians were the direct ancestors of the eastern Slavs.[185] It was a small step from there for Russian alternative writers to insist that the Scyths were not just Slavs, but Russians.

Alternative writers have a common set of myths and heroes. They relate the mythology surrounding each and every lost or mysterious civilization to the history of Russia. For alternative historians, some form of Slavic state existed for millennia and its traces are to be found everywhere from India in the east to the Viking world in the west. The fact that ethnic names such as Slavs and Russians are relatively new on the world historical stage in comparison with, for example, the Egyptians and Sumerians, does not intimidate writers of alternative history. They explain it by the fact that, historically, outsiders have always attached a multitude of names to the occupiers of the Russian lands. Ancient sources and modern scholars have named various tribes—including Aryans, Scythians, Tauroscythians, Sarmatians, Cimmerians, Alans, Goths, Roxalans and Huns—who lived on the steppe in past eras. To use a modern analogy, the twentieth-century inhabitants of the Russian Empire and the Soviet Union comprised a hundred ethnic groups of Slavic and non-Slavic peoples. Around its Slavic core, a great civilization—the Russian Empire and its successor, the Soviet Union—was built. Is it not likely that such an entity existed in the past as well?

---

[185] P. Shul'ts, *Tavro-skifskaia ekspeditsiia v Krymu* (Simferopol': Sovetskii Krym, 1946) and P. Shul'ts, *Mavzolei Neapolia skifskogo* (Moscow, 1953).

Part Three: Fomenko, the Terminator

There are, it must be acknowledged, several versions of alternative ancient history. Fomenko's version is distinctive because he tackles the whole chronological framework of ancient history. Fomenko is most at home in his original field of mathematics. Diacu has captured the confidence that comes from the mastery of mathematics and mechanics when he wrote that:

> No science is 100 percent exact; each involves certain approximations. But if there is one science that comes closest to perfection, it's celestial mechanics [which] has been able to forecast the return of comets, discover new planets, and guide rockets into space. No mission has ever failed because of it, and no eclipses have ever occurred at any time other than those it predicted.[186]

The approach to the problem of Russia's missing ancient history championed by Fomenko is to rewrite chronology, that is, to replace our existing timelines with a 'new chronology'. Using arguments developed by earlier critics of conventional chronology and dismissive of techniques such as carbon dating, Fomenko claims that it is only by reference to astronomical data that dating is possible. Using his methods, Fomenko came to the conclusion that history was at least one thousand years shorter in duration than the standard books maintain. Critics who have maintained their sense of humor have labeled Fomenko as 'the terminator' because so many accepted periods, events and personalities are expunged from his version of the past.

Fomenko was not the first scientist to cast doubt upon the dating of ancient history. Isaac Newton himself was one of many experts dissatisfied with the conventional wisdom. In Russia, Nikolai Morozov (1854–1946) developed the proto-type of Fomenko's new chronology. Morozov was a Socialist Revolutionary in his youth whose grandfather was a distant relative of Peter the Great. From 1881 to 1905, Morozov was in prison and used his time to study chronology, mathematics, chemistry and the Bible.[187] For Fomenko, it was Morozov who 'first created a scientific understanding of chronology and introduced important new methods of scientific chronological analysis'. Morozov would have been right at home among the alternative writers of the

---

[186] Diacu, *The Lost Millenium*, p. 95.
[187] For an account of Morozov, see *Nikolai Aleksandrovich Morozov 1854–1946*, vstupitel'naia stat'ia Semena Vol'koficha (Moscow: Nauka, 1981), and Semen Vol'fkovich, 'Nikolai Aleksandrovich Morozov, ego zhizn' i trudy po khimii', *Priroda* 11 (1947).

post-Soviet period. Such was his hatred of the West that Morozov believed that the Mongols actually struck Russia from Europe, and not from the Orient, as was commonly believed. Fomenko has noted, with some pride, that, in 1946, Morozov and Joseph Stalin were two of only three honorary members of the USSR Academy of the Sciences.[188]

In 1924–1932 Morozov published his last and most comprehensive work, the seven-volume *Khristos* where he elaborated upon his criticisms of conventional chronology and attacked Christianity. Morozov claimed with good reason that ancient sources used by historians were rarely originals. Instead all we have are copies of copies. For Morozov, these were most likely written during the Renaissance. The so-called Dark Ages that linked classical civilization to the Middle Ages were understandably opaque to the early moderns. According to Morozov, these centuries never existed. They were a figment of the West's imperial imagination.

Fomenko read the works not only of Morozov, but also of Immanuel Velikovsky (1895–1979), the Russian-born popular writer who confirmed the strangeness of ancient history. In the modern world, there is more or less continuous progress in civilizational terms, even if it is a team effort with sometimes Europe, sometimes the Arab world and sometimes Eurasia or China leading the way. In the ancient world, there are puzzling gaps and apparent circles where the otherwise curious and competent human race seems to have fallen backwards.[189] Velikovsky's notion that celestial catastrophes might explain the dark and stagnant periods of ancient history was not good enough for Fomenko.

For Fomenko, the principal villain of the false, pro-Western chronology is Scaliger, or Joseph Justus dell Scala (1540–1609), the most celebrated scholar of his era. A student of astronomy and history, Scaliger applied textual criticism to ancient Roman works, wrote about ancient astronomy and attempted to make sense of the often contradictory chronology found in the

---

188 Fomenko, *History: Fiction or Science*, p. 16.
189 Fomenko is not the first scientist to question world chronology. Isaac Newton (1643–1727), the great English mathematician and scientist, wrote *The Chronology of Ancient Kingdoms Amended* in which he took issue with the chronology of the ancient Greeks and used astronomy to recalculate well-known events. Thus, Newton thought that the siege of Troy needed to be moved two hundred years forward from 1183 BCE to 965 BCE. Newton concluded that national vanity caused the Greeks, Latins, Babylonians, Assyrians, and Egyptians, to extend the time lines of their histories.

work of Greeks, Romans, Persians and Egyptians. Morozov and Fomenko believe that Scaliger was the author of the problem, and not its solution. The examples cited by Morozov and Fomenko famously include the account of the Peloponnesian War by our only eyewitness, Thucydides. Thucydides noted three eclipses in the first, eighth and eighteenth years of the war. Looking at this evidence, scholars, including Scaliger, found the starting point for the Peloponnesian War in 431 BCE. The problem is that Thucydides described a full eclipse when stars were visible during the day in the first year of the war; but we now know that the eclipse of 431 BCE was partial over the southern half of Greece. Thucydides might have been using poetic license in his account, may have witnessed the eclipse further north from Athens, or the date might be wrong.

Morozov and Fomenko reviewed sequences of eclipses in a wide variety of periods and decided that the eclipses that Thucydides sighted could only have taken place in the eleventh or twelfth centuries, more than fourteen hundred years later. Emboldened by his new chronology, Fomenko was soon able to make a series of startling claims. Fomenko finds it incredible that a grammatically complicated and factually rich account such as that of Thucydides, the only one we have detailing the greater part of the Peloponnesian War, could have emerged in the fifth century BCE 'when writing materials were scarce and expensive—the Mesopotamians use styluses to scribble on clay, the Greeks are not yet familiar with paper, and write on pieces of tree bark or use sticks for writing on wax-covered plaques'.[190] Thucydides would have had more congenial writing materials if he wrote his history at a much later date.

As for Roman history, Fomenko was just as skeptical of the dates for Augustus as he was about ancient Greece. Why was the name of Tacitus, the celebrated historian of Rome, seldom mentioned before the Italian Renaissance? Here, Fomenko repeats a suggestion already made in the nineteenth century, that the works of Tacitus were a modern forgery. Tacitus was a historical duplicate for Poggio Bracciolini (1380–1459), the Renaissance writer who provided such detailed descriptions of the Rome of his day. Why, asks Fomenko, do medieval Italians refer to the fourteenth century as the trecento or three hundreds and the sixteenth century as the cinquecento or five hundreds? The Italians wisely ignored a millennium that

---

[190] Fomenko, *History: Fiction or Science?*, p. 98.

did not exist.[191] As for the Roman Empire, in general, it was great but nowhere near as long-lived as traditional ancient history claimed. Augustus ruled Rome from 1175 to 1205 CE according to Fomenko and not a millennium earlier as conventional chronology suggested.

Fomenko praised Morozov but the pupil found his teacher to be a flawed genius whose works needed substantial correction. Morozov criticized world chronology only for the periods before the sixth century AD. Morozov, in Fomenko's opinion, underestimated the extension of world chronology by one thousand years. As Fomenko argues, Scaliger's history loops backwards on three occasions, thus creating three chronological shifts of 330 years, 1050 years, and 1300 years. As a consequence the same event is potentially replayed three times. Morozov and Fomenko agree that the Biblical events are much younger than we think. Morozov dated them to the third to fifth centuries CE.[192] According to Fomenko, the main events of the Bible took place in the eleventh and twelfth centuries, which gives a difference of one thousand years compared to Morozov's calculations, and 1800 years compared to Scaliger's chronology.

For Fomenko, historians and scientists alike tended to be conservative and supportive of the status quo. They failed to ask the radical questions.[193] Fomenko's conviction that astronomy and mathematics should always trump politically biased written sources as evidence led him to decode horoscopes from Egypt that suggested its ancient greatness too was seriously overrated. The real ancient Egypt flourished for just three hundred years between 1100 and 1400 CE. Happily for modern historians, Fomenko believes that most dates from the seventeenth century to the present are more or less correct. Happily for Russian nationalists, conventional ancient history that marginalized Russia turns out to be a mix of falsehood and misdating.

Fomenko dazzled his readers not just with his knowledge of astronomy, but also his application of statistical analysis. The method here was to look at the dating, for example, of the reigns of a succession of popes and kings to

---

191 Fomenko, *History: Fiction or Science?*, p. 25.
192 Nikolai Morozov, *Otkrovenie v groze i bure: Istoriia sozdania Apokalipsisa*, ed. by V.Sablin, (Moscow: Bylœ, 1907); *Proroki. Istoriia vozniknovenia bibleiskikh prorochestv, ikh literaturnoe izlozhenie i kharakteristika* (Moscow: ob. Sytina, 1914); *Khristos. Istoriia chelovecheskoi kultury v estestvonauchnom osveshchenii*, VII volumes (Moscow-Leningrad: 1924–1932).
193 Nosovskii and Fomenko, *Bibleiskaia Rus'*, I, pp. 92–104.

see patterns in the length of reigns. Because, statistically, no real patterns emerged from about 1700, the presence of statistical correlations of this type in our lists of various popes, kings, and emperors from the more distant past might suggest that we are dealing with the same popes, kings and emperors known by different names in different ages. Having found his list of historical suspects, Fomenko was soon claiming that professional historians had failed to notice countless phantom rulers who were the duplicates or even triplicates of the original.

While no supporter of Christianity and a critic of Biblical chronology, Fomenko willingly plundered the Biblical stories for useful information. Just because the Old Testament of the Bible was wrongly dated did not mean that its contents were of no historical value. The Biblical story of Gog and Magog is an example. The image of Gog and Magog, the terrifying devils from the north, has long resonated with Russian readers. The Book of Ezekiel makes reference to 'northern' peoples who are fierce warriors and to a Prince of Rosh, whose homeland sounds suspiciously like Russia.[194] According to Genesis 10:2–4, Magog was one of the sons of Japeth. According to Ezekiel 38:1–4, Gog came from the land of Magog, was a chief prince of Meshech and Tubal, and seems to have had an army of 'horsemen, all of them clothed in full armor, a great company...wielding swords'. Ezekiel 38:15–23 maintains that Gog was connected to 'the uttermost parts of the north', a land of 'many peoples', 'all of them riding on horses, a great host, a mighty army'. Revelations 20:6–10 suggests that Gog and Magog comprised innumerable hordes, Satan's armies who made war against the camp of the saints.

For modern anti-Semites it is especially appropriate that Gog and Magog seem to have been at war with the people of Israel. Fomenko notes that medieval Byzantines concluded that the Prince of Rosh referred to in Ezekial was a Russian and wrote the Prince of Ross, not Rosh. Leo the Deacon, the Byzantine writer who lived in the second half of the tenth century, wrote in his *History* about the march of Grand Prince Sviatoslav from Kiev against Byzantium. According to Leo, 'Many know that this people are a mighty, warlike, brave and inconsiderate host. Divine Ezekiel told of the coming of people of Gog and Magog, the prince of Ross'.[195] For Fomenko, it is clear that the Biblical story is based in fact. It just needed to be interpreted cor-

---

194 Nosovskii and Fomenko, *Bibleiskaia Rus'*, I, pp. 144–146.
195 See Boris Grekov, *Kievskaia Rus* (Moscow, Leningrad: 1944), p. 622.

rectly. The Prince of Rosh was Russia's Grand Prince. Gog, Magog in their different forms is a reference to the Russians, Tatars and Mongols, peoples who created the great empire of Magog. Meshekh is Mosokh, the legendary founder of Moscow according to medieval authors. Tubal is a reference to the river Tobol in Western Siberia, which remains one of the traditional centres of Russian Cossackdom.

The legends about Gog and Magog spread to the East, further evidence for Fomenko of how widespread the reach of the Russian Horde once was. In the Koran there is an account of how Alexander the Great built a wall to keep the fearsome Gog and Magog away. On a map of Palestine drawn by Matthew of Paris there are walls blocking the northern lands where Alexander had locked up the allegedly barbaric Gog and Magog. The commentary to the map states that this is the place from where the Tartars came from. Thus, Fomenko concludes that Gog and Magog were Tartars for the West and Russians for Byzantium. Tatars and Russians were one and the same mighty horde that had conquered the ancient world.

Medieval artists portrayed ancient places and individuals in the settings and dress of their own era. For most historians, this was simply a fantasy on the part of medieval art but for Fomenko these artists were painting what they saw. Fomenko notes that there are sixteenth century depictions of Jesus and Pontius Pilate that portray the trial as if it took place amid typically medieval surroundings. Pilate has even been painted wearing headgear that looks like a Turkic turban, sits on soft pillows, while his warriors wear medieval plate and chain armour. In the background there are two and three-story stone buildings with chimneys. Later in the nineteenth century, it was more likely that the scene of Jesus' trial would be depicted as we imagine it today with Pilate looking like a conventional Roman senator sitting on a hard stone chair. Is it not more likely, Fomenko argues, that earlier depictions closer to the real events in time, were more accurate? It might seem to a modern reader that drawings or paintings from the medieval period are obviously inaccurate or anachronistic. From Fomenko's perspective if ancient and early modern times were one and the same then these artists are eyewitnesses describing exactly what they saw. Fomenko notes that the famous medieval pictures that we have of Christ's birth, crucifixion, and resurrection usually suggest a fertile and well-watered land. Strong evidence, in Fomenko's view, that important events described in the Bible did not take place in Palestine.

Part Four: The Hyperborean Exodus

Fomenko has inspired many followers and imitators but it must be said that, in the realm of ancient history, most alternative historians have preferred to move in a different direction. They have sought to extend Russian history by thousands, sometimes millions of years. Alternative history is very interested in the mythologies, folklore, and ancient literature that suggest that advanced civilizations once flourished on or near 'Russian' lands. Here the most popular topics of conversation are Hyperborea, Plato's northern utopia, Shambhala, the advanced civilization of ancient Tibet, and Atlantis, the fabled Atlantic island.

Many alternative historians cite Plato's description of Hyperborea, the northern land or continent that Plato thought lay 'to the north of Thrace', as the original Russian homeland. Described by ancient writers as a land of eternal spring 'beyond the northern wind (boreus)' or across some mysterious 'frozen seas', Hyperborea was the ancient Greek equivalent of Eden before the fall. Given that the modern Russian Empire and Soviet Union has claimed sovereignty over the central and eastern Arctic coastline for centuries, Hyperborea becomes part of Russia for alternative history.[196] Of course, the 'north' is not a precise location and many popular accounts, and especially those emerging from Scandinvavia, have claimed the Hyperboreans as their ancestors.

The suggestion that Hyperborea was a utopia whose descendants degenerated as they moved farther away from their Russian motherland has energized alternative historians, and an army of like-minded occultists and mystics, to locate more precisely this ancient homeland. Due credit for the popularity of Hyperborea should be given to Helena Blavatskaia (1831–91), the Russian-born giant of late nineteenth-century mysticism, occultism and a founder of the Theosophical Society. Blavatskaia's account of humankind's seven 'root races' included the Hyperboreans of the Arctic north. This idea of primordial and superior races existing in the distant past has provided inspiration for racial thinking across Europe. Hyperborea's northern location is especially attractive to Russian nationalists.

The most northerly point from Thrace is the Taimyr Peninsula, deep in the Arctic Circle and as far north as the Russian landmass extends in the direction of the North Pole. As unlikely a home as the contemporary inhospitable

---

[196] See Shnirelman, 'Russian Response'.

Taimyr Peninsula might appear, alternative historians often make the claim that not just Russians, but all ancient nations and ethnoses have descended from Taimyr, a temperate paradise, it seems, before the most recent ice age. Another favoured location of Hyperborea is the Kola Peninsula, which also extends deep into the Arctic Circle. The newly installed Soviet government launched a pioneering expedition to the Kola Peninsula in 1921–23. Alternative historians claim that the fantastic evidence uncovered by this expedition–a gigantic black-rock figure of a man, pyramids, traces of paved roads and other wonders–was later concealed in the archives of the Cheka. The tradition of amazing discoveries in the deep north continued even after the collapse of the Soviet Union. Valerii Demin (1945–2006), a tireless promoter of Hyperborea, attracted considerable publicity in 1997 when he organized an expedition to the Kola Peninsula; the expedition claimed to have found the remnants of paved roads, an ancient observatory, and an engraving on a rock wall that allegedly illustrated a hyperborean plane under attack from a laser cannon.[197]

While the critics label these ideas as preposterous, alternative historians have enlisted the aid of non-Russian literary sources to bolster their case for a northern home for humanity. Especially important in this regard is Sanskrit because it is ancient, Indo-European and, allegedly, contains references to a primordial northern home. The Indian writer who is most often cited in this regard is Bal Gangadhar Tilak (1856–1920) whose 1903 book, *Arctic Home in the Vedas*, claims that the most ancient Vedic hymns described the exodus from the Arctic. The Vedas, we are told, clearly indicate that the Polar Star was right above the head of these early 'Aryans': one

---

197 For Demin's prodigious contribution to alternative history see Valerii Demin, *Otkuda ty, russkoe plemia?* (Moscow: Veche, 1996); Valerii Demin, *Tainy Russkogo naroda* (Moscow: Veche, 1997); Valerii Demin, *Giperboreia—utro tsivilizatsii* (Moscow: Veche, 1997); Valerii Demin, *Zagadki Russkogo severa* (Moscow: Veche, 1999); Valerii Demin, *Tainy zemli russkoi* (Moscow: Veche, 2000); Valerii Demin, *Giperboreia: istoricheskie korni russkogo naroda* (Moscow: Veche, 2000); Valerii Demin, *Zagadki russkikh letopisei* (Moscow: Veche, 2001); Valerii Demin, *Zvezdnaia sud'ba narodov Rossii* (Moscow: Veche, 2001); Valerii Demin, *Rus' giperboreiskaia* (Moscow: Veche, 2002); Valerii Demin, *Zagadki russkogo mezhdurech'ia* (Moscow: Veche, 2003); Valerii Demin, *Drevnee drevnosti: rossiiskeia prototsivilizatsia* (Moscow: Veche, 2003); Valerii Demin, *V poiskakh kolybeli tsivilizatsii* (Moscow: Veche, 2004).

day lasted all summer, and one day lasted all winter.[198] Tilak claimed that Hyperborea existed until the earth's climate cooled and the last ice age drove the Hyperboreans south. There are, as one alternative historian puts it, 'innumerable descriptions pertaining to the Arctic still preserved in the monumental works of ancient Indian literature'.[199] The now frozen north was once the cradle of many nations.

Theories of cataclysmic events in the earth's history abound in the alternative literature. Velikovsky, the father of 'catastrophe theory' claimed that fluctuations in the Earth's orbit caused many 'near misses' with Venus and Mars. Few scientists take these claims seriously, but alternative historians are very attracted to celestial catastrophes. Pavel Globa (1953–) is a popular writer and astrologist who claims that about 26 thousand years ago a cosmic catastrophe caused by the destruction of the planet 'Phaeton' changed the axis of the earth's rotation. This in turn caused the ice age that forced the Hyperboreans from their idyllic, temperate home.[200] Others consider that an earthquake destroyed the continent of Arktida and forced the Hyperboreans to begin their migration south. Their science, mathematics, astronomy and written sources were mostly lost during the migration but enough of these Indo-European proto-Slavs escaped the dying Northern Motherland to build civilizations that stretched from India to Crete. Alternative History fills in the gaps surrounding the migration from the North Pole as the Hyperboreans moved southwards into both Asia and Europe. Siberia, the escape route from the increasingly frozen and inhospitable Hyperborea, has become the original Middle Earth or Middle Kingdom, the staging post for the future migrations of the earliest civilized peoples westwards and eastwards. Russian nationalists, including the supporters of Fomenko, venerate the famous excavations at Arkaim. Citing speculation from Russian archaeologists that the remains of twenty more cities are to be found in and around Arkaim, Russian alternative historians assume the Slavic origins of

---

198 B. Tilak, *Arkticheskaia rodina v vedakh*, translation by Guseva, (Moscow: Fair-Press, 2001).
199 B. Tilak, *Arkticheskaia rodina v vedakh*, translation by Guseva, (Moscow: Fair-Press, 2001), V. Lapenkov, *Istoriia Netraditsionnoi Orientatsii, Legendy i Mify Vsemirnoi Istorii*, (Moscow: Bystrov, 2006), p. 13.
200 See, for example, P. Globa, *Zhivoi Ogon'. Uchenie drevnikh Ariev* (M: 1996). *O chem molchit Luna* (Moscow: 1991).

Arkaim.[201] It should be noted that Tatars and Bashkirs view Arkaim as part of their heritage.

Some otherwise conventional scholars have lent their authority to the quest for Hyperborea. Natalia Guseva (1914–2010) and Svetlana Zharnikova are specialists on Indian culture who have blurred the lines between conventional and alternative history with their learned treatises about the Hyperborean migration.[202] Guseva and Zharnikova advocate, for example, Sanskrit origins of the names of the Siberian Rivers. 'The Ob' River is often described both as the escape route for the Hyperboreans and the point at which these travelers separated, with one branch heading to the Caucasus and Asia Minor and the other towards the Far East and Tibet.[203]

Part Five: History as Hoax

In the world of Alternative History, there are many sources of doubtful provenance, but one especially important literary forgery. This is the so-called Veles Book (*Vlesovaia kniga*), arguably the most successful hoax invented in Russia since the publication of the notorious *Protocols of the Elders of Zion*.[204] The Veles Book is allegedly a record, carved on wooden planks, of the Hyperborean refugees as they travelled across the southern steppe fighting off their enemies and regaining their civilizational strength. The Veles Book is crucial for many alternative historians because, without it, there are no written sources for the period before Kiev Rus, a strange state of affairs if the Slavs really were so ancient and so remarkable.

For conventional scholars, it was Christianity that gifted the Slavs their alphabet thanks to the efforts of Byzantine missionaries in the ninth century. Bark writings and church chronicles can be traced back only to the tenth and eleventh century. Alternative history claims that the Veles Book turns

---

201 See Viktor Mair and E. Kuzmina, *The Prehistory of the Silk Road* (University of Pensilvania Press, 2007); also Mikhail Demidenko, *Po Sledam SS v Tibete* (St-Petersburg: Olma-Press 2003).
202 See, for example, Natalia Guseva, *Slaviane i Arii. Put' bogov i slov* (Moscow: Fair-Press, 2001) *Russkii Sever – prarodina indo-slavov: iskhod predkov ariev i slavian* (Moscow: Veche, 2003); Svetlana Zharnikova, *Arkhaicheskie Korni Traditisionnoi Kultury Russkogo severa* (Moscow: MDK, 2003), *Zolotaia Nit'* (Vologda: 2003).
203 This is a very old idea that is being reanimated in alternative history. See V. Peredolskii, *Bytovye ostanki ilmentsev* (Moscow: 1893) - one of the original texts that alternative historians are borrowing from.
204 Veles refers to an important Slavic deity associated with cattle, wealth and magic.

this scholarship on its head. The contents of the Veles Book were first revealed to a wider public only in 1957 when the Russian émigré and eccentric folklorist Iurii Miroliubov (1892–1970), along with the editorial board of an obscure San Francisco journal, published 'translations' of the strange 'writing' found on these wooden planks. As Miroliubov told the story, the original planks were found in a house in southern Russia during the Civil War of 1918–20 and then hidden away by a secretive White officer. This treasure disappeared altogether during World War Two and all that remained were a poor-quality photograph of one of the planks and Miroliubov's translations. No serious scholar regards the Veles Book as anything other than an obvious forgery that was created in the nineteenth or twentieth centuries. Its provenance can be reliably traced only as far as Miroliubov himself; one scholar has noted that Miroliubov seems not only to have forged the script, but also to have borrowed the plot of the story of how he came across his archaeological treasure from the classic Jack London story *Tri serdtsa* (*Hearts of Three*), which was very popular in the Soviet era.[205]

The *Veles Book* is a key source for almost all alternative historians despite the fact that its invented Slavic language, with its mix of modern Russian, Czech and Polish words, is utterly incredible as a legitimate source.[206] The supporters of the Veles Book claim that it contains all sorts of evidence about how advanced were the ancient Aryans who escaped from Hyperborea. To the delight of Neo-Pagans, the religion of the Hyperborean refugees anticipated Christianity by thousands of years. The Veles Book reveals that the Hyperboreans were both monotheistic and embraced the concept of a trinity. Rather than Christianity having been brought to Russia in the ninth century as traditional historical accounts suggested, the Orthodox faith emerged organically from its very Russian and very ancient pagan predecessor. Of course, this was not a story that the powerful Orthodox Church and its Romanov patrons wished to entertain and hence the suppression of all knowledge of the Veles Book's existence until recent times.

Alexander Barashkov (1964–), (pseudonym Asov), a former Communist, Komsomol functionary and socialist realist author, is currently the most successful populariser of the Book of Veles in Russia. Asov is a ubiquitous

---

205 See Khlebnikov, *Teoriia zagovora*, p. 413.
206 On the improbability of the Veles Book, see A Alekseev, 'Opiat' o "Velesovoi knige"', *Russkaia literatura*, 1995, No. 2, pp. 248—264, and O. Творогов, 'Chto zhe takoe «Vlesova kniga»?', *Russkaia literatura*, 1998, No 2, pp. 77–102.

presence on YouTube documentaries and his speculations have found their way into various textbooks and teaching aids. Asov is a master of occultist and apocalyptic hocus-pocus and claims to be the reincarnation of Bus Kresen', a pagan priest who lived in the 7th century.[207] However astonishing these claims, Asov and his version of the Veles Book are a publishing triumph.[208] The Veles book is popular not just in Russia, but in Ukraine as well. For Ukrainian neo-pagans, the Veles book is an especially important 'discovery' given the absence of other written sources from the pre-Christian period.

The Hyperboreans may have migrated through Siberia, but they were remarkably Russian in appearance, according to alternative history. The Hyperboreans were 'tall, slender, blonde, and blue-eyed' just like their Aryan offspring.[209] For evidence of these claims, alternative historians often invoke the authority of Gumilev, who argued that even the Borjigin clan, whose descendants included Genghis Khan, comprised tall, white-skinned, fair-haired and blue-eyed people.[210]

Of course, the 'white' people of central Asia were mostly likely the remnants of the Hyperborean exodus and/or evidence that white-skinned Aryans were responsible for the great civilizational achievement of the steppe. The hostility of alternative historians and their audience to any suggestion that Russia or its people are Asian rather than European in part reflects uncertainties over Russia's mixed ancestry and in part is a response to the chacterization of Russia as Asiatic so popular among Russia's critics.

Part Six: Civilizations East and West

It is not just the frozen north that represents a possible ancestral home for the Russians. Not just Hyperborea, but also the myth of Atlantis has undergone a spectacular renaissance in Russia since the collapse of Communism. Speculating about mythical places such as Atlantis is not simply a

---

207 For an analysis, see 'Kuda idut mastera folk-history? *Novaia Gazeta*, 10-06-28 (retrieved March 11, 2013).
208 http://members.cox.net/veles/Spisok.htm www.universalinternet-library.ru
209 http://hyperbor/narod/ru/www/graal/htm Novgorodov
210 Gumilev, *Drevniaia Rus i velikaia step'*, pp. 395, 398. Dmitrii Ilovaiskii, the popular anti-Western nineteenth century historian also emphasized that Genghis Khan was most probably of European appearance. See Dmitri Ilovaiskii, *Stanovlenie Rusi* (Moscow: Charli, 1996) p. 499.

Russian obsession. Dozens of books appear on the topic of Atlantis in English each year. What is most striking about alternative ancient history in Russia is how often the great civilisations of the distant past turn out, on close inspection, to be Russian.

Vladimir Shcherbakov (1938–2004), a Soviet-era radio physicist and science fiction writer, is Russia's most prolific writer on Atlantis. For Shcherbakov, Atlantis was the cradle of human civilizations on both sides of the Atlantic and gave Russia its name. The Atlanteans were originally leopard-worshiping tribes known as Russes, Raseny, or Rusichi and it was they who gave Russia her name.[211] The Russian Atlanteans facilitated a great trans-Atlantic civilisational exchange of peoples and ideas. How else, alternative history asks, are we to explain the similarity of the images of the deities found in the Mayan ruins at Palenque and the images of the Slavic pagan gods such as Dazhbog?[212] Atlantis becomes the explanation of why the ancient cultures of Asia Minor, Cyprus and Crete in the east and the civilizations of Mexico and Peru in the west followed similar trajectories.

As for the 'mystical' East, there is a bewildering amount of information available to modern-day Russians that was not available in the Soviet period. This was especially so when it came to the Buddhist world, which, in the European imagination of the Enlightenment and Romantic periods, attracted attention as a potential alternative source of wisdom.[213] The mystical speculations of writers such as Madame Blavatskaia and the Roerichs are now well known in Russia. In the 1920s and 30s, it was not just German racial theorists who hoped to find evidence of a remarkably advanced civilization based in Tibet and Mongolia. Amateur philosophers, travelers, explorers, and pilgrims from Russia and elsewhere held similar ambitions long preceding the schemes that drove German expeditions to Tibet in the 1930s.

In the 1920s, Soviet authorities became interested in the far-fetched claim of Alexander Barchenko that the legendary Buddhist kingdom of Shambala not only existed, but also was likely to provide clues about useful techniques of mind control. Tibet and Mongolia were considered vital to Soviet geopolitics in the battle for influence in central Asia. The Buryat and Kalmyk

---

211 Shcherbakov, *Potomki Synov Leoparda*, V. Shcherbakov, *Vse ob Atlantide* (Moscow: 1990).
212 A. Asov, *Atlantida i drevniia Rus* (Moscow: AiF, 2001), p. 19.
213 Znamenski, *Red Shamhala*, pp. 168–69.

peoples were Buddhists, the latter having fled China to Russia to escape persecution in the seventeenth century. Soviet authorities hoped to use their Buddhists as a revolutionary wedge aimed at the East.[214] Mongols reputedly considered Russia, and especially her Siberian territories, as a part of Shambhala (or even Shambhala itself), a source of light from the East and the place whence the world would be reborn.

Shambhala lives on in Russia's post-Communist imagination. Ernst Muldashev (1948–) made his name as a celebrated eye surgeon before achieving remarkable success as a popular writer. He has traveled the world in seach of lost civilisations and his books have print runs of hundreds of thousands of copies. According to Muldashev's comparisons of eye pupils around the world, the Earth was populated from Tibet in consecutive waves. In this migration, the Russians occupied a special place. He claims that Himalayan Yogis explained to him that Russia has a 'pink aura' and that 'Russians are able to hear an intuition that comes directly from God. It was not by chance that one sixth of the world's surface has been given to the Russian Life Force (*Russkaia Zhiznennaia Sila*)'.[215]

Hyperborea, Atlantis, and Shambhala are mysterious places whose provenance stretches back into history. A more recent ancestor is the world of the steppe north of the Black Sea. Yet here too the discoveries of alternative historians are no less amazing. For two decades, Yuri Shilov (1949–) and Anatoly Kifishin (1935–) have enjoyed great popularity with their attempts to show that the Black Sea steppe was the original home of Slavic, and, for that matter, world civilisation. Shilov studied archaeology in the Soviet era but was unable to defend his doctoral thesis at the Kievan Institute of Archaeology. He worked in various academic capacities in the 1970s and 80s before reinventing himself, after the Soviet collapse, as, in his own words, a 'charismatic scientist'. His most spectacular claim is that around 7000 years BCE the Tripol'e culture established the first state on earth, Aratta, on what is now the territory of modern Ukraine. Shilov insists that Aratta, not Hyperborea, was the birthplace of law, writing, governance and Indo-European or 'Aryan' civilisation.[216] The evidence for Aratta is obscure and the claim is without any corroboration in the scientific literature.[217] By

---

214 Znameskii, *Red Shambhala*, pp. 110–111.
215 Muldashev, *Mysticheskaia Aura Rossii* (Moscow: 2008).
216 http://www.neplaneta.ru/secrets_history.shtml
217 Shnirleman, 'Russian Response', p. 43.

2013, Shilov had published nearly thirty books on this topic and, like Asov and Fomenko, is a ubiquitous presence on YouTube.[218]
Kifishin was drummed out of the Soviet archaeological academy for claiming that Sumerian, the world's oldest written language, originated in Ukraine.[219] While an academic pariah, Kifishin achieved a revenge of sorts when he published a voluminous and popular account of *Kammenaia mogila* (Stone Tomb), the burial mound that lies just to the north of Crimea near modern Melitopol. It was discovered in the nineteenth century and dates to 2400–2000 BCE. Kifishin claims to have found at *Kamennaia mogila* dozens of carved stone tablets, evidence of the oldest library on earth.[220] His conclusion is that the Slavs of Aratta, the builders of *Kamennaia mogila*, were the nucleus of the Aryan people, and therefore of all human civilisation. In both Russia and Ukraine, Scyths are a major prize in the competition for ancestors. Nationalists on all sides claim that Scyths had an advanced civilization, that the Scyths raided Asia because Europe was too poor in that era to produce worthwhile booty, that the Roman historian Jordanus described Attila the Hun as the ruler of all Scyth barbarians, and that Byzantine writers referred to Prince Sviatoslav of Kiev Rus as leader of the Tauro-Scythian raiders. Archilles, the Greek hero, was supposedly born at Myrmidon in Scythian territory. Alternative historical documentaries tell us that, in 1954, ironically the year that Khrushchev separated Crimea from Russia and gifted it to Ukraine as a reward for the Ukrainian sacrifices in the Great Patriotic War, Soviet archaeologists unearthed in Crimea the semi mummified remnants of a noble Scythian woman, and her gold buried in a deep catacomb; a golden tablet with the depiction of a Scythian quiver; a text telling the story of Achilles's biography from his divine birth to his death in a Trojan war; and inscriptions of the sun that resemble those in use in the pagan religion of the early Slavs.
Shilov and Kifishin are critical of the idea that Russians originally migrated from the north through Siberia to the southern steppe. They point out that the oldest kurgans in the world have been discovered in Ukraine and that

---

218 See, for example, Shilov's film '*Po sledam Velesovoi knigi*', recently filmed in India and Ukraine.
219 Igor Diakonov, the leading Russian specialist on Sumer, exposed Kifishin's idiosyncratic translations of ancient languages as a fraud.
220 http://www.mesogaia.il.if.ua/shilov09.htm

they are far older than Arkaim.[221] Thus, the original Aryan homeland was the Ukrainian steppe where an egalitarian warrior society reminiscent of the Cossacks created a mighty civilisation.[222] For Shilov, Aratta's descendents sailed from Ukraine to Troy in 2400–2200 BCE and, between 1700 and 1100 BCE, sent expeditions to Etruria where they left behind the Etruscan language.[223] Worryingly, the Ukrainian Ministry of Education and Science has recommended as teaching aids books that rely upon the wisdom of Shilov and Kifishin.[224]

Of course, a Ukrainian nationalist might say that all of this proves only the greatness of Ukrainians. Russian nationalists brush aside such objections; everything Slavic is Russian, including Ukraine itself. Kifishin himself in 2012 received a prestigious prize in the Kremlin for his contributions to inter-Slavic unity and his 'outstanding achievements in the study of the ancient written memorials of humanity and personal bravery in defending the interests of patriotic science'.[225]

For many Russians, there has always been a natural affinity with the allegedly barbarian Scyths, the northern neighbours of the ancient Greeks. Russian and Ukrainian writers compete for the Scyths as their Russian ancestors. The Scyths themselves had no written language, but they were most likely an Indo-Iranian-speaking group and their semi-nomadic pastoralist economy is often contrasted with the economy and culture of the Slavs, who were sedentary farmers.[226] Of course, alternative historians do not accept the distinction between nomadic Scyths and Slav farmers, and nor do they acknowledge a link between the Scyths and the Iranian language. But where is the proof of the Scyths' connections to the Slavs? Fortunately, a picture is worth at least a thousand words. The images of the Scythian 'ideal type' left to us on various artifacts depict warriors that closely resemble latter-day Cossacks, Russian peasants and nobles, or so alternative historians assert. They depict spear-throwing horsemen dressed in a shirt covered in pea-shaped circles, and wide pants with stripes along the sides. Alternative historians claim that this was the prototype of the standard dress

---

221 http://www.neplaneta.ru/secrets_history.shtml
222 Victor Shnirelman, 'Russian Response', p. 43.
223 http://clarino2.narod.ru/troia.htm
224 Lapenkov, *Istoriia Netraditsionnoi Orientatsii*, p. 162.
225 http://www.cnsr.ru/eng/news.php?id=487
226 Shnirelman, 'Russian Response', p.39. Anthony, *The Horse, the Wheel, and Language*, p. 51.

of the latter-day Cossacks. The gold coins found in their burial sites is evidence not just that the Scyths were mounted warriors and hunters like the Cossacks, but that their civilization was much more advanced than the ancient Greeks allowed.

Figure Two: A Scythian warrior with allegedly Slavic dress and hairstyle
Source: Google Pictures

Alternative history insists that, like the Cossacks, the Scyths were a military democracy, comprising expert cavalrymen. As was the case with the Cossacks, there were both sedentary and nomadic Scyths. The nomadic Scyths moved often as they looked for new pastures; many Cossacks did the same. Other Scyths were more sedentary, lived in fortified towns, and migrated much less frequently. Meanwhile, Scyth farmers produced grain surpluses, which they stored in gigantic granaries, and then exported to the Greek world. There was, we are told, equality between Scyth men and women, with the latter performing military service; the mummified remains of Scyth women dressed as warriors have been found in the steppe kurgans, a practice that may have given rise to Herodotus's tales of Amazonian warriors. Byzantine sources report that the Kiev Rus' raiding party led by Prince Sviatoslav in the mid-tenth century contained female warriors. Herodotus described Scythian rituals such as baptism by the sword, which matched descriptions of Slavic baptisms in medieval church chronicles. The ancient Greeks, who watered down their wine, noted that the Scythians enjoyed their alcohol in a purer form, further evidence, it would seem, that, culturally, the Scyths were the forerunners of modern Russians.

Part Seven: The Russian Tower of Babel

As countless works of alternative history will attest, the Slavic language is the trunk, and not just one of the branches, of the Indo-European language tree. Here, Russian alternative historians are experiencing fierce competition from the champions of other ethnic groups within the former Soviet Union. For example, Mirfatykh Zakiev, a Chairman of the Supreme Soviet of the Tatar ASSR and professor of philology who has published hundreds of scientific works, argues that proto-Turkish is the starting point of the Indo-European languages. Zakiev and his colleagues claim to have discovered the Tatar roots of the Sumerian, ancient Greek and Icelandic languages and deciphered Etruscan and Minoan writings.[227]

Of course, alternative historians in Russia cannot accept any of this. In the world of alternative history, the spatial and temporal reach of Russia is matched only by its civilizational achievements. Slavic, and, increasingly, Russian, turns out to have been the most ancient of all the world's languages.[228] Alternative writers claim to have solved just about every mystery connected to the history of languages, especially Indo-European (Aryan) languages. For example one of these linguistic mysteries is Etruscan. Conventional historians consider that the Etruscans arrived in Italy from Asia Minor and used a version of Greek. For alternative historians, Etruscan, like Sanskrit or Sumerian, was part of the Slavic language group.

The Phaistos Disc, the clay artifact from Minoan Crete dating to the second millennium BC, has defied expert analysis for decades. Gennadii Grinevich (1938–) has had no difficulties establishing that the Cretan system of writing was derived from ancient proto-Slavic runes. According to Grinevich, the Cretans were a sophisticated people, although his translations suggest that they were deeply concerned with bodily functions. He has found endless

---

[227] V. Lapenkov, *Istoriia Netraditsionnoi Orientatsii*, 23. I. L. Izmailov, *Zvezda Povolzhia*, 17–21 (169–173), April–May, 2003.

[228] Genadii Grinevich, *Praslavianskaia pis'mennost': rezultaty deshifrovki*, vols one and two (Moscow: Obshchestvennaia pol'za, 1993, 1997).

references to vomit, semen and other fluids disgorged from these early Russians. It is a measure of the reach of alternative history that Grinevich's mistranslations have become part of popular culture in present-day Russia. Valerii Chudinov (1942–), a Soviet-era philosopher and academic, is one alternative writer who thinks that Grinevich is guilty of a great many errors. Chudinov, who, in 2012 alone, published four books and reprinted eight others, specializes in runes, a type of writing usually associated with the early Germans and Scandinavians. Runes, according to Chudinov are the earliest Russian writing; he claims to have read over three thousand runic inscriptions found on coins, monuments, household items, the Veles Book, and in just about every archaeological dig.[229] Like many other popular accounts of the ancient past, Chudinov believes that the ancients were remarkably advanced and invented such modern wonders as jet engines, which were subsequently lost to history. Chudinov claims that there are Russian inscriptions on the Moon and Mars.[230] Fantastic as it may seem that this type of claim has any credibility with readers, it must be remembered that Russia itself was a land of peasant carts and space travel in the Soviet era.

A 'greatness syndrome' is at work within alternative history; they compete with each other to astonish their readers. Iurii Khlestkov (1942–), a teacher at MIFI and a specialist in the field of relative electro-dynamics and gravitational theory, tells us that 'RA' is the original and distinctive combination of sounds for the ancient Aryans. It was associated with the Sun and the Universe and was the chief deity of the ancient Slavs as it was for many other ancient peoples. 'Ra' evolved into the 'Ru' in Russia. This means that the Russians are the sons of the Sun and the Universe.[231] How could it be otherwise, the skeptical reader might ask.

Part Eight: Good versus Evil

There are countless books establishing a new genealogy for an imagined Russian empire, and revealing the plot against it that lies behind its decline in more modern times. Victor and Dmitrii Kandyba are a father-and-son

---

229 V. Chudinov, *Runitsa i tainy arkheologii rusi* (Moscow: Veche, 2003).
230 V. Chudinov, *Runitsa i tainy arkheologii rusi*.
231 Ui. Khlestkov, *Ura. Smyslovoi slovar basovykh slov ruskkogo iazyka* (Moscow, TOO Novina: 1996). For more on the importance of 'Ra', see See V. Istarkhov, *Udar Russkikh Bogov*, (Moscow: 1999)

team who championed the cause of hypnosis before achieving further success by writing books that explore Russian history in the spirit of neo-paganism. Predictably, Russia was central to a cosmic cycle of civilizational rise and fall and an endless battle between good and evil that began no less than eighteen million years ago.[232] The heroes of this story are Russian 'supermen' who, according to Kandyba, built their first city, Troy, about ten thousand years BCE and soon after wrote the Book of Veles. By 5000 BCE, Russian civilisation was flourishing in Europe, the Aegean and China. By 500 BCE, this Russian Empire expanded to create new civilizations in Japan, Vietnam and Korea. In the 400s AD, Russians marched against Rome, conquered the Indian Gupta dynasty, and then created their new capitals in Kiev and Novgorod. Disaster struck in the twelfth century with the arrival of evil Mongol invaders. In the twentieth century, a massive international conspiracy against Russia brought the Communists to power and resulted in the virtual genocide of the Russians. While the Russians showed signs of revival in World War Two, it fell once more into the hands of criminals in the 1980s. Nonetheless, it is the Russians who are fated to 'eliminate evil from the earth and to restore God's kingdom'.[233]

After the collapse of the Byzantine Empire in 1453, Russian churchmen proclaimed that Russia's mission was to be a Third Rome and to restore the fortunes of Christianity. Pagans like Kandyba view Russia in much the same way. For Kandyba, Russians are warriors of the purest type, in contrast to the treachery and depravity of their enemies; he recommends the use of nuclear weapons to win the war against evil. This is remarkable stuff, but just as remarkable is the fact that Kandyba has been able to team up with a conventional historian, Petr Zolin, an academic with a doctorate in history, to write his books.[234]

All of this might be dismissed as a harmless carnival of ideas, were it not for the more sinister undertones and explicit racism of much alternative history. Kifishin and Shilov have described how hordes of proto-Semites from the East forced the Aryans/Indo-Europeans northwards into the glacial regions; vivid pictures of this struggle are to be found everywhere in the remains of

---

232 Kandyba, V, *Istoriia ruskogo naroda* (St-Petersburg: Lan', 1996).
233 See Victor Shnirelman, 'Ancient Wisdom and Ethnic Nationalism: The View From Eastern Europe', *The Pomegranate*, 9.1 (2007). p. 58.
234 Viktor Kandyba and Peter Zolin, *Istoriia i ideologia ruskkogo naroda* II volumes (St-Petersburg: Lan', 1997); Viktor Kandyba, *Zapreshchennaia Istoriia* (St-Petersburg: Lan', 1998).

Ice Age Europe. The proto-Slavic names of the Celtic Gods are, it seems, testimony to the pluck and resilience of the proto-Slavs, who refused to surrender to the Semite menace and eventually fought their way back into history.[235]

Alternative history is full of warning about the Jewish threat to Russia. Yuri Petukhov (1951–2009) was a Soviet-era defence engineer, who, as Communism collapsed, reinvented himself as a dystopian science fiction writer, and, in the 1990s, as a self-described 'ethno-historian' and 'ethno-philosopher'. Like many of his alternative brethren, Petukhov travelled widely in search of the original Indo-European, that is, Aryan, homeland. He inspected well-known archaeological sites and acquainted himself with conventional scholarship. Darwinian evolution made no sense to Petukhov. Instead, the peoples of the world descended from a Russian 'superethnos'. The Russian people today are, figuratively, just the crowning tip of a gigantic iceberg that stretches far back into history.[236] Uniting the most ancient civilisations including Egypt, Sumer, the Harappa culture from the Indus Valley and Chatal-Uiuka in Asia Minor is the fact that they were creations of the Rus, who were also the people described in the Bible as living before the 'flood', speaking the one language and the creators of human civilization. Russians dominated the 'Scythian-Siberian world' and much else besides. Petukhov claims that more than two-thirds of all place names in the Aegean, the Balkans, Apennines and Mediterranean coastline have an obvious Slavic source. Over the last four thousand years, Russians vacated these lands in favour of their junior Slavic brothers, a category that Petukhov thinks includes the Greeks, Italians, Germans, Balts and other nations. Like many other alternative historians, Petukhov has found in the ancient past a monumental struggle between Jews and non-Jews. The original homeland of the Rus turns out to be Palestine. Moses was in fact Mosokh,

---

235 See Ui. Shilov, *Djerela* (Kiev: Aratta, 2002), and A. Kifishin, *Drevnee Sviatilishche Kamennaia Mogila* (Kiev: Aratta, 2001).

236 See, for example, Iurii Petukhov, *Vechnaia Rossiia* (Moscow: Molodaia Gvardiia, 1990); Iurii Petukhov, *Dorogami Bogov* (Moscow: Mysl', 1990); Iurii Petukhov, *Kolybel' Zevsa: Istoriia Russov ot antichnosti do nashikh dnei* (Moscow: Mysl', 1998); Iurii Petukhov, *Gibel' Rossii* (Moscow: Mysl', 1999); Iurii Petukhov, *Istoriia Russov 40.000 let do nashei ery* vol. I (Moscow: Mysl', 2000); Iurii Petukhov, *Russkaia Khazaria* (Moscow: Mysl', 2001); Iurii Petukhov, *Tainy drevnikh russov* (Moscow: Veche, 2001, 2002, 2003); Iurii Petukhov, *Rusy drevnego Vostoka* (Moscow: Veche, 2003);

the legendary founder of Moscow. Much later, younger tribes of proto-Semites pushed out the Rus from the Holy Lands.[237] Shortly before his death in 2009, Petukhov was involved in legal proceedings where he was accused and found guilty by a Moscow court of xenophobia and inciting violence; this, of course, has not prevented his books selling in the millions of copies and new editions continuing to appear after his death.

Part Nine: Local Heroes and Family Feuds

Often, there are also local pressures that drive forward the writing of alternative history. Nikolai Novogorodov (1948–) is well known as a Siberian 'Fomenko'. He argues that Alexander the Great did not invade India, but rather invaded Siberia and that traces of the invasion are to be found in the Hellenistic toponomy of Novgorodov's home region.[238] Novgorodov focuses upon the Siberian city of Tomsk, whose historical prestige has been overshadowed in recent years by Arkaim. Fortunately, local researchers led by Novgorodov have made some remarkable discoveries.[239] Novgorodov trumpeted Tomsk's connection to the legend of the Holy Grail. According to Novgorodov, the European area where the legend of the Grail spread is identical to the area once inhabited by the Goths. Novgorodov's analysis of the sources, archaeological evidence, and linguistical data points to the Siberian origin of both the Goths and the Grail legend. He notes that various European maps placed Prester John's legendary kingdom on the right shore of the Ob' river, referring to it as *Grustina*. During a conference dedicated to developing the tourist trade in Siberia, Novgorodov made an announcement that the ruins of a three-thousand-year-old city had been found under Tomsk, much to the delight of local dignitaries and business people.[240] Conventional scholars often toil away for decades with no remarkable discoveries to their credit. The world of alternative history is one of instant gratification.

Alternative history is not a unified movement and alternative historians routinely squabble with one another and compete for the honour of making the

---

237 Petukhov, *Rusy drevnego Vostoka* (Moscow: Veche, 2011).
238 N. Novgorodov, *Sibirskii Pokhod Alexandra Makedonskogo* (Tomsk: Agraf-Press, 2006).
239 See Novgorodov, *Sibirskaia Prarodina: v poiskakh Giperborei* (Moscow: Belye Al'vy, 2006).
240 See Lapenkov, *Istoriia netraditsionnoi orientatsii*, pp. 113–14.

most remarkable claim. Zharnikova, for example, notes that Shambala and Atlantis have no precise location. By contrast, 'Hyperborea is real… and we are its descendants'.[241] Such an argument for Hyperborean speculation does not impress Shilov who has written that the 'Arctic theory' is a patriotic tease for amateur historians and pseudo-scientists that, sadly, distracts from the 'holy facts and true problems of our national history'.[242] Neo-pagans have condemned Fomenko, Asov, Chudinov, Grinevich and other alternative history for discrediting the cause with their wild claims.[243] Critics of Neo-paganism object to the fact that 'occultists' have turned Arkaim into a place of pilgramage and distracted attention from the real history of Russia's civilisational achievement. Still others blame the standard textbooks where 'Russian history starts as if from a zero, from Slavic settlements of the seventh century, the Second Act so to speak. … As a result, our semi-educated people are producing, constructing, and consuming folklore about Etruscans as if they are ethnic Russians. They are filling the void with answers that cannot be found in conventional textbooks'.

Conclusion

According to alternative history, these lost civilisations and legendary stories are at the very least evidence that the ancients believed that something important and foundational to civilization had occurred not in relatively recent Ancient Greece and Rome, but in the lands that would later belong to the Russian Empire. Russia's geography has encouraged alternative historians to imagine a vast empire in the past. These imaginings are a useful and, arguably, an indispensible part of present-day Russian claims to lands that stretch from Siberia and Tibet in the east to the Baltic and Black Seas in the west, and from the steppe in the south to the Arctic coastline in the north. One Soviet citizen, cast adrift politically, economically, and socially after the collapse of Communism, complained that the authorities had left its citizens to their own devices. It was, he noted, like leaving a house pet in the forest to fend for itself.[244] Alternative writers are helping the former

---

241 See Lapenkov, *Istoriia netraditsionnoi orientatsii*, p. 13.
242 http://www.mesogaia.il.if.ua/shilov03.htm
243 Соглашение "О жрецах славянских" от 23 мая 2012 года", retrieved March 11, 2013.
244 Oushakine, 'Stop the Invasion', p. 72.

house pets to restake their territory in every corner of Russia's spatial and historical forest.

It is unlikely that alternative historians will achieve the total victory they are seeking in their contest with the professional historians. On the other hand, a partial victory is within their grasp. There have been heavyweight Soviet-era historians, who have moved in a more 'patriotic' direction since the collapse of the Soviet Union. Perhaps the most famous Soviet expert on the origins of the Slavs was Boris Rybakov (1908–2002). Rybakov, whose scientific publications date back to 1932, argued in the post-Soviet period that not only the Scyths, but also Tripol'e culture was a Slavic culture even though most experts see no evidence of the Slavs until thousands of years later.[245] Gennadii Zdanovich, the Soviet archaeologist who led the excavations at Arkaim, has suggested that Arkaim proves that the Slavs and the steppe peoples share a common ancestry.[246] All of this is music to the ears of Alternative History, proof that they are on the right side of history.

---

245 See Boris Rybakov, A. Sakharov, A. Preobrazhensky, B. Krasnobaev, *Istoriia otechestva* (Moscow: Prosveshchenie, 1993).
246 See Victor Shnirelman, 'Russian Response. Archaeology, Russian Nationalism, and the "Arctic Homeland"' in Philip L. Kohl et al, *Selective Remembrances : Archaeology in the Construction, Commemoration, and* Consecration *of National Pasts* (Chicago: University of Chicago Press, 2007), p. 46.

Chapter Five: Vikings and Slavs

'Moderately wise a man should be, not too crafty or clever.
A learned man's heart whose learning is deep seldom sings with joy.'

The Havamal, Viking poem

Part One: Nestor the Normanist and Russophobe

The passions of the alternative historians have to be understood in the context of the oldest debate in Russian history, the dispute over the Viking origins of Kiev Rus. According to the standard accounts, Vikings came to Russia in search of silver in the ninth century. They established trade with Byzantium and the Arabs along the Dvina, Dnieper, and Volga rivers that connected the Baltic, Black and Caspian Seas. Known as Varangians to the early Slavs, these Viking or Norman raiders evidently impressed the warring Slavic tribes because, according to the early Church chronicles, the Slavs asked the Varangians to establish peace and good governance in their lands. The invitation of the Slavs to a certain Rurik and his kinfolk, the 'Rus', in 862 led to the establishment of Kiev Rus, the first state in the lands that would later become the Russian Empire. With its princes ruling vast areas from Novgorod in the north to Kiev in the south, from Galich in the west to Moscow in the east, Kiev Rus was arguably the largest state in medieval Europe. Kiev Rus in the ninth century was bordered by Turkic peoples to the east, notably the Khazar kaganate on the Black Sea coast and the Bulgar khanate of the middle Volga. Further to the south was Byzantium and further to the southeast was the Abbasid caliphate. Kiev Rus had the disadvantage of having no natural frontiers, but also the advantage of sitting adjacent to the trade routes that linked Asia, Byzantium and Europe.

Kiev Rus remains a matter of great pride to Russians as well as Ukrainians and Belalrusians, a land of 'international commerce, flourishing cities, 'democratic' institutions and cultural achievements'.[247] Gumilev thought that Kiev was the third richest city of the era after Constantinople and Cordoba.[248] For Slavophiles, Kiev Rus was a cradle of East Slavic, and, therefore,

---

[247] Charles Halperin, *Russia and the Golden Horde: the Mongol impact on modern medieval history* (Bloomington: Indiana University Press, 1985), p. 10.
[248] Gumilev, *Drevniaia Rus' i velikaia step'*, p. 269.

Russian civilization. For Eurasianists, Kiev Rus was an early example of the strength of the relationship between the early Slavs and their nomadic neighbours who lived along the southern steppe.

Outside of Russia, historians have been less impressed by Kiev Rus. In the West, the tendency until recently was to view Russia as 'a backward, Asiatic, or medieval society until the reforms of Peter the Great' in the seventeenth and eighteenth century.[249] According to Halperin, the golden age of Kiev was much exaggerated.[250] In reference to the reign of Iaroslav the Wise, a high point of Kievan civilization, one Western account concluded that Kiev Rus's 'literary culture—almost entirely borrowed—bears little comparison with the elite intellectual pursuits which might be found in the centers of Greek and Latin learning. Despite the triumphal image building, Kiev was not Constantinople'.[251] Norman Davies exceeded these polite rebuffs with his claim that this was the 'most downtrodden province of Christendom'.[252]

There remains heated controversy about the origins of Kiev Rus. For the protagonists in this debate, the question was whether Kiev Rus was a legacy of the early Slavs or a creation of Viking conquerors. The so-called Normanist viewpoint suggested that Vikings from Scandinavia gave Russia her name and established the first state in the lands that would become the Russian Empire. Anti-Normanists rejected this account, arguing that a Russian state existed before the Vikings and that the Viking ascendancy was much exaggerated. In the nineteenth century, the controversy became a key element in the struggle between Slavophiles and Westerners, especially for the former who came to believe that knowledge of the past was the key to shaping Russia's future.[253] This historical battle continued in the twentieth century with the official history of the Stalin era taking up the cause of anti-Normanism in place of the Slavophiles.

At the heart of the matter is the variety and complexity of the source material, comprising, as Davies put it, 'Slavic and Byzantine chronicles...Old

---

249 Michael C. Paul, 'The Military Revolution in Russia, *1550–1682*', The *Journal of Military History* 68: 1 (January 2004): p. 9.
250 Halperin, *Russia and the Golden Horde*, p. 10.
251 Simon Franklin and Jonathan Shepard, *The Emergence of Rus, 750–1200*, (London: Longman, 1996), p. 244.
252 Norman Davies, *Europe: a history* (Oxford: Oxford University Press, 1996), p. 457.
253 Joseph Black, 'The State School Interpretation of Russian History: A reappraisal of its genetic origins', *Jahrbucher for Geschichte Osteuropas* 2:173:511.

Norse literature, comparative German and Turkic (Khazarian) mythology, runic inscriptions, Scandinavian and Friesian law codes, Danish and Icelandic annals, Arab geographies, Hebrew documents, even Turkic inscriptions from Mongolia'.[254] The basic source for the history of Kiev Rus is the *Povest vremennykh let*, or, as it is better known in English, the *Russian Primary Chronicle*. Allegedly written by the monks Nestor and Sylvester in the early twelfth century, the *Primary Chronicle* describes important events from the ninth to the twelfth centuries, most famously the invitation to the Varangians to come to rule over Russia.

A crucial passage in the *Primary Chronicle* recorded under the year 862 how:

> The four tribes who had been forced to pay tribute to the Varangians—Chud, Slavs, Merya and Krivichi drove the Varangians back beyond the sea, refused to pay them further tribute, and set out to govern them. But there was no law among them, and tribe rose against tribe. Discord thus ensued among them, and they began to war one against the other. They said to themselves, 'let us seek princes who may rule over us, and judge us according to custom. Thus they went overseas to the Varangians. These particular Varangians were known as Rus, just as some are called Swedes, and others Normans and Angles, and still others Gothlanders, for they were thus named. The Chud, the Slavs, the Krivichi and the Ves then said to the Rus 'our land is great and rich, but there is no order in it. Come reign as princes, rule over us.' Three brothers with their kinfolk were selected. They brought with them all the Rus and migrated. The oldest, Riurik, located himself in Novgorod; the second, Sineus, in Beloozero; and the third, Truvor, in Izborsk. From these Varangians the Russian land received its name. Thus those who live in Novgorod are descended from the Varangian tribe, but earlier they were Slavs. Within two years, Sineus and his brother Truvor died. Riurik gathered sole authority into his own hands, parceling out cities to his own men, Polotsk to one, Rostov to another, and to another Beloozero. The Varangians in these cities were the colonists, while the first settlers in Novgorod were Slavs, in Polotsk Krivichi, in Beloozero Ves, in Rostov Mer, and in Murom Muromians. Riurik had dominion over all these folk.[255]

From this passage, it would seem that Russia obtained its name from a Varangian tribe, the Rus, whose kinfolk were Swedes, Normans, Angles and Gothlanders. It is stated just as clearly that Slavic peoples along with other presumably Finnic and Baltic peoples of the Novgorod region invited foreign

---

254 Davies, *History of Europe*, p. 656.
255 The translation comes from Samuel Hazzard Cross and Olgerd P. Sherbowitz-Wetzor (ed.), *Russian Primary Chronicle: Laurentian text* (Cambridge: Medieval Academy of America, 1973), pp. 144–45.

intervention as a means of ending their civil war. Varangians were the active state-builders, warriors and colonists while Slavs needed to be saved from themselves.

From the early eighteenth century, historians pieced together evidence from Byzantine, west European, Arab and Persian sources to confirm that the Rus referred to in the *Primary Chronicle* were most likely from Scandinavia. In the West, the war is declared over and a moderate and modified version of Normanism triumphant. Normanists see little more than wounded pride in the more extreme statements of anti-Normanism. As Geoffrey Hosking has put it, 'in the past there was a lively historical debate about the identity of the Rus, but today there does not seem to be much doubt that they were Scandinavian Vikings or 'Varangians' as the Slavs called them.[256]

Hosking is certainly correct to state that Normanists dominate the debate in the West. Hosking's suggestion that 'it is not unknown for relatively primitive peoples to accept a ruler from a higher culture' is unlikely to win over anti-Normanist writers inside Russia, who will not countenance the idea that the Slavs of that era were more backward than the notoriously brutish Vikings.[257] Starting with Lomonosov in the mid eighteenth century, there has been a consistent and virulent Anti-Normanism, at the core of which is the suspicion that Normanism is a key element in the plot against Russia.

Ironically, it was the educational reforms Peter the Great put in place that would elevate the Swedes, whom the founder of modern Russia vanquished on the battlefield, to place of pride in the story of Russia's origins. Peter the Great not only defeated Sweden in the war for control of the Baltic sea-lanes, but he established centers of learning, notably the Academy of Sciences in St. Petersburg in 1725, that would take charge of writing Russia's history. The establishment of St. Petersburg's Academy of Sciences was entrusted to Laurentius Blumentrost, Peter the Great's physician. Born in Russia of German parents, Blumentrost presided over an academy dominated by scholars born outside of Russia. The first four presidents were Germans, a microcosm of the German-dominated political establishment of the mid eighteenth century. At that time, three-quarters of the fifty-seven individuals appointed to the Academy spoke German as their first lan-

---

[256] Hosking, *Russia and the Russians*, p. 30.
[257] Hosking, *Russia and the Russians*, p. 31.

guage.[258] A similar pattern emerged after Moscow University was founded in 1755 with foreign-born scholars playing key roles. Lectures took place in Latin because none of the professors spoke proficient Russian, while Russian students did not speak German.[259] Despite the language problems, many Russian academics would subsequently praise the work of their German predecessors; others suspected a German plot against Russia.

For alternative historians, the German cultural invasion known as the Academy of Science was an especially significant development because now, for the first time, history would be written in the modern form that has reached us in the present day. The fabrication of Russian history, that is, the writing out of history of the Russian Horde and its replacement with the myth of first Viking and then Mongol conquerors of Russia, can be dated from this period.

The first of the German scholars to make a contribution to Russian history was S.H. Bayer (1694–1738), a philologist by training and one of the first appointments to the St.-Petersburg's Academy of Science. Bayer had expertise in a great many languages. The striking exception was Russian. Even so, Bayer, in *De Varagis*, argued that the Varangians were clearly Vikings. Bayer found the answer to the rapid expansion of Kiev Rus in the political and military energy generated by the arrival of Scandinavian warriors in the area stretching from Novgorod to Kiev.

Bayer not only deflated the pretensions of the Russians to have been a great medieval power. He also deprived the Slavs of the Scyths, describing them as people from Asia, and therefore not Slavs. Bayer's lack of expertise in Russian language later fuelled claims that foreigners were not competent to deal with Russian history. Critics derided Bayer for concluding that the Kievan Rus' princes Vsevolod, Olga, Vladimir and Svyatoslav were Scandinavian Vikings on the basis of their supposedly 'Germanic' names.[260] Kliuchevskii commented acidly:

---

258 Edward Thaden, 'V. N. Tatishchev', German Historians and the St. Petersburg Academy of Sciences,' *Russian History* 13:4 (Winter 1986): 3, pp. 67–98, 371.
259 Beliavskii, *M. V. Lomonosov i osnovanie Moskovskogo universiteta K 200 letiiu MGU* (Moscow: 1956), p. 77.
260 Mikhail Lomonosov, *Trudy po russkoi istorii, obshcestvenno-ekonomicheskim voprosam i geografii*, 1747–1765, vol. 6 (Leningrad: USSR Academy of Sciences, 1952), p. 30.

Foreign historians-academics had to deal with the Norman question, when the circumstances were against them. Knowing little or no Russian language at all, they nevertheless eagerly seized an opportunity to work with that (Norman) theory. Bayer did not even know that Sinopsis' was not a historian.[261]

Sinopsis was a popular history that first appeared in 1674 written by Innokentii Gizel who was then archimandrite of the Kievan Cave Monastery. It traced the Russians back to the Biblical flood. Bayer had a more secular approach and bolstered his case with strong evidence from non-Russian sources. The Byzantine document, *De administrando imperiia* was written by the Emperor Constantine VII Porhyrogenitus (913–959) to assist in the education of his son. On the basis of a source known to him but not to us, Constantine provided a bilingual list of the names of the seven Dnieper rapids in Slavic and in Rus, implying that the two languages and therefore the peoples who spoke them were distinct entities. Constantine's list of Rus names contained a majority of names that seem to Normanists to be clearly Scandinavian in origin. For many subsequent commentators, this was decisive evidence in favour of the Norman theory.[262]

Gerard Fredrick Mueller (1705–1783) was the second of the German historians to work in Russia. Arriving in Russia in 1725, Mueller painstakingly learnt the Russian language and was, by most accounts, an excellent historian. Mueller noted the lack of sources in the Russian central archives. Between 1733 and 1743, Mueller travelled through Siberia, collecting and copying chronicles. He brought back with him thirty-eight copies of various chronicles, the famous Mueller portfolio.[263]

In 1748 Mueller received Russian citizenship, the title of Russia's historiographer, and an obligation to write Russian history.[264] The following year, Muller presented an oration to the Empress entitled *De origine gentis et nominis Russorum*. Mueller argued that Russia acquired its name from the Finnish word for Swedes, *ruotsi*. It is a claim that still has supporters.[265] Mueller also used the treaties signed in 911 and 945 between the Byzantine

---

[261] Vasilii Kliuchevskii, *Neopublikovannye proizvedeniya* (Moscow: Nauka, 1983), p. 120.
[262] See, for example, A D Stokes, 'Kievan Russia' in Robert Auty and Dimitrii Obolensky (eds), *An introduction to Russian History* (Cambridge: Cambridge University Press, 1976), p. 52.
[263] Kliuchevskii, *Neopublikovannye proizvedenia*, p. 191.
[264] Vernadsky, *Russkaia istoriografia*, p. 51.
[265] Franklin and Shephard, *The Emergence of Rus*, pp. 28–30.

emperors and the princes of Kiev to show that the Rus, in Mueller's opinion, had names with obviously Scandinavian origins.[266]

The third of the German historians was August von Ludwig Schloezer (1735–1800). Schloezer was invited to Russia by Mueller and worked there between 1761 and 1767. He served as an honorary member of St.-Petersburg's Academy of Science after he returned to Germany in 1768. There is general agreement that it was Schloezer who undertook the first systematic study of the Russian chronicles. Schloezer's shining achievement was the preparation for publication of the *Russian Primary Chronicle*, the crucial source that has served as a foundation for the writing of the history of Kievan Rus. Schloezer also was involved in preparing for publication the Radzivill Chronicle, famous for its six hundred miniatures and dated to the fifteenth century. It was Schloezer who emphasized the importance of the *Primary Chronicle*, claimed that it was the work of the monk Nestor and argued most strongly that the Varangians must have been Scandinavians. Unlike Mueller, Schloezer did not think that the Varangians were Swedes specifically but instead saw them as being of mixed Scandinavian or Germanic origins.

While Nestor's authorship of the *Primary Chronicle* is often questioned, the *Primary Chronicle* itself remains the most widely used source for the history of Kiev Rus. The Soviet historian Priselkov, echoing Gumilev, wryly remarked that Nestor was clearly an ultra-Normanist.[267] Schloezer, meanwhile, did not endear himself to future generations of Russian patriots when he commented famously in one of his later works published in Germany that:

> Even if it is offensive for Russian patriots, their history... is not as ancient as Greek and Roman, and is even younger than that of Germans and Swedes...the wild, crude and dispersed Slavs became public people only with the help of the Germans, whose fate it was to spread the fruits of civilization in the North-Western and North-Eastern worlds.[268]

Bayer, Mueller and Schloezer together established the basic features of what might be called 'strong' Normanism. The claims that the Varangians

---

266 Walter Gleason, 'The course of Russian History According to an eighteenth Century layman,' *Laurentian University Review* 10:1 (1977): p. 21.
267 Mikhail Priselkov, *Istoriia Russkogo letopisaniia XI–XV vekov* (Moscow: 1940), p. 39.
268 Anti-Normanists invariably stress this statement as evidence of German bias. See Tolz, *Russia*, p. 52.

were Scandinavian, that the Rus were a sub-group of the Varangians and that it was Riurik and his offspring who established the Kiev Rus state lies at the heart of standard Western and, to a lesser extent, Russian accounts of Russia's origins. It is now clear that the claims of the early Normanists were overstated. By the twentieth century, it had become apparent that Viking influence upon Russian politics or culture was not as great as Schloezer imagined. Instead, modern Normanists tend to look upon the Varangians as a catalyst for a new and important phase in Russian history without insisting that this was the first example of statehood in Russian history or that Russian politics and language are deeply indebted to Scandinavians, the key claims of Schloezer.[269] As Hosking has put it, 'together, the 'Viking-Slavs' formed a kind of tribal super-alliance with its centre at Kiev'.[270]

Part Two: Slavs as State Builders

The eighteenth-century debate highlighted divergent ways of conceiving what Russia was. German historians tended to look upon the relationship between Scandinavia and Russia as if the two regions were distinct in the manner of modern states. Schloezer believed that here was a case of a more advanced Scandinavian or German culture lifting the backward Slavs out of their benighted and primitive pre-state existence, much as was happening thanks to German education of the culturally backward Russians at the imperial court.

The Normanist thesis came under attack on at least three occasions. In 1749–50, it was Lomonosov. In the second half of the nineteenth century when Slavophilism and Pan-Slavism were strong currents among the Russian reading public, anti Normanism revived in the works of Dmitrii Ilovaisky (1832–1920), Stepan Gedeonov (1818–1878) and Mikhail Hrushevskii (1866–1934).[271] Finally in the Soviet era, and especially after the Great Pat-

---

269 See, for example, David Christian, *A history of Russia, Central Asia, and Mongolia*, p. 334.
270 Hosking, *Russia and the Russians*, p. 34.
271 Dmitrii Ilovaisky, *Istoriia Rossii; Razyskania o nachale Rusi* (Moscow: 1882); Stepan Gedeonov, *Variagi i Rus* (St-Petersburg: 1876), and 'Otzvyki iz issledovanii o variazhskom voprose', *Zapiski Akademii Nauk* 2 (1862); Mikhail Hrushevskii, *Kievskaia Rus* (St-P: 1911).

riotic War, it became standard practice to criticize Normanism. This was the literature with which Fomenko and many of the alternative writers grew up. The Soviet political leadership, fanatically opposed to bourgeois nationalism in theory but pragmatically Russo-centric in practice, presided over a massive rewriting of Russian history from an anti-Normanist perspective. The chief exponents of Anti-Normanism in the Soviet era included Boris Grekov (1882–1953), Mikhail Tikhomirov (1893–1965), Boris Rybakov (1908–2002), Peter Tretiakov (1909–1976), Lev Cherepnin (1905–1977), Vasilii Mavrodin (1908–1987), Arsenii Nasonov (1898–1965), Alexander Udal'tsov (1883–1958) and M. Priselkov (1881–1941).[272] Anti-Normanists have attempted to prove that the *Primary Chronicle* was contradictory, that foreign sources relied upon by Normanists were ambivalent, that advocates of Normanism were biased, that people called the Rus lived in Russia but not in Scandinavia long before 862, that Russia was urbanized and agricultural with only isolated evidence of Scandinavian presence or a trade and plunder culture, and that Slavs were as capable as Vikings of having achieved military feats such as raids on Byzantium or the Caspian ports.

The problem is that patriotically minded activists as well as historians want answers to questions for which the existing sources are simply not adequate. Even the staunchest supporter of Normanism would acknowledge that there is room for doubt about the claims made in the *Primary Chronicle*. For example, historians have pointed to the coincidence that the invitation sent to the Varangians, as recorded in the *Primary Chronicle*, resembles the history of other peoples, notably invitations sent to the Saxons by the Britons, and that the story of three brothers coming to a foreign land echoes many legendary texts. Historians mostly agree that the *Primary Chronicle* is a compilation of earlier chronicles, that at least some of the information pre-

---

272 Boris Rybakov, *Obrazovanie drevnerusskogo gosudarstva* (Moscow: 1954), *Drevnie Russy* (Moscow: 1951); *Kievan Rus'* (Moscow: Progress, 1984); Boris Grekov, *Kievskaia Rus* (Moscow-Leningrad, 1944); Mikhail Tikhomirov, *Rossiiskoe gosudarstvo XV–XVII vekov* (Moscow: 1973), and *Russkaia kultura X–XVIII vekov* (Moscow: 1968); Peter Tretiakov, *Vostochoslavianskie plemena* (Moscow: 1953), and *U istokov drevnerusskoi narodnosti* (Leningrad: 1970); Lev Cherepnin, *Istoricheskie uslovia formirovania russkoi narodnosti do kontsa XV veka* (Moscow: 1957), and *Russkaia Istoriografia do XIX veka* (Moscow: 1957); Vasilii Mavrodin, *Proiskhozhdenie russkogo naroda* (Leningrad: 1978); Arsenii Nasonov, *Russkaia zemlia i obrazovanie territorii Drevnerusskogo gosudarstva* (Moscow: 1951), and "K voprosy ob obrazovanii drevnerusskoi narodnosti," *Vestnik AN SSSR* 8 (1951); Mikhail Priselkov, *Istoriia Russkogo letopisania XI–XV vekov* (Moscow: 1940).

sented there is not historically reliable²⁷³, and that it is impossible to date with any precision the time of its writing.²⁷⁴ Few Western historians think that Vikings first established a permanent presence in Russia as late as 862 as the *Primary Chronicle* suggests.

The *Primary Chronicle* suggests that a mere twenty years after Riurik arrived in the north, the Varangian warlord Oleg (Hilga/Helga) in 882 conquered Kiev from Askold and Dir, the mysterious Varangians who already ruled Kiev according to the *Primary Chronicle*. Recent Western accounts suggest that it is likely that the *Primary Chronicle* is simply wrong about these early dates and that, on the basis of archaeological evidence, that Kiev did not even develop, let alone become the capital, until well into the tenth century.²⁷⁵

The detailed story of Russia's baptism, which took place over the years 985–89 according to the *Primary Chronicle*, seems to be an example of how chronicle writing served ends other than a purely factual record of events. At some point in the 980s the Kievan Prince Vladimir decided to reject his murderous, pagan and polygamist past and to become a Byzantine-style Christian. According to the *Primary Chronicle*, Vladimir received ambassadors from Catholics, Muslims, Orthodox Christians and Jews. After he had listened to their testimonies, Vladimir decided to send his own people to witness the different religions and then report to him. Eventually, Vladimir ruled out Islam because it prohibited alcohol and pork, chose Orthodox Christianity for the beauty of its service and married his sister to the Byzantine emperor at Korsun.

Critics have long argued that this was a strange undertaking given that Vladimir should have known very well the differences among the world's religions. He already knew of the Muslim Volga Bulgars, his eastern neighbours since the ninth century. The relationship with the Latin West had also been established long before Vladimir became the Prince of Kiev. In 959, Russian ambassadors visited Emperor Otto asking to send an archbishop and priests to Russia.²⁷⁶ There were Byzantine churches in the south of Russia including Kiev whose remnants are still scattered along northwest

---

273 For examples see Franklin and Shepard, pp. 106–107, which describes obvious latter-date interpolations that have found their way into the chronicle.
274 Henryk Paszkiewicz, *The Making of the Russian Nation* (Connecticut: Westport, 1963), p. 111.
275 See Christian, *Russia, Central Asia and Mongolia*, p. 343.
276 Bushkov, *Rossiia I*, p. 49.

Crimea. Kiev Rus had a long and complex relationship with the Khazar Khanate, whose elite practiced Judaism. As most historians would acknowledge, Kiev and Byzantium chose one another as the alliance of choice after Vladimir's father Sviatoslav obliterated the Khazar Empire in 965.[277]

It is not enough for anti-Normanists to show that the *Primary Chronicle* was fanciful about certain issues. There needed to be an alternative explanation of how Russia received its name, who the Rus and the Varangians were and why confusion about their identity flourished subsequently. The suggestions made by anti-Normanists as to who the Rus were if they were not Scandinavians seem almost endless. There are references to a people called Rus, or at least something like Rus long before 862 when according to the *Primary Chronicle*, Riurik and his Rus arrived. The Bavarian Geographer, an anonymous description of 'Cities and Lands North of Danube' dating to 850 mentions *Ruzzi* living next to Khazars and Hungarians. There is the testimony of Constantinople's patriarch Photius who in 867 described a people called 'Rhos' who surpassed all other nations in cruelty.[278] Such cruelty could as easily have been the calling card of Slavs as of Vikings, so the anti-Normanists claim.

Artamonov came to the same conclusion as Vernadsky, that the Rus from Novgorod were the descendants of the Rosomon tribes who fought against the Goths and allied with the Huns. They lived alongside the Slavs, but were different in language and customs until the tenth century when they merged completely. Earlier, the West knew these people as *Rugi*.[279] Novosel'tsev argued that the process of merger between the Rosomon (Rugi) and the Slavs began in the ninth century, a protracted and difficult process.[280] Kuz'min also identified Russes and Rugi: he claimed that Rugi were part of the Roman Empire in 307. For him these Rus or Rugi were not Germans but 'northern Illyrians' who originally hailed from the southern Bal-

---

277 Christian, *Russia, Inner Asia and Mongolia*, pp. 345–47.
278 Paszkiewicz, *The Making of the Russian Nation*, p. 110.
279 Mikhail Artamonov, *Istoriia Khazar* (St-Petersburg: 2002), p. 366.
280 Anatolii Novosel'tsev, *Vostochnye istichniki o vostochnykh slavianakh i Rusi VI–IX vekov/Drevnerusskoe gosudarstvo i ego mezhdunarodnoe znachenie* (Moscow: 1965), pp. 355–419.

tic but were eventually pushed south toward the Balkans and northeast toward lake Ilmen' by the Goths.[281]

Rybakov and Nasonov came to the conclusion that neither the term Rus nor the Rus land represented a single tribe or area. Rybakov's hypothesis suggested that in the fifth or sixth centuries AD along the mid Dnieper the tribes that we know from the *Primary Chronicle* as Polyane, Severyane and Ulichi united to form a powerful entity known as Ros. These early Ros or Rus in the period before the ninth century resembled Turkic nomads because of their close association with the steppe. Ethnic differences between the Slavs and the Rus described by observers are so miniscule according to Rybakov, that they could not be distinguished.[282] Therefore, according to Rybakov, when the *Primary Chronicle* referred to the Rus land or Rus, it described the territory populated mostly by eastern Slavs.[283]

Nasonov also argued for the existence of a tribal union called Rus, but for him the emergence of such a union occurred in the ninth century when Slavic tribes paid tribute to the Khazars; according to Nasonov, Polyane and Severyane were the ancestors of the Rus. Nasonov took the view that the term 'Rus land' has a more ancient history than Kiev Rus'.[284] Tretiakov argued that the nucleus of the future Russians formed before Christian times on the mid-Dnieper, later incorporating the tribes of Polyane, Severyane and Ulichi, while tribal formations bearing the name 'Ros' were known in northern Black Sea region as early as the times of the Gothic chieftain Germanarikh.[285]

Still other writers have sought answers to the origins of the term 'Rus' in the Iranian language where there are words such as rauka, ruk, that mean 'to shine', or 'the light'. The Ossetians have rux and roxs—whitish.[286] Padalka

---

281 Apollon Kuz'min, *Padenie Peruna. Stanovlenie Khristianstva na Rusi* (Moscow: 1988), pp. 133–139.
282 Boris Rybakov, 'Problema obrazovania drevnerusskoi narodnosti,' *Voprosy Istorii* 9 (1952): p. 127.
283 Rybakov, *Obrazovanie drevnerusskogo gosudarstva*, p. 126 and *Drevnie Rusy*, p. 125.
284 Arsenii Nasonov, *'Russkaia Zemlia' i obrazovanie territorii Drevnerusskogo gosudarstva* (Moscow: 1951), p. 97.
285 Peter Tretiakov, *Vostochnoslavianskie plemena* (Moscow: 1953), p. 162.
286 Oleg Trubachev, 'Rus, Rossiya; Ocherk etimologii nazvaniya,' *Russkaia Slovesnost'* 3 (Moscow: 1994): pp. 67–70; Kaitiko Bzaev, *Proiskhozhdenie etnicheskogo termina "Rus"* (Valdikavkaz: IR, 1995), p. 112; Valentin Krasnopevtsev, *Varvary-berbery i zagadochnaia Rus'* (Pskov: 2001), p. 150; Alexander Shakhmatov, 'Nazvanie Rus''

has argued that 'white' is not simply a color but a symbol for leadership, the hegemony that the Rus enjoyed in the ancient Slavic world. As Padalka would have it, Scyths gave their name to a multitude of different tribes that had in common the same mode of living on the southern steppe, and who became known to the outside world as Sarmatians and Alans, then Anty and Venedy, and finally as Slavs.[287]
According to Grekov, Rus was the term for northern Slavs and Ros for the southern Slavs, and the socio-cultural collision between the north and the south provided the competing terms of Russia and Rossiia that still exist to this day.[288] While Normanists could cite evidence from the Arab traveler, Ibn Rusta, that the Rus 'have no landed property, nor villages nor cultivated lands', Grekov did his best to prove that the reverse was true.[289] Grekov devoted much of his research to proving that the ruling class of Kiev Rus was accustomed to taking tribute from a basically agricultural society that was quite different from the war and-trade-based society that early Normanists imagined.
For Tikhomirov, the Rus were included among the northern nations in the *Primary Chronicle* in error. The compiler of the *Primary Chronicle* found the name Rus in northern Scandinavian sagas written long after the foundation of Kiev. These sagas mention the Rus alongside Swedes and Normans, causing the chronicler to mistakenly identify the Rus as natives of Scandinavia. According to Tikhomirov, a twelfth-century Icelandic map placed Rus next to Sweden, Gothland and Norway, to the east of Scandinavia.[290] Therefore, the Rus and the Scandinavians could not have been the same people, but the Rus were identified as Varangians by the compiler of the *Primary Chronicle* because they were grouped in the same sentence with other northern nations.[291]

Drevniia Rus' (Moscow: 2005), pp. 31–38; N. Zharvin, *K voprosy o proiskhozhdenii etnonimov 'Rus' i Slaviane'* (Moscow: Noosfera, 2003), p. 183; G. Kovalev, 'K proiskhozhdeniiu imeni Rus': est' li alternativa?' *Nestor: Istoriko-kulturnye issledovaniia* 3 (Voronezh, 1995), pp. 45–59; Mikhail Tikhomirov, 'Proiskhozhdenie nazvanii Rus' i Russkaia zemlia,' *Russkoe Letopisanie* (Moscow: 1979), pp. 22–45.

287 L. Padalka, *O proiskhozhdenii slova 'Rus'* (Poltava: 1915), p. 103.
288 Boris Grekov, *Kievskaia Rus'* (Moscow: 1944), p. 47.
289 Quoted in Hosking, *Russia and the Russians*, p. 33.
290 Mikhail Tikhomirov, 'Proiskhozhdenie nazvanii Rus i Russkaia Zemlia', *Russkii Narod*, (Moscow: Kuchkovo pole, 2001), pp. 236–237.

To reinforce his argument Tikhomirov cited passages from the *Primary Chronicle* that demonstrate the confusion of the chronicler about the connection of Rus to the foundation of Novgorod. Thus, one entry from the *Primary Chronicle* specifies that 'Rus appeared from those Varangians, Novgorodians, that is people of Novgorod from the Varangian clan, although they were Slavs before'. At another point, the *Primary Chronicle* describes 'Polyane...whom we call Rus'. Since Polyane dwelled in the Kievan region, it is clear to Tikhomirov that Rus was the name of the Kievan domain, and that the Polyane adopted the name Rus in recognition of their homeland, while Novgorodian Slavs and Varangians came to be known as Rus only after they settled in Kiev.

Tikhomirov argued that other examples from the *Primary Chronicle* corroborate this view. According to the *Primary Chronicle*, Oleg, the founder of Kiev, was referred to as a Rus prince upon his ascension to the Kievan throne. When Oleg arrived in Kiev, he brought with him Varyags and Slovenes and others, who only then started to call themselves Rus. For Tikhomirov it is obvious that the Slav princes hired mercenaries, including Scandinavians, who later acted on behalf of their rulers and presented themselves as Rus as they went about their diplomatic and military tasks.

For Udal'tsov there is no doubt as to the southern or Kievan origin of the word Rus. The nucleus Ros-Rus could be encountered in works of Jordanes and Procopius, sixth-century writers connected to the Byzantine court.[292] Parkhomenko too believed that the term Rus originated in the south, around the Black and Azov seas. As for Scandinavians in the Russian north, the term 'Rus' is unequivocally encountered only in 1167, and, therefore, far too late to be connected to the origins of its use in the lands of Russia.[293] Other writers link the name of the Rus to geographic locations in the south. Vernadsky agreed with those who pointed to the river called Rus or Ros, a tributary of the Dnieper south of Kiev.[294]

For Fomenko, the chronicles have clearly been misinterpreted. Varangians refer not to the Vikings but to *vragi*, the Russian word for enemies just as

---

[292] Alexander Udal'tsov, 'Osnovnye voprosy etnogeneza Slavian', *Sovetskaia etnografia* VI–VII (1947): p. 168.

[293] Vladimir Parkhomenko, *U istokov russkoi gosudarstvennosti* (Leningrad: 1924), p. 107.

[294] George Vernadsky, *The Origins of Russia* (Oxford: Clarendon Press, 1959), p. 212; Paszkiewicz, *The Making of the Russian Nation*, p. 117; Stender-Petersen, *Varangica*, 16, 85–87, p. 243.

the Mongol-Tatars was a generic reference to the horrifying invasion and did not designate a specific tribe. Riurik is most likely a corruption of Iurii and refers to Iurii Danilovich, the fourteenth-century prince of Moscow and Grand Prince of Vladimir.[295] More plausibly, Gumilev has argued that it is obvious that Russia boasted a proud and ancient history long before we hear of Varangians. Gumilev endorsed those who claimed identification between the Rus and Rugi. For all these mainly twentieth century writers, Russians received their name from ancestors called Rus or its equivalent, but, importantly, these ancestors were not Scandinavians. The early Russians were descended from an ancient ethnos known under many names—rogi, rugi, rutsi, ruyany, rosy, or ruthenians, long before the Varangians made their appearance. Their success in conquering a vast territory explains the instability in the spelling of their name.[296]

In the West, a moderate Normanism is adopted almost everywhere. In Russia, Normanism is under constant attack, as it has been since the Stalin era. For the consensus of scholarly opinion in the West, the point is not that the *Primary Chronicle* is infallible but that its general story fits with what is now known from non-Slav sources and from archaeological discoveries. The *Primary Chronicle*, a medieval source written by Orthodox Slavs and hailing the achievements of pagan Norsemen, represents one powerful argument for the Normanist thesis. Other texts pointed to the Scandinavian presence in Russia and the association of Rus and Vikings. Arab sources reported the Rus burning their boats as part of funereal proceedings, as Vikings often did. Viking swords have been found in south Russia and Byzantine coins on the river Kama dating to the sixth century. From the Byzantine, Jordanes, it is known that Rus were travelling widely to trade in fur at this time. Given the scale of this sea-faring trade and military operation, these warriors seem to resemble closely the Vikings active in Western Europe.[297]

Nonetheless, a great many readers of Soviet literature about Kiev Rus have received the strong impression that there is no credible argument for Normanism whatsoever. As Rybakov put it, 'the sum total of the Normanist assumptions in the course of two centuries is insufficient not only to call Normanism 'a theory', but even a hypothesis, because it offers no analysis.'[298]

---

295 Nosovskii and Fomenko *Novaia khronologiia Rusi*, p. 114.
296 Gumilev, *Drevniaia Rus i velikaia step'*, p. 126.
297 Christian, *Russia, Central Asia and Mongolia*, p. 335.
298 Rybakov, *Kievan Rus*, p. 12.

Deeply frustrating to anti-Normanists is the fact that, seemingly, Westerners apparently knew that there was no basis for their claims. According to Rybakov, the 'leader' of the Normanists, Stender-Petersen, acknowledged in 1960 in an academic speech that Normanism as a scientific construction was dead because all of its basic pillars had been disproved. Nevertheless, this Danish scholar urged historians to create a neo-Normanism.[299] Pseudo-history is quick to repeat this apparent evidence of Western duplicity and dogmatism.

For anti-Normanists, the proposition that Vikings were state builders simply defies logic. Kiev Rus had many connections with its non-European neighbours to the south, including people from the Turkic steppe, the Byzantine Empire and Bulgaria. Anti-Normanists argue that in comparison to these advanced states, the Vikings were barbarians who failed to build cities even in their homeland or to leave any tangible legacy in Russia. Lomonosov's hypothesis that the Vikings who found their way to Kiev Rus were hired mercenaries of the Slavs flourishes in the popular literature today.

Anti-Normanists point out that no researcher has found reference to a tribe called the Rus living in Scandinavia at the time specified by the *Primary Chronicle*. Yet there are many references to Rus living in the lands of Kiev Rus' long before 862. The names of individuals seem fluid and it is impossible to know if two names have been attached to the one person. Khazar sources suggest that in the 940s the Rus army of Helgi attacked Tmutorkan, the Black Sea base of the Khazars, and it seems possible that this Helgi was Prince Oleg who captured Kiev.[300]

As for the ethnicity of the Rus princes, descriptions suggest natives of Russia and not Vikings. A Byzantine eyewitness described Sviatoslav, the Kievan prince and classic Rus warrior/adventurer of the tenth century as a medium-sized man who was snub-nosed, had blue eyes, thick shoulders, bushy eyebrows and a savage appearance. Sviatoslav described himself not just as Rus, but as a Tauridian Scyth.[301] More importantly for Fomenko, Sviatoslav boasted a Cossack-style shaven head and forelock and a golden earing to distinguish his high birth. At his meeting with the Byzantines in 971, Sviatoslav crossed the river in a 'Scythian' boat dressed in a plain

---

299 Rybakov, *Kievan Rus*, 13.
300 See Christian, *Russia, Central Asia and Mongolia*, p. 343.
301 See Boris Grekov, *Kiev Rus*, trans. by Sdobnikov (Moscow: Foreign Languages Publishing House, 1959), pp. 620–21.

white garment and, like Cossack atamans, did not try to distinguish himself from the men he led. Alternative writers routinely quote this passage from Johan Tzimiskes, the Byzantine emperor, as evidence that the Rus Sviatoslav, far from resembling a Swede, seemed to have much more in common with steppe peoples in terms of appearance, and, in terms of horsemanship and attire, with the Cossacks of more recent times.[302]

It is the Vikings not the Slavs who have a reputation for boat building and piracy. But, as David Christian points out, the Rus depended upon the excellent canoes with the Greek name of *monoxyla* made by Slav craftsmen.[303] As for the seafaring of the Rus, there is no doubt as to the scale and effectiveness of maritime operations. As Gumilev tells the story, around 790 the Rus stormed Sudak in Crimea, and then moved to the southern shore of the Black Sea. In 840, the Rus took Amastrida in Asia Minor and in 852 Kiev.[304] In 909, Rus boats launched attacks in the Caspian Sea and, in 913, a huge flotilla of five hundred ships with the permission of the Tsar of the Khazars entered the Caspian once more.[305] In 941 the Russians fought for four months against the Byzantine Emperor Constantine while three yeas later Igor led a land and sea army against Byzantium.[306] If these were mainly Viking pirates, how could it be that these warriors rapidly disappeared from history, leaving virtually nothing to Russian politics, military organization or culture? The numbers of Rus sailors were impressive if ancient sources and the guesses of modern historians can be believed; in 913 there may have been five hundred Rus ships on the Caspian, with one hundred warriors on each ship. The Soviet historian Mavrodin considered that there were 20,000 warriors since according to the chronicles an average Russian boat could take forty warriors.[307] Gumilev thinks that there were from 35,000 to 50,000 warriors.[308] Later, the Cossacks proved adept at seamanship, raiding the Turkish fort of Azov, the Turkic coast of the Black Sea and earning comparisons to Moroccan pirates of the Mediterranean.

---

302 Vernadsky, *Origins of Russia*, pp. 276–77.
303 Christian, *Russia, Central Asia and Mongolia*, p. 344.
304 Gumilev, *Drevniaia Rus i velikaia step'*, p. 161.
305 Gumilev, *Drevniaia Rus i velikaia step'*, p. 188.
306 Gumilev, *Drevniaia Rus i velikaia step'*, p. 196.
307 Vasilii Mavrodin, *Ocherki po istorii feodalnoi Rusi* (Leningrad: 1949), p. 47.
308 Gumilev, *Drevniaia Rus i velikaia step'*, p. 198.

Even the staunchest Normanists had to admit that the numbers of Varangians in Russia were probably limited. It follows logically that there was a significant number of experienced sailors among the Slavs who either learnt that trade from the Vikings or evolved largely without help from Scandinavia. In 965 the Russians under Prince Sviatoslav did not dare to attack the Khazars who dominated the steppe with their cavalry, and instead built boats in the land of Viatichi, set sail down the Volga, attacked Khazaria from the rear to destroy Itil, the Khazar capital. As Gumilev stated, the power of the Rus of the tenth century was in the boats.[309] If Slavs built the boats and crewed them, it seems likely that they could also have been commanders and navigators.

For Normanists, it is irrelevant that the *Primary Chronicle* is almost certainly wrong about when the Rus first made their appearance in Russia. The point is that there is indisputable and extensive evidence about the Viking presence in Kiev Rus. As Paszkiewicz put it, even if the Povest' did not exist, we should still have to recognize Rus' as Norsemen'.[310] Vikings were already active almost everywhere in Europe and the Middle East before their arrival in Kiev Rus and were the most feared warriors of this era.

The fact that ambassadors calling themselves Rhos turned out to be ethnic Swedes gave Normanists reason to claim that this was proof that the Rus were in fact ethnic Swedes. However, for anti-Normanists, the fact that the ambassadors were detained should attract attention, not the fact that they were Swedes. Louis's logic seems to have been that if a person had called himself a Rus, how could he be a Swede?[311] If the Rus were known in Western Europe to be Vikings then Louis should not have been surprised. Baumgarten argued that the Byzantine Emperor had not realized that the Rhos were Swedes when he offered them safe passage. Anti-Normanists dismiss this argument as impossible to believe.[312]

For anti-Normanists, the Swedes who appeared at Ingleheim as ambassadors for the Rus had simply been hired by the Russians or were Vikings integrated into Kiev's army, who took upon themselves a Rus identity.[313] As Lomonosov had put it, the Varangians were 'northern soldiers' and not an

---

309 Gumilev, *Drevniaia Rus i velikaia step'*, p. 211.
310 Paszkiewicz, *The Making of the Russian Nation*, p. 114.
311 Sergei Lesnoi, *Istoriia Rusov* (Paris: 1953), pp. 43–44.
312 Sergei Lesnoi, *Istoriia Rusov*.
313 Vernadsky, *Origins of Russia*, pp. 199–200.

ethnic group.³¹⁴ Normanists have dismissed such claims as highly unlikely. It would be the first example, Thomsen claimed, of Vikings offering their services as ambassadors to a foreign power. If there were a relationship between Vikings and Slavs in Kiev, it was more likely that the latter served the former, according to Thomsen. Normanists cite too the testimony of Liutprand of Cremona who described the Rus who attacked Constantinople as a people known to the Germans as *Nordmanni*.³¹⁵ Anti-Normanists counter that the same Liutprand testified that his understanding was that the etymology of the term for the Rus referred to the blonde-reddish color of the warriors' hair and so his testimony is at best contradictory.³¹⁶

Anti-Normanists claim that Constantine, who listed the names of the Dnieper rapids in Slavic and Rus, was often wrong about names. For example, Constantine suggested an identical name in Russian and Slavic for the first Dnieper rapid, Essupi, which is unlikely to be the case if Slavonic and Rus were two very different languages. Secondly, the Byzantine Emperor suggested that the name Gelandri was of Slavonic origin, when Scandinavian etymology seemed a better explanation for it. Meanwhile, other scholars have suggested not Scandinavian, but Iranian or even Greek etymology for the names of the Dnieper rapids mentioned by Constantine.³¹⁷

The descriptions of some Arab observers suggested that the Rus merchants who travelled to Arab lands were in fact Scandinavians, judging by their customs such as burying the dead in their ships.³¹⁸ Not so, say the anti-Normanists who find their own Arab sources to paint a different picture. They point to the fact that Ibn-Khurdadhbih (d. 912) claimed that Rus merchants, 'who belonged to the Slavonic people', and paid a tithe to Constantinople or the Khazar Kaganate³¹⁹ used Slav eunuchs as interpreters. For anti-Normanists the fact that Slavonic eunuchs were used as interpreters is evidence that the merchants were themselves Slavs. This same writer, whose work describes the trade routes of his era, referred to Rus as a place

---

314 Lomonosov, *Trudy po russkoi istorii*, 6, p. 203.
315 Hilda Davidson, *The Viking Road to Byzantium* (London: Allen and Unwin, 1976), p. 59.
316 Lesnoi, *Istoriia Rusov*, pp. 37–38.
317 See Lesnoi, *Istoriia Rusov*, 52–56 and Abrashkin, *Predki russkikh v etom mire*, pp. 376–377.
318 Basil Dmytryshin, *Medieval Russia* (Holt, Rinehart and Winston, 1973), pp. 11–17.
319 Boris Rybakov, 'Problema obrazovania drevnerusskoi narodnosti v svete trudov Stalina', *Voprosy Istorii* 9 (1952): p. 44.

of many towns, an unlikely home for the nomads of the sea. Another Arab writer of the ninth century, Al-Jakhaini, wrote that Ruses lived in three clans. The first was adjacent to the Bulgars and had a ruler in Kiev. Thus, anti-Normanists respond, Kiev was known to the Arabs as the capital of the Rus long before the invitation to Riurik in 862.[320]

The proponents of Normanism argue that it was the quick absorption of the tiny Scandinavian ruling class by the mass of Slav underlings that caused a fairly rapid dying out of Scandinavian names. Anti-Normanists are sceptical and argue that history usually shows the reverse. Tikhomirov, the giant of Soviet anti-Normanism, argued that in Bulgaria, Turkic princes managed to maintain their hereditary names, culture and language for at least two centuries despite living among a majority Slav population.[321]

In part, Tikhomirov's confidence comes from the comparative levels of civilization in Scandinavia and Russia. He has counted 271 towns in Russia at a time when Scandinavia was much less developed.[322] Lesnoi claimed that he found over two hundred more towns in the chronicles and evidence only of seven cities in total in Scandinavia.[323] Why the Vikings would have needed sophisticated settlements to achieve their political and military goals is not clear. Witnesses described them as expert in setting up temporary bases for their trading activities. At the same time the Vikings called medieval Russia *Garda/Gardariki*, the place of many cities/towns, a sign that Russia was older than Scandinavia in civilizational terms, or so anti-Normanists aver.

Anti-Normanists point to the fact that the names of Russian cities such as Novgorod, Smolensk, Kiev, Polotsk belong to the Slavonic language group, and appeared long before the Varangians were invited to cross the Baltic. The assumption here is that the city is the bearer of culture, and that the Varangians, even if they were of Scandinavian stock, appeared in Russia only after the cities were founded and named, producing little, or no impact on Russia. Anti-Normanists, starting with Lomonosov, emphasize that the Russian language is virtually free of Scandinavian borrowings as compared

---

320 Tikhomirov, 'Proiskhozhdenie nazvanii Rus' i Russkaia Zemlia', *Russkii Narod*, p. 249.
321 Tikhomirov, 'Proiskhozhdenie nazvanii Rus' i Russkaia Zemlia', *Russkii Narod*, p. 241.
322 Mikhail Tikhomirov, *Drevnerusskie goroda* (Moscow: 1956).
323 Lesnoi, *Istoriia Russov*, p. 689.

to heavy borrowings from the Tatar, Finnish or Polish languages, a conclusion that stands up well in the light of modern research.[324]

For anti-Normanists the sheer volume of alternative suggestions is proof not of the individual weaknesses of each of these arguments but of their collective strength in the war against the Norman myth. Nor do they regard as damaging to their case the fact that some foreigners seemed to know the Rus as Viking warriors. Kiev Rus like present-day Russia was a mixed horde. What anti-Normanists cannot accept is that Slavs/Russians played a subordinate role to a foreign band of conquerors and state builders. Thus, while Russians are happy to proclaim themselves free of any suggestion of racism or an obsession with biological races, the 'Russianness' of the original inhabitants of the lands that came to form Russia was a matter of furious debate that gained momentum in the Stalin era. When Lomonosov first attacked Mueller, the Normanist controversy had no name. It was an elite parlour game fought out by dueling intellectuals. Even the Slavophile revival of anti-Normanism in the nineteenth century remained confined to a small group of interested readers in a largely illiterate peasant society. The Stalin era democratized reading, inflamed passions about history of a patriotic variety and gave its readers the impression that there was only a single historical truth. Alternative historians are keen to finish the job.

The strategy adopted by anti-Normanists operates at different overlapping levels. The church chronicles are unreliable. The Vikings showed no sign of higher civilization naming no cities, imparting few customs or even words to the Slav underlings and seem to have bred into the basic Slav mass within a generation or two. When the Scandinavian burial ground at Gnezdovo near Smolensk yielded the oldest Russian inscription (*goroushna* or mustard), Normanists claimed that this was evidence of just how quickly the Vikings were able to learn the Slavic language. For anti-Normanists, this is too fantastic to be believed. Why were the Vikings so keen to learn the language of a conquered people. If there were so few Normans, how then could the Rus have launched massive raids against the likes of Byzantium with as witnesses tell us tens of thousands of warriors. The Chronicle provides several examples of Scandinavians hired by Rus princes to take part in military campaigns and civil wars so logically it would seem that the Rus spotted by the likes of Louis the Pious were simply armed ambassadors

---

324 Lomonosov, *Trudy po russkoi istorii* VI, 173.

serving the more culturally advanced Slav rulers of Rus. As Hosking has put it, 'together, the 'Viking-Slavs' formed a kind of tribal super-alliance with its centre at Kiev'.[325] Anti-Normanists will not rest until the terms are reversed and this super-alliance is understood as one in which the Vikings served merely as the hired mercenaries of a Slav state.

Part Three: Western Plot (1)

Anti-Normanists believe they have demolished the Normanist position point by point and have been persecuted for their trouble. Fomenko cites the exasperated criticism of the historian S. Stroev who argued that Normanism is simply the accumulation of falsehoods repeated so often by well-paid professors that they attained the status of conventional wisdom. Zagoskin, writing near the end of the nineteenth century expressed the same sentiment, that those 'who protested against the Norman theory were ridiculed and accused of vandalism: it was 'scientific terror', and it was extremely difficult to struggle against it'.[326] Conventional historians acknowledge that Normanism flourished outside of Russia after World War Two partly because of Cold War hostility to Russia.[327] Fomenko and his supporters take such statements as their starting point, arguing that it is pointless to battle such entrenched and obviously biased dogma and academic thuggery as Normanism in the usual manner.

For many patriotic readers of Russian history, the debate had reached a dead end. The nuances, endless corrections and failure to prove the case definitively have indeed been deeply frustrating. To be a shining light alternative history, it is necessary to be bold in attacks upon enemies and ingenious in uncovering the details of plots against Russia. With the defection of Ukraine and Belarus in 1991, present-day Russia has lost some of its claim to the history of Kiev Rus. The major centres of Kiev Rus, with the exception of Novgorod the Great, are now located in Ukraine, not Russia. One way to deal with this issue was to write Kiev Rus out of history altogether, a task that the journalist Kungurov has set himself. For Kungurov, Bayer, Mueller, and Schloezer did not invent the Normanist hypothesis, but simply

---

325 Hosking, *Russia and the Russians*, p. 34.
326 Mikhail Zagoskin, *Istoriia prava russkogo naroda* I (Moscow: 1899), pp. 336–337.
327 Christian, Russia, *Central Asia and Mongolia*, p. 334.

developed an existing narrative penned by Innocent Gizel in his famous chronicle, *Sinopsis*.

According to Kungurov, Gizel, Polish but fanatically Orthodox, invented Kiev Rus after he visited Moscow in 1654.[328] Gizel ardently supported the idea that the future Ukraine should be incorporated into the Muscovite state, and was appointed as an archbishop of the Kievan *Lavra* in 1656. The legend about Kievan Russia was born in 1674 when *Sinopsis* was published. The first mass-produced historical textbook in Russia's history, with twenty-five editions before 1861, *Sinopsis* was written on the Romanov's orders, and the following generations of historians accepted its basic storyline.[329]

Bayer, Mueller, and Schloezer made their contribution by suppressing the majority of the writings of patriots such as Lomonosov. Later, the Austro-Hungarian Empire employed a divide and rule policy to maintain its territorial reach; a key part of this strategy was inventing the modern idea of Ukraine. The Soviet Union completed the process of Ukrainianisation and paved the way for an independent Ukraine. For Kungurov, the Mongol Yoke was invented as a convenient method of demonising Moscow as an Asiatic power. According to Kungurov, there has been a concerted effort to persuade the Ukrainians that they are Europeans and that the Russians are Asiatics, that Ukrainians are much older than Russians, that Russians are the eternal enemy of Ukraine, and that the Russians adopted Christianity and their alphabet from Ukraine.

For Kungurov, the Ukrainians stole the name 'Rus' together with the Slavic language. As for Kiev, it was a medieval backwater that has revealed very little archaeology. This was not surprising because it was well known that the rapids of the Dnieper rendered the river non-navigable at the time when Kiev Rus was said to exist. The Volga was the real transit point between Russia, Byzantium, and the Arab world. Moscow with the Golden Ring of fortresses was the home of the Volga horde, a Finnish-Slavic-Turkic entity. Kungurov insists that even in the nineteenth century, Ukrainians and Belarusians considered themselves as Russian.[330]

---

328 Alexey Kungurov, *Kievskoi Rusi ne bylo, ili chto skryvaiut istoriki* (Moscow: Eksmo, Algoritm, 2011).
329 Kungurov, *Kievskoi Rusi ne bylo*, p. 185.
330 Kungurov, *Kievskoi Rusi ne bylo*, pp. 412–413. It is worth noting that Kungurov is prone to radical claims even about modern history. He doubts, for example, that Stalin ordered the massacre of Polish officers at Katyn and blames Gorbachev for meekly accepting this Western 'lie'.

Part Four: Western Plot (2)

Fomenko takes a different approach to Kungurov. While scholarly anti-Normanism dissects the Normanist position piece by piece in its efforts to refute it, Fomenko attempted a knockout blow by proving, he claims, that the very chronicles relied upon were forged as part of the German plot against Russian history. From Lomonosov to the Stalin era, anti-Normanists devoted themselves to meticulous source criticism. Fomenko claims that this was itself the source of the problem. If the *Primary Chronicle* can be discredited, the Normanist position, in Fomenko's view, would have collapsed centuries ago. To achieve this goal, Fomenko set himself the task of proving that we have no certain knowledge of the provenance of any chronicle earlier than the eighteenth century and that the real Ur-source of the chronicles we do have is the Radzivill chronicle that was fabricated by Schloezer and his allies in the middle of the eighteenth century.

Hostility towards Germany and its designs upon the Slav lands was a popular theme in Russia long before the emergence of Hitler. As the Slavophile Khomiakov put it:

> German scientists have investigated every little phenomenon or tribe on the face of this planet except for the Slavs. Whenever they deal with the Slavs, their mistakes are so obvious, blindness is so great, that there is no explanation to it. Nations also have emotions, exactly as individuals do, and sometimes these emotions and passions are far from being noble. Perhaps the Germanic instincts are based on a hostility that they do not admit to, a hostility that is found on fear of the future, or the remembrances of the past.[331]

There are of course many conventional writers who note excessive Germanic influence in the political and cultural life of Russia in the eighteenth century. As one Western historian put it, Russian history following Peter the Great is usually described as a 'rapid succession of monarchs and the influence of foreigners and intriguers who used high government office for personal gain'.[332] The future American sociologist Pitirim Sorokin put it more dramatically when he complained that in the period between Peter the Great and Alexander the First, 'Teutons literally flooded into Russia, and in the end their presence was much more damaging to the country than even

---

[331] Bocharov, Efimov, Chachukh, Chernyshev, *Zagovor Protiv Russkoi Istorii,* p. 17.
[332] Daniels, *Tatishchev,* p. 3.

the Tatar wars'. For Sorokin, 'the otherwise great German civilization' with few exceptions exported only its social excrement to Russia.[333]
For Fomenko and his allies, the German scholars were brutal thugs in the pay of Western governments. As for Mueller's claim that that the historian knew no 'fatherland, faith or ruler', this was sheer hypocrisy.[334] Why, asks Fomenko, is Russian history in essence a product wholly of foreign writers who wrote its basic outline in the eighteenth century? The answer is that the Romanovs wanted it this way and not because of Russian cultural backwardness, as critics of Russia have sometimes suggested. Thus, Tatishchev is a shining example of a fine historian whose works mysteriously failed to find a publisher. Why? According to Fomenko, the reason was that Tatishchev, unlike his rivals, was a Russian.[335]
Conventional historians tell the story of foreign authorship of Russia's past rather differently. When Tatishchev died in 1750, his historical work was still in manuscript form.[336] He wrote an English colleague, Jonas Hanway, in the hope that the latter might arrange to have his work published through the Royal Society in London. Hanway found Tatishchev's request inconvenient and nothing came of Tatishchev's efforts to publish his work. The manuscript was left in the archives of the St. Petersburg Academy until 1768 when Mueller, starting with a copy of the manuscript provided by Tatishchev's son, began the task of editing what would appear in 1784 as *Istoriia rossiiskaia s samykh drevneishykh vremen*. Four volumes were produced with financial assistance provided by Catherine the Great herself. A fifth volume was uncovered and published by Pogodin in 1848.[337] Schloezer, meanwhile, praised Tatishchev, as 'the father of Russian history'. It was also Schloezer who would ensure that Lomonosov's work was published posthumously.
For Western writers, the German scholars continued their scientific work despite the fact that the Romanov government hindered them and favored Russians. It was in fact the Germans who were the recipients of vicious academic attacks from Lomonosov. Lomonosov fell foul of the authorities in

---

333 Pitirim Sorokin, *Teoriia natsional'nogo voprosa* (Moscow: 1994), p. 49.
334 For a positive account of Mueller see Edward C Thacen, *The Rise of Historicism in Russia* (New York: Peter Land, 1999), pp. 28–30.
335 Nosovskii and Fomenko, *Novaia khronologiia Rusi*, pp. 20–22.
336 Elizabeth Koutaissoff, 'Tatishchev's 'Joachim Chronicle'', *University of Birmingham Historical Journal* 3:1 (1951): pp. 52–63.
337 Elizabeth Koutaissoff, 'Tatishchev's 'Joachim Chronicle'', pp. 52–63.

the Academy because of drunkenness, brawling and the threats and insults that he routinely hurled at those Academy members with whom he disagreed.[338] About Bayer, Lomonosov expressed the view that the German 'looks like an idolater priest who, having poisoned himself with henbane and altered his mind by spinning around on one foot, shouts vague, dark, wild and incomprehensible answers'.[339] Rather than a martyr, Lomonosov comes across in these accounts as an intelligent but unattractive figure whose vanity and prejudice often got the better of him. Lomonosov did his best to enlist the support of the government in his battle with Mueller and other foreign academics[340]. Karamzin and Kliuchevskii more or less apologized for Lomonosov's intemperate outburst against the scholarly and well-intentioned Mueller.[341]

Nonetheless, thanks in part to Fomenko, a new generation of Russian readers will learn of how the history of Russia was compromised from the outset by German historians. After World War Two when Stalinist historiography took a particularly patriotic and anti-German turn, the story of Lomonosov's battle against German influence was told in emphatically dark terms. Fomenko utilizes this literature extensively. His chief source for the story of Russian intellectual life in the eighteenth century is a 1950s Soviet account by Beliavskii that is virulently anti-German.[342] Fomenko demonstrates his peculiar method of historical research by claiming that this Soviet era source is very rare, and thus full of suppressed and valuable knowledge.

How does Beliavskii tell the story? For the first thirty years of its existence (1726–1755), the Academy's gymnasium did not train a single student capable of entering the Academy of Sciences. The Academy's professorship came to the conclusion that 'the only way out of this situation is to draft students for the Russian Academy in Germany, because it is clearly impossible to train Russians'.[343] Rebelling against the alleged German dictatorship over the academy, some Russian students and teachers protested in Senate demanding reforms. The Senate appointed a commission to investigate, headed by Count Iusopov and it condemned the protests as a 'rebellion

---

338 Black, *Mueller*, p. 86.
339 Mikhail Beliavskii, *M.V. Lomonosov i osnovanie Moskovskogo Universiteta. K 200 letiiu MGU* (Moscow: 1956), p. 60.
340 Tolz, *Russia*, pp. 47–50.
341 For an account see Black, *Mueller*, pp. 203–205.
342 Beliavskii, *Lomonosov*.
343 Beliavskii, *Lomonosov*, p. 77.

against authorities', and arrested Russian academicians. Vindicated, the German academics remained at the head of the departments and continued to draw their inflated salaries.

It seems that the conditions of academic life in the eighteenth century resembled those of Stalin's Russia. Beliavskii noted how one of the Russian members of Academy's staff, Gorlitskii, was sentenced to death after having spent two years chained in jail, for his stubbornness and disrespect toward the Iusupov commission. Others, such as Grekov, Polyakov, Nosov were publicly whipped and sent to Siberia, while Popov, Shishkarev and others were kept under arrest till the future decision made by the next President of the Academy.[344] For Stalinist writers, the German-dominated government of the Romanovs favored Bayer, Mueller and Schloezer. Despite Lomonosov's protests to Empress Catherine II, Mueller's intrigues resulted in the appointment of Schloezer, Lomonosov's rival, as professor of Russian history in the Academy of Science. Schloezer held a very low opinion of Lomonosov, stating that the Russian scientist 'was an ignoramus who did not know anything except for his chronicles'.[345]

These same German authorities were so infuriated by Lomonosov's defiant behavior that they ordered him to be arrested as well: members of the commission demanded the execution of Lomonosov on account of 'his disrespectful attitude toward the commission's members and the German land', or that at the very least he should be whipped, and his property and rights confiscated and cancelled. After having spent seven months in prison Lomonosov was released, but had to publicly read and sign an admission of guilt written by Mueller. In 1763, Empress Catherine the Great fired Lomonosov from the Academy on the basis of another report. Mueller and Schloezer were busily seeking out Lomonosov's historical archives to plunder it both to help their own careers and to distort what it was that Lomonosov had written.

Lomonosov's works were allegedly confiscated and disappeared after his death. None of his original works, including the documents and comments that Lomonosov intended to publish, nor the manuscripts of the second and third parts of *Drevniaia Rossiiskaia Istoriia* have reached us in their original form. Mueller and Schloezer edited the version we have today and it is therefore almost certainly only a pale reflection of the original.

---

344 Beliavskii, *Lomonosov*, p. 82.
345 Beliavskii, p. 64.

Reading the accounts of the Stalin era and their repetition in Fomenko and comparing them to the more scholarly literature leaves the reader with the impression that completely different events are being described. Western accounts describe Lomonosov as a difficult personality and ungrateful towards those who tried to help him. Bayer remained on good terms with Tatishchev even after Tatishchev's fall from grace, and helped Tatishchev with his research.[346] Black records that Lomonosov received a pension and Gorlitsky was promoted, not sentenced to death. Those who wanted to help Lomonosov included Mueller.

Russian readers of Fomenko and other alternative historians are left with the impression that ill-intentioned foreigners wrote a history of Russia without collaborating with local Russian historians. Meanwhile, the openly pro-German court of the Romanovs rewarded its hand picked propagandists with good salaries, hereditary titles, and the prestige of pioneering historical studies in Russia.[347] It was therefore predictable that a 'pro-German' theory about the origins of the first Russian state, where 'incompetent' Russians invited Scandinavian-Germanic princes to rule over their lands, should have taken hold in the eighteenth century.

For Fomenko, Tatishchev and Lomonosov's conclusions are tamer than might have been expected of someone who took such a brave stand against foreign control of the Russian academy. Fomenko has embellished the story of the plot against Tatishchev who spent his last years in internal exile towards the end of his life after he was found guilty of financial misbehaviour. In St.-Petersburg, the authorities were not really interested in corruption allegations against Tatishchev but instead warned the bureaucrat turned historian that he would be suspected of political freethinking if he pressed on with his publications. Tatishchev's history was not an original of his work and it was the German, Mueller, who readied the work of Tatishchev for publication. Mueller himself acknowledged that he edited the deceased Tatishchev's diaries and copies of his book in order to prepare them for publication.[348] For Fomenko, the original of Tatishchev's work, as well as the documents that Mueller had worked with, conveniently disappeared. Mueller's revision of Tatishchev's did not contain an account of the Slavs prior to the invitation to Riurik. What we know today as 'Tatishchev's

---

346 Thaden, *The Rise of Historicism* in *Russia* (Peter Lang, 1999), pp. 27–28.
347 Beliavskii, *Lomonosov*, pp. 82–84.
348 Thaden, *The Rise of Historicism in Russia*, p. 31.

information', the sources known only to Tatishchev and now lost to modern historians, was destroyed by the German clique. In this way, Mueller brought Tatishchev's conclusions sufficiently into line with his own, or at least rendered them so ambiguous that latter-day historians were in the end divided over whether Tatishchev was even anti-Normanist at all.[349]

The question for Fomenko then becomes; if it is so obvious that the Normanist position is hopeless, why did Normanism enjoy such success? Not all Russian academics were suppressed. How could Russian patriots such as Karamzin, Soloviev or Kliuchevskii have been fooled? The answer is that Schloezer's account of the *Primary Chronicle* has won them over. The fact that it was German historians who edited the *Primary Chronicle*, made the claim that the Varangians were Vikings and for nearly a century were in possession of some of the most important documents pertaining to early Russian history has led to the destruction of the true history of Russia. Schloezer all but succeeded in his attempt 'to destroy the Russian national history school with open support from the Russian court'.[350] Having suppressed the Russian version of Russia's ancient history, what did the plotters do next? They rewrote the Russian chronicles and then claimed the doctored versions as centuries-old originals.

Fomenko's biggest claim concerns the Radzivill Chronicle. To prove that important parts of the record of early Russian history were written by German academics in the eighteenth century, it is necessary to show that there were no extant chronicles that can be reliably traced back beyond the eighteenth century. This is not an easy task but Fomenko uses the works of established historians to attempt to prove that we have no direct proof of the existence of early Russian chronicles.

Kliuchevskii wrote that, in the seventeenth century, neither the Tsar's nor the Patriarch's libraries contained any information on the history of Russia.[351] According to the decree of Tsar Alexis of 1657, a church cleric named Kudriavtsev was charged with the task of seeking out chronicles in the central archives. After sixteen months of work he was unable to produce a single document. Kliuchevskii held a low opinion of Muscovite history writing and concluded that 'in old Muscovy neither the people nor their minds, nor the documents were ready for such an undertaking.' Fomenko embel-

---

349 Nosovskii and Fomenko, *Novaia khronologiia Rusi*, pp. 28–29.
350 Nosovskii and Fomenko, *Bibleiskaia Rus'* II, pp. 319–23.
351 Kliuchevskii, *Neopublikovannye proizvedeniia*, pp. 188–191.

lishes Kliuchevskii's account by adding that Kudriavtsev's work was actively sabotaged. How else could the decree of Alexis be disobeyed? Fomenko concluded not just that this particular researcher failed in his mission but either few original chronicles existed in the seventeenth century or the chronicles were hidden by church and governmental authorities.

Fomenko next cites the opinion of Morozov, the imprisoned polymath who devoted years to his idiosyncratic reading of the major chronicles. In his book *Khristos*, Morozov compared the styles and grammatical structures of the three earliest Russian Chronicles—Laurentian and Troitsko-Sergiev and Radzivill chronicles—each of which contains as its core the *Primary Chronicle*.[352] Morozov was surprised to discover that, apart from minor changes in style, their texts were absolutely identical.

This fact surprised Morozov because the conventional wisdom stipulated that the chronicles were discovered separately and in locations that were remote from each other—Suzdal, the Moscow region and Konigsburg. If they were copies from a more ancient original, it is still unclear why they did not have more textual differences relating to important, local events. Fomenko built on this idea to conclude that the anonymous writer of the Troitsko-Sergiev as well as the Suzdal' monk Lavrentii used the 1767 Radzivill chronicle to create their own chronicles.[353] Thus the earliest Russian chronicle first appeared six hundred years later than was originally thought.

For conventional historians, this is, to say the least, an astonishing claim. It was usually considered that the Radzivill Chronicle was a product of the fifteenth century, making it one of the oldest extant chronicles but certainly not the oldest chronicle.[354] Highly valued because it is a rare illustrated medieval chronicle with 617 miniatures and drawings, it contains most of the details found in the *Primary Chronicle*. According to Fomenko, all records of the *Primary Chronicle* are altered copies of the Radzivill chronicle.[355]

---

352 Nosovskii and Fomenko, *Novaia khronologiia Rusi*, 25; Nikolai Morozov, 'O russkoi istorii', v. VIII, *Khristos* (Moscow-Leningrad: Russia's Academy of Sciences archive, Gosizdat, 1924–1932).
353 Nosovskii and Fomenko, *Novaia khronologiia Rusi*, p. 26.
354 Leonid Milov, 'K voprosu o podlinnosti Radzivillovskoi khroniki', *Kritika Novoi Khronologii*, p. 8.
355 Nosovskii and Fomenko, *Imperia: Rus', Turtsia, Kitai, Evropa, Egipet. Novaia matematicheskaia khronologiia drevnosti*, p. 18.

To build the case he reminds the reader of how little public access there has been to the Radzivill chronicle. The original may have been owned by the hetman of Vilnius, whose brother Boguslav transferred the chronicle to Konigsberg's library. Although the conventional wisdom states that the Radzivill Chronicle was widely known and used as early as the middle of the sixteenth century, historians acknowledge that the proof is indirect.[356] In 1711, during his visit to Konigsberg, Peter the Great saw what he assumed to be an original and ordered that a copy be made for his personal library. In 1758, Konigsberg was overrun by Russian troops and the Radzivill Chronicle became a war trophy, delivered to the Library of Russian Academy of Sciences. Schloezer worked with the chronicle, which was reprinted in Germany in 1802–1809. A Russian edition perished in the fire of 1812. While the task of publishing a complete set of Russian chronicles got under way in 1841, it was only in 1902 that the Radzivill Chronicle was published and without the transcription of the text.[357] The complete Radzivill chronicle saw the light of day only in 1989.[358]

The Radzivill Chronicle provides ideal material for a conspiracy theory. Because of the presence of watermarks, historians believe that the chronicle's binding dates to the eighteenth century. The chronicle's page numbers follow the Arabic system that was normal for Russia in the eighteenth century. The first three pages have been marked with the letters a, b, and c, while the remainder have Arabic numbers in the upper right hand corner.[359] Fomenko suggests to his readers that they should be deeply suspicious of an allegedly fifteenth-century manuscript that did not have the Church Slavonic numbering commonly in use before the seventeenth century. Conventional historians accept that the original markings were in Church Slavonic and that much later, in the eighteenth century Arabic numbers were added for the convenience of modern readers. More likely, claims Fomenko, that the chronicle we view today is an eighteenth-century creation.

Shakhmatov pointed out a major discrepancy in the text of the Radzivill Chronicle, where according to the text flow, page 236 should have been fol-

---

[356] Nosovskii and Fomenko, *Novaia khronologiia Rusi*, pp. 23–31.
[357] Sovetskii Entsiklopedicheskii Slovar', *Sovetskaia entsiklopedia* (Moscow: 1984), p. 1028.
[358] 'Radzivillovskaia Letopis", *Polnoe Sobranie Russkikh Letopisei* 38 (Leningrad-Moscow: Nauka, 1989), p. 3.
[359] Nosovskii and Fomenko, *Novaia khronologiia Rusi*, pp. 30–36.

lowed by pages 239–243, then 237, 238, and 244.[360] It seems that at some point the pages were mixed up. Shakhmatov speculated that at least two pages are missing altogether.[361] Since both Arabic and Church Slavonic page numbers ignore the obvious confusion of the pages, the conclusion that Fomenko has drawn is that the page numbers were added only after the binding of the chronicle. Having evaluated the quality of the paper and the presence of watermarks on the manuscript, Fomenko confidently asserted that the Arab page numbers were the originals, and the Church Slavonic numbers were added later in a clumsy attempt to establish the historical legitimacy of the text.

The plot thickened for Fomenko once he realized which topics are discussed in the pages that are in dispute. Fomenko claims that someone, most likely Schloezer himself, has omitted two pages, while adding one page under the Arab number 8 and Church Slavonic number 9 to the first book of the chronicle. The forger has changed the page numbers in order to create space for an extra page. These pages stand out from the rest of the book—one can clearly see the changes in numbers, while the corners of the inserted page are torn.

It is the allegedly inserted page that contains the story about the invitation to the Varangians. Thus Fomenko alleges that proof of the theory first put forward by Bayer finds its confirmation in an obviously doctored chronicle of the eighteenth century. Fomenko triumphantly noted that without the page detailing the Varangian invocation, Riurik appears in the chronicle as an obviously Slavic prince.[362] Fomenko's forensic triumph is trumpeted everywhere in the literature of the alternative writers.[363] Without the doctored chronicle, anti-Normanism would have been able to show that either there were no important Vikings, or if there were Vikings, then they simply served the Russian princes and they left nothing of value to Russian history. For Fomenko, the find is so significant that if earlier generations had known about the forged chronicle, there would have been no Westerner/Slavophile divide in Russia.

---

360 See Alexander Shakhmatov, 'Opisaniie rukopisei. Radzovillovskaia ili Konigsbergskaia letopis'', *Stat'i o texte i miniatiurakh letopisei* 2 (St. Petersburg: 1902).
361 Nosovskii and Fomenko, *Novaia khronologiia Rusi*, pp. 32–34.
362 Nosovskii and Fomenko, *Novaia khronologiia Rusi*, pp. 35–36.
363 See, for example, Guts, *Mnogovariantnaia istoriia Rossii*, pp. 73–83.

Thus, according to Fomenko, the allegedly 'ancient' sources of Russian history, and Russian history as we know it today, were written during the era of Peter the Great and his successors—the most pro-western and anti-Russian monarchs. First Karamzin, then Soloviev, Kliuchevskii, Liubavski, Pogodin and others accepted the lie and Normanism became widespread and accepted. Russian historians became weighed down under the voices of previous authority whose starting point, in the view of Fomenko, was as narrow and unconvincing as the histories that have appeared.

Milov is one conventional academic who has offered a point-by-point critique of Fomenko. Milov criticizes Fomenko for his amateurish approach to the problem. According to Milov, Fomenko should have thoroughly studied leading scholars in the field–Tatishchev, Shakhmatov, Priselkov, Bestushev-Riumin, Nasonov–before making wild claims about the *Primary Chronicle*'s validity.[364] For Milov, Fomenko has displayed breathtaking ignorance and arrogance in regard to the Russian chronicles. Russian historiography boasts at least ten generations of historians who have dealt systematically with the chronicles and ancient texts.[365] Those historians were professionals, Russians as well as Germans, and it is highly unlikely that they would have missed such a sensational discovery as the forging of the Radzivill chronicle in the eighteenth century.[366]

Milov noted that Fomenko claimed support from Kliuchevskii but that Fomenko uses the famous historian out of context. Kliuchevskii noted the failed attempt of the priest, Kudriavtsev, to find and compile chronicles in the middle of the seventeenth century.[367] Fomenko interprets Kudriavtsev's failure as evidence that no chronicles existed until the middle of the seventeenth century. Yet, Kliuchevskii wrote elsewhere that Russian chronicle writing began in the eleventh century in such seats of princely power as Kiev, Chernigov, Novgorod, Smolensk, Polotsk, and Vladimir.[368] Milov points out that the mistake to which Fomenko is so attentive came to prominence at the beginning of the twentieth century. The young Shakhmatov discovered the text discrepancy and suggested that Church Slavonic numbers were inserted after two pages were omitted, or lost. Milov insists that there

---

364 Leonid Milov, 'K voprosu o podlinnosti Radzivillovskoi khroniki', *Sbornik Russkogo istoricheskogo obshchestva* (Moscow: Russkaia Panorama, 2000), pp. 31–47.
365 Milov, pp. 31-47.
366 Milov, pp. 31-47.
367 Kliuchevskii, *Neopublikovannye proizvedeniia*, pp. 188–190.
368 Kliuchevskii, *Sochineniia* I, pp. 74–89.

was no justification for such a claim. Milov does not deny the page mix up that had been noticed practically by all the researchers in the field. However, according to Milov it was not a conspiracy, but a mistake made in an earlier version. Given the difficulties under which church chroniclers wrote, there should be no surprise about this sort of textual problem.

Milov argues that the unknown binder of the Radzivill chronicle was not very numerate in Slavonic. Therefore he had missed ten pages, indicating page number 200 after 189, instead of 190. In order to reinforce his claim, Milov invokes the opinion of other experts who also preferred the fact that the linear textual story of the chronicle was disturbed in the ancient past as compared to the plot or conspiracy theory favoured by Fomenko. Milov also points to the Troitsky Chronicle where the omissions in the text are identical to that of the Radzivill Chronicle. There are similar omissions and problems with many medieval documents. Therefore, for Milov, identical omissions discovered in different chronicles are a sign not only that they are historically accurate, but also that the mistake was made in the old proto-chronicle that does not exist today. In this respect Milov points out that the Radzivill chronicle was used to restore parts of the text of the Laurentian chronicle, while the events of 1206 that are fully preserved in the Laurentian chronicle are missing from the Radzivill chronicle.

It might be thought that wild claims would have discredited Fomenko. But it seems the reverse has occurred and Fomenko remains a folk hero to those inclined towards alternative history. Fomenko has suggested that a great deal remains hidden from the Russian public. Among the yet unpublished works of ancient Russian literature are for example the Novgorodian Karamzin Chronicle[369] and the unpublished *Litsevoi Svod*, which is reputed to contain nine thousand pages of information and sixteen thousand miniatures describing history from the alleged creation of the world up to the year 1567.[370] Fomenko is sure that the latter work will turn out to be the oldest example of Russian literature.

Pseudo-historians have pronounced themselves pleased that conventional history is, in their view, moving slowly in their direction. Alternative writers express some satisfaction that Russian textbooks are beginning to see the light. Instead of focusing upon the comings and goings of states, Russian

---

369 *Pamiatniki Literatury drevnei Rusi, XII vek* (Moscow: Khudozhestvennaia literatura, 1980), p. 540.
370 *Sovetskii Entsiklopedicheckii Slovar'*, p. 718.

pedagogy is making better use of archaeological evidence to take a longer view of Russian history. Sakharov and Buganov argue that the first ancestors of modern humans appeared on Russian territory 300,000–400,000 years ago.[371] The genealogy of these early people may in fact extend back millions of years. The roots of the Slavs are traced back to the Neolithic revolution and Indo-Europeans, at least six thousand years. This textbook gives information on the Scythians and their state, as well as detailed information about Scythian military feats as if these developments were part of the history of Russia. Other textbooks suggest that Kiev was founded in the fifth or sixth centuries AD long before any Vikings. [372] Yet another textbook dates the history of Russia one thousand years before the arrival of the Varangians. [373]

---

[371] A. Sakharov and V. Buganov, *Istoriia Rossii* (Moscow: Prosveshchenie, 1995).
[372] Boris Rybakov, A. Sakharov, A. Preobrazhensky, B. Krasnobaev, *Istoriia otechestva* (Moscow: Prosveshchenie, 1993).
[373] Alexander Novosel'tsev, *Istoriia Rossii s drevneishikh vremen* (Moscow: AST, 1996).

Chapter Six: Farewell to the Mongols: Fomenko and his 'Horde'

'Russia still struggles against the legacy of backwardness, ignorance, servility, submissiveness, deceit, cruelty, oppression, and lies imposed by the terrible Mongols.'

Harrison Salisbury

Part One: Mongols—Demons or Phantoms?

For alternative historians, the conventional story of Kiev Rus, like so much else in Russian history, is a hollow shell deeply encased in mythology. It will not surprise the reader to learn that, for alternative history, much the same is true of the Mongol era too. For those who believe that the past is some sort of guide to the future, Kiev Rus was crucial to Russia's sense of identity. The Rus, whoever they were, gave Russia not just its name, but its first state and its Orthodox faith. After 1991, the heartland of Kiev Rus no longer fell within Russian or Soviet territory but instead came to rest in the territory of the independent states of Ukraine and Belarus. For many Russians, these developments have thrown into focus the period of Russian history that followed Kiev Rus, the Mongol era. Without Ukraine, the Mongols and other steppe peoples from the East seem much more important to the history of the lands that now comprise the Russian Federation. History and pseudo-history alike have engaged in a reevaluation of the Mongols.

Attitudes towards the Mongols have changed in recent decades. Earlier accounts tended to adopt a hostile attitude vividly expressed by one Western writer who wrote that the Mongol invasion 'may be truly described as one of the most dreadful calamities which ever befell the human race'.[374] This view was reinforced during the Cold War when it was often assumed that Soviet totalitarianism occurred because Russia was located too far to the East. Harrison Salisbury, for example, wrote of Russia's struggle to overcome the 'legacy of backwardness, deceit, submissiveness and lies imposed by the

---

[374] Edward Browne, *A History of Persian literature under Tartar Dominion* (Cambridge: Cambridge University Press, 1920), p. 4.

Mongols'.[375] While more recent accounts still find in Russia a history of backwardness and lies, they are less inclined to blame it on the Mongols.

Instead of violent barbarians who bequeathed little to history apart from the tactics of ruthless terror, the Mongols have received more and more recognition as state-builders, traders and as a crucial conduit between the civilized East and the uncivilized medieval West.[376] David Christian, for example, has described the Mongols as the high water mark of pastoralism in the history of inner Eurasia, the rivet that held together the world system of the thirteenth and fourteenth centuries.[377] His account placed Russia squarely within that history of Eurasia. In Russia, revisionist histories written by Gumilev helped to improve the standing of the Mongols, a task undertaken earlier in the century by the Eurasianist, Trubetskoi.

The story of the Mongol invasion of Russia is usually told this way. In the beginning of the thirteenth century, there emerged from the Mongolian steppes an energetic and talented warlord, Genghis Khan, who created a huge, disciplined and powerful army out of Mongolian nomads and neighbouring tribes, promising 'to conquer the entire world to the last sea'. David Morgan has argued that the Mongols were motivated by the search for booty and, on this occasion, channelled their warlike nature into external conflict rather than the debilitating internal wars typical of nomad history. The logic of sustaining long-distance war and rewarding allies necessitated more complex and systematic methods of extracting booty or tribute from the peoples they conquered.[378]

Christian has noted the increasing sophistication of nomadic confederations in the Mongolian steppes. By the time of the Mongols, nomad political and military organization closely resembled the states established by sedentary peoples.[379] Having conquered their neighbours, including the powerful Chinese Empire, the invading hordes turned westward, and advanced more than five thousand kilometres. The Mongols destroyed the Central Asian kingdom of Khwarezm, the Christian kingdoms of Armenia and Georgia, the Muslim Bulgars on the river Volga and finally approached the southern borders of Kiev Rus' in 1223.

---

375 Harrison Salisbury, *War Between Russia and China* (New York: Norton, 1969), p. 31.
376 See, for example, Janet L. Abu-Lughod, *Before European hegemony: the world system A. D. 1250–1350* (Oxford: Oxford University Press, 1991), pp. 3–4.
377 Christian, *Russia, Central Asia and Mongolia*, pp. 426–27.
378 David Morgan, *The Mongols* (London: Basil Blackwell, 1986), pp. 62–64.
379 Christian, *Russia, Central Asia and Mongolia*, p. 150.

In the initial battle with the Russians on the river Kalka, the Mongols destroyed the armies of Kiev Rus and their allied Polovtsy. Lacking manpower or perhaps satisfied with the initial outcome, the Mongols headed back to Mongolia, only to return in 1237–40 with incredible force.[380] The Mongols sacked and burned the most important Russian cities, sparing only Novgorod. Unlike previous steppe nomads with whom the Russians were familiar, the Mongols made their presence permanent by establishing their base at Sarai on the Volga river.[381] Under Batu Khan, the Mongols founded a new state, the Kipchak khanate or Golden Horde, on the Volga and collected tribute from lands that stretched in an arc from the Middle East to western Russia.

In 1241 Batu Khan moved through Poland and the Czech lands to reach the Mediterranean and threaten Western Europe. Only the death of Genghis's successor, Ogedei, brought an end to this westward march and caused Mongol leaders to return to their homeland to settle the succession, saving Europe in the process. Meanwhile, the irruption of the Mongols set in motion other steppe peoples, including Seljuk and then Ottoman Turks who for centuries would dominate the eastern part of the Mediterranean.[382]

How did Genghis Khan establish such a powerful force? *The Secret History of the Mongols*, the main source for much of the detail of this early period, was written after Genghis Khan's death in 1240 and describes a rare combination of military and political talents.[383] The population was divided into military units, each with one thousand warriors, whose strength lay in horsemanship and mounted archers. Each commander was well known to Genghis Khan who expected all males from the age of fifteen to be ready for military duty. Genghis Khan was far-sighted enough to recruit imperial administrators, tolerated different religions, encouraged commerce, and established a code of laws known as the Great Yasa.

---

380 George Vernadsky, *Kievan Russia* (New Haven and London: Yale University press, 1973), pp. 235–239.
381 Morgan, *Mongols*, p. 135.
382 Davies, *Europe: a history*, p. 297.
383 See, for example, Francis Woodman Cleaves (ed), *The Secret History of the Mongols* (Cambridge: Harvard University Press, Mass, 1982); Rashid ad-Din, *Sbornik letopisei*, translated by Iu. Verkhovskii (Moscow-Leningrad: Academy of Sciences USSR, 1960); Boris Vladimirtsov, *Chingiz-Khan* (Moscow: 1922); Wilhelm Barthold, *Chingiz-Khan* (St-Petersburg: 1991), pp. 856–862.

The Golden Horde is the name that the Russians gave from the seventeenth century to the Kipchak Khanate, or Horde.[384] This entity formed after 1240 in the territory adjacent to the Volga River and incorporated areas once ruled by the Bulgars, Polovtsy/Kipchaks, Khwarezm and Kiev Rus. The Mongols appointed provincial and town governors, and taxed the population. Tax collectors known as *baskaki* were accompanied by armed detachments ready to deal with those brave or foolhardy enough not to accept the rule of the Mongols.

With Mongolian military help, the defeated Russian princes fought amongst each other, trying to outmaneuver competitors for the title of Grand Prince and Mongol favorite. Kiev was weakened by the Mongol onslaught and came under the influence of Lithuania, which remained independent of Mongols. For much of the Mongol period, Vladimir was the centre of Russian affairs. In 1380, a stronger Russia, with a newly emerged political center in Moscow under the leadership of Dmitrii Donskoi, defeated Mamai and his Tatar troops. The contest continued for another hundred years until, in 1480, Ahmad retreated from Russian lands having been stared down by the troops of the Moscow Grand Prince, Ivan the Third.[385]

The largest continental empire in the history of mankind stretched from Beijing in the East, westwards along the Central Asian trade routes to the Volga and into Europe itself, overshadowing the Russian lands. From Sarai, Mongol khans plundered Russia, levying taxes in the form of a tithe, ten percent of everything, including the population. While formally governed by Russian princes, the local population had to endure the burden of double taxation, supporting their Russian and Mongol overlords. The Mongols appointed Grand Princes of Russia who received the *iarlyk* enabling the holder to extract tribute. Moscow grew more influential and became the principal successor state of the Golden Horde because it voluntarily acted as the conqueror's surrogate. For critics of Russia in the West, Moscow and the Tartars (sic) were inseparable. Davies described Ivan the Third, the Moscow Grand Prince who threw off the Tatar yoke as 'an exponent of Tartar fi-

---

[384] Donald Ostrowski, *Muscovy and the Mongols. Cross-cultural influences on the steppe frontier, 1304–1589* (Cambridge: Cambridge University Press, 1998), xiii.
[385] George Vernadsky, *History of Russia* III (New Haven: Yale University Press, 1952), pp. 258–263.

nancial, military and political method who used the shifting alliances of khans and princes to replace the Tartar yoke with a Muscovite one'.[386]

Part Two: Interpretations

Ostrowski has identified five principal views or models, Russian and non-Russian, that historians have used to explain the relationship between Moscow and the Mongols. The first contends that Moscow, and, by extension, Russia, was *sui generis* and developed for indigenous reasons with little outside influence. This was the predominant view of much Russian and Soviet history. For most Imperial and Soviet historians, the Mongols were a curse and the Russians victims of an unprovoked attack. Uncivilized in comparison to the Slavs, Mongols came out of nowhere and made little positive impact upon Russia even if they caused its development to fall behind that of Western Europe. Soloviev considered the Mongols to be barbarians who bequeathed nothing of value to Russia.[387] The Soviet-era historians, Grekov and Iakubovsky argued that:

> The Russian state with Moscow at its head was created not with the assistance of Tatars, but in the process of a hard struggle of the Russian people against the yoke of the Golden Horde.[388]

Soviet historiography mostly considered that the Mongol Empire worked to the detriment of the Mongol people as well as the Russians. Their ruling dynasties were parasitical, and their conquests had a negative effect on the development of the various sedentary peoples subjugated by the Mongol war machine.[389] In 1944, Stalin's Central Committee even passed a decree declaring that the Golden Horde was both 'reactionary' and 'parasitic'.[390]

---

386 Davies, *Europe*, p. 461.
387 Soloviev, *Istoriia Rossii s drevneishikh vremen* volume II, p. 489; volume IV, p. 179.
388 Boris Grekov and Alexander Iakubovsky, *Zolotaia Orda i ee padenie* (Moscow-Leningrad, 1950), p. 256; also Arsenii Nasonov, *Mongoly i Rus* (Moscow: 1940).
389 Nikolai Merpert, Lev Cherepnin, Vladimir Pashuto, 'Chingiz khan i ego nasledie', *Istoriia SSSR* 5 (1962): pp. 91–110; I. Maiskii, 'Chingiz khan', *Voprosy Istorii* 5 (1962): pp. 74–83; Vadim Kargalov, *Mongolo-tatarskoe nashestvie na Rusi XIII vek* (Moscow: 1966), *Narod-bogatyr'* (Moscow: 1971), *Sverzhenie Tataro-Mongolskogo iga* (Moscow: 1973), and *Konets ordynskogo iga* (Moscow: Nauka, 1980).
390 Viktor Shnirelman, *Who Gets the Past? Competition for Ancestors among Non-Russian Intellectuals in Rusia*, p. 7.

Ostrowski groups with these writers the best-known Western historian of medieval Russia, Edward Keenan, who argued that Byzantine influence upon Russia was a mythology for which there is no contemporary evidence.[391] Keenan's argument that Byzantine influence in Moscovy was a latter-day invention is an indication of the suspicions that serious scholars of Russian history harbour about the sources for Russian history prior to the era of Peter the Great.

Many scholars have rejected the indigenous model but in different ways. The second and third models identified by Ostrowski comprise those writers, Russian and Western, who think that Moscow/Russia are entirely derivative of other cultures. Obolensky, for example, saw Moscow as having borrowed its beliefs and values from Byzantium. Other writers underscored the importance of the Mongols. Karamzin, the most popular of Russia's nineteenth century historians, admitted that without the Mongols, Kiev Rus was likely to have perished because of internecine princely feuds.[392] Karamzin considered that Moscow, which grew in strength as a Mongol surrogate, 'owed its greatness to the khans'.[393] Kostomarov emphasized the role of the khans' decrees in strengthening the authority of the Muscovite duke within his realm.[394]

Trubetskoi firmly rejected the notion that the term 'yoke' was applicable to Russian-Mongol relations.[395] For Trubetskoi, 'the Russian state was an inheritor, the successor, the continuation of the historical work and legacy of Genghis Khan'.[396] The Muscovite dukes became genuine Russian rulers only after they gathered the Tatar lands.[397] Writing in the West, Vernadsky tried to show that the Mongols left an important legacy in Russia in terms of politics and law even if their overall impact represented a heavy burden.[398]

A fourth model identified by Ostrowski tried to combine Byzantine and Mongol influence. Thus, Russia's attachment to Byzantium could be explained

---

391 See Ostrowski, *Mongols and Muscovy*, pp. 4–6.
392 Nikolai Karamzin, *Istoriia gosudarstva rossiiskogo*, vol. V, (St-Petersburg: 1851–1853), p. 223.
393 Karamzin, *Istoriia gosudarstva rossiiskogo*, vol. V, pp. 365–384.
394 Nikolai Kostomarov, 'Nachalo edinodershavia v drevnei Rusi', *Sobranie sochinenii* V (St-Petersburg: 1905), pp. 41–47.
395 Nikolai Trubetskoi, *The Legacy of Chengiz-Khan and Other Essays on Russia's Identity*, pp. 182, 185, 189.
396 Trubetskoi, *The Legacy of Chengiz-Khan*, pp. 163, 167, 175, 180.
397 Trubetskoi, *The Legacy of Chengiz-Khan*, p. 185.
398 Trubetskoi, *The Legacy of Chengiz-Khan*, p. 344.

in terms of its need to find something Russian about Russia following centuries of Mongol domination. The fifth model comprises those who, from Karl Marx to Alexander Yanov, see Russia as undergoing stages of development similar to those of Britain, France or Germany. These writers emphasise economic developments rather than superficial changes in the elites of the emerging Russian state. It would be fair to say that the first three models presently attract the greatest interest from scholars.

One trend that is clear in both Western and Russian scholarship is that the relationship between Russia and the Mongols was more of a partnership, symbiosis or interrelationship than was previously thought. Fennell, Vernadsky and most Soviet historians represented an older view when they argued that Moscow was instinctively hostile to the Tatar khanates, allying with the Crimean Khans, for example, only in times of need in the face of a common enemy like the Lithuanians. More recently, Western writers like Halperin, Ostrowski and Christian have noted the links between not just Moscow but Kiev Rus and their nomadic neighbours.

Halperin noted that the term Kagan or emperor was used by the Turks and applied not just to the leader of the Khazars but to the prince of Kiev as well. According to Halperin this seems to be the only case of the application of this title to a non-nomadic people. Russians dealt with Turkic peoples without the aid of interpreters and Turkic of some sort must have been the *lingua franca* of the steppe.[399] The Mongols and their empire connected Russia to the outside world.[400] It was only in the reign of Ivan the Terrible in the middle of the sixteenth century that Moscow's policy toward the East became one of conquest.

For Halperin the medieval world was one of 'mixed Christian and Islamic societies'. Russia's church chroniclers misled future generations of historians because they were silent about the fact that Russians and Tatars intermarried, shared institutions and together launched military campaigns.[401] According to Halperin, a similar process of forgetting about an earlier relationship would take place among the Turks. Thus, the 'widespread use of Christian soldiers, farmers, artisans, and bureaucrats in the early Ottoman empire' was passed over in silence not just by Russian chroniclers but by Ottoman writers as well.

---

399 Charles Halperin, *Tatar Yoke* (Slavica Pub, 1986), p. 24.
400 Halperin, *Russia and the Golden Horde*, pp. 5–28.
401 Halperin, *Russia and the Golden Horde*, p. 7.

Ostrowski emphasized a strong Mongol influence on Muscovy in terms of administration and military organization.[402] He has argued that medieval Russia was an amalgam of Byzantine theoretical and philosophical concepts, legal concepts derived from Kiev Rus, and Mongol/Islamic governmental structure and administration.[403] The church chroniclers gave the impression that the leaders of Russia had thought in negative terms about the Tatars since time immemorial or at least since the initial invasion of the mid thirteenth century. Ostrowski has pointed out that in reality there is not much evidence of official hostility towards the Tatars before the Orthodox Church in Moscow finally broke with its elder brother, the Byzantine Church in the fifteenth century. Byzantium treated the Tatars as a 'valuable ally and trading partner'.[404] An anti-Tatar ideology came to suit the rulers of Moscow thereafter and evidence of cooperation with the Tatars was written out of history.

Part Three: Fomenko Russifies the Mongols

While plainly aware of the debates of the professional historians, Fomenko and many of his readers were convinced that conventional history lacked all credibility on the issue of the Mongols after years of lies, silences and gaps in official histories. While his conclusions were speculative, Fomenko's premise, that there was something wrong with Russian history, struck a chord with the Russian public. For Fomenko, the Mongol/Tatar invasion was a poorly named and deliberately twisted fantasy of Romanov historians. Rather than a Mongol invasion, the real history was the civil wars that broke out occasionally within the Russian Horde, this great Slav-Turk Empire.

Fomenko's ideal type of an invasion and conquest seems to be the Nazi blitzkrieg of 1941–45 when the German invaders made a systematic effort to destroy the Soviet state, eradicate all political or cultural independence and reduce the population to slave labour. Soviet writers certainly gave their readers the impression that the Mongols operated in much the same way as modern conquerors. This picture was simply wrong. It is now clear to historians that the Mongols chose not to impose an occupation of this kind and left Russia, so long as it paid tribute, semi-independent. Alternative histori-

---

402 Ostrowski, *Muscovy and the Mongols*, p. 35.
403 Ostrowski, *Muscovy and the Mongols*, p. 15.
404 Ostrowski, *Muscovy and the Mongols*, p. 164.

ans argue that the story of the Tatar yoke is yet to be exposed as another of the lies told by official history.

Fomenko and his allies follow their usual pattern of argument, pointing to the paucity of reliable sources from the medieval period, the obvious inaccuracies and forgeries that abound in the sources that do exist, the plot on the part of Church and State in Romanov Russia aimed at extirpating all traces of a Russian alliance with Turks or Moslems and the strange resemblances among the array of characters described in conventional accounts of this period. Alternative history cites indiscriminately the works of Russian and Western historians to highlight problems in the conventional account. It then offers its own reconstructions as if they are at least as plausible as anything that the flawed conventional wisdom can offer.

As ever, the sources really do present a challenge to conventional history. Many latter-day writers chose to view the first Russian state as a golden age or paradise that fell victim to its own pride and was then punished by demonic invaders in the shape of the Mongols. The Orthodox Church, the Romanovs and Slavophiles all had reason to celebrate the East Slavic successes story and medieval power of Kiev Rus. Russian historians idealized Kiev Rus as a centre of Christianity, as a civilized place where commerce and popular institutions flourished only to be destroyed by warlike and unchristian Mongols. The problem is that the evidence of the Tatar yoke is not as strong as ealier readers were led to believe. According to Halperin, the church chroniclers were so stunned by Russia's ill fortune that they adopted the 'ideology of silence', pretending that the conquest had not occurred.[405] For Fomenko, their silence about the conquest is comprehensible in terms of fact and not discourse. The conquest never happened.

As Abu-Loghod has put it, 'the Mongols left only a modest primary record that is focused largely on campaigns, dynastic successions and conquests'.[406] It seems likely that Russia was a peripheral issue to the original Mongols even though the Mongol era endured longer in Russia than most other places. According to Fennell, the basic sources for the Russian reaction to the Mongols comprise what he describes as four 'princely' chronicles (Lavrent'evskii, Novgorod First, Ipat'evskii and Sofiiskii First) that conveniently provide information, albeit in latter-day editions, from all the affected

---

[405] Halperin, *Russia and the Golden Horde*, p. 8.
[406] Janet L. Abu-Lughod, *Before European hegemony: the world system A. D. 1250–1350* (London: Oxford University Press), pp. 25–26.

areas, Kiev, Chernigov, Galicia, Smolensk, Rostov and Vladimir.[407] On the other hand, there is much that is not known about the Golden Horde, in part because Tamerlane's fourteenth-century raiding party destroyed the archive at Sarai.[408]

Initially, the chroniclers portrayed the Mongols as ruthless and barbaric nomads from the eastern steppe, strangers to the lands of Kievan Rus, who established their rule suddenly and with great force. As not only Russian but also Georgian and Armenian chronicles put it, following the 'clouds of Tatars not an eye was left to weep'.[409] According to the Russian chroniclers, 'in those times there came upon us for our sins, unknown nations. No one could tell their origin, whence they came, what religion they professed. God alone knew who they were.' It seems powerful evidence that the Mongols did indeed come from far away if the Russians, who knew so many steppe peoples, regarded them as complete strangers.

Not so, counters Fomenko. The chronicles are the mouthpieces of the church and are mostly latter-day inventions intended to demonise non-Christians whenever possible as horrible and strange. All the evidence we have, claim the alternative writers, points to familiarity to the point of contempt among those who fought in Russia during the so-called Mongol era. The chroniclers even called these people Tatars, the name they bestowed upon other steppe peoples.

Historians outside of Russia have long acknowledged the difficulty in using church chronicles for an account of the Mongols. Ostrowski identified three distinct periods of chronicle writing and in each case the attitude towards the Mongols appears to have been determined mostly by political considerations. From 1223 to 1252, the chroniclers were plainly hostile to the Tatars, the 'godless Moabites' from the East. In 1252, the Mongol surrogate, Alexander Nevsky became Grand Prince of Vladimir and, for the next two hundred years, barely a harsh word is to be heard from the chroniclers about the Tatars. It was as if there were no invaders. The Tatars who do appear in the chronicles are occasional interlopers and not occupiers.[410]

---

407 John Fennell, *The Crisis of Medieval Russia, 1200–1304* (London: Longman, 1983), p. 65.
408 Halperin, *Russia and the Golden Horde*, p. 44.
409 Haining, 'The Vicissitudes of Mongolian Historiography', *The Mongol Empire and its Legacy*, p. 334; Alfred Rambaud, *History of Russia, from the earliest times to 1800*, trans. by L.B. Lang, H.A. Bolles (Boston: 1882).
410 Ostrowski, *Muscovy and the Mongols*, pp. 147–50.

Finally, from the middle of the fifteenth century as the power of the Golden Horde waned and the Moscow church stood alone as the last outpost of Orthodox Christianity, the modern view of the Mongols as horrible heathens rapidly gained ascendancy. For Ostrowski, it is clear that, for two hundred years, Russians and Tatars were joint administrators of the 'Tatar' yoke. Only nearing the end of the Mongol period was the 'Church concocted virtual past of Rus' princes trying to free the Rus' lands from the Tatars' invented.[411] Halperin argued that the chroniclers could not bring themselves to describe the Mongol occupation or the Russian defeat. Ostrowski preferred to call it a conspiracy of silence, involving the deliberate falsification of sources, with the aim of smoothing the trading and diplomatic relationship between the Mongols on the one hand, and the Rus and Byzantium on the other.[412]

Part Four: Gumilev and the steppe

Conveniently for Fomenko and his allies, a ready-made bridge already existed to cross the murky waters that the patriotic history of the Soviet and post-Soviet world. Among modern exponents of the new burst of patriotic history in Russia, Lev Gumilev is probably the most famous and certainly the most important.[413] Until his death in 1992, Gumilev maintained a foot in both camps with a reputation among conventional and alternative historians. He has won acceptance among conventional scholars to the point where he writes textbooks, has scholarly works translated into foreign languages and has a university named after him.[414] On the other hand he is highly regarded among the writers considered in this thesis, partly because he claims to have added a scientific dimension to nationalism with his theory of ethnoses. Shnirelman has pointed out that in putting forward his concept of the ethnos, Gumilev was unable or unwilling to escape the constraints of Soviet anthro-

---

411 Ostrowski, *Muscovy and the Mongols*, p. 163.
412 Ostrowski, *Muscovy and the Mongols*, p. 145.
413 Lev Gumilev, *Drevniaia Rus i velikaia step'* (Moscow: Mysl', 1992); *Poiski vymyshlennogo tsarstva* (Moscow: Tanais, 1994); *Chernaia legenda* (Moscow: Ekopros, 1994); *Ot Rusi k Rossi* (Leningrad: 1989); *Etnogenez i biosfera zemli* (Leningrad: 1989); *Geografiia etnosa v istoricheskii period* (Leningrad: 1990); *Otkrytie Khazarii* (Moscow: AST, 2000); Chtob svecha ne pogasla (Moscow: AST, 2001); *Tysiacheletie vokrug Kaspia*, II volumes (Moscow: AST, 2002).
414 Viktor Shnirelman and Sergei Panarin, 'Lev Gumilev: His Pretensions as founder of Ethnology and his Eurasian theories', pp. 1–18.

pology. The Soviet concept of the ethnos, championed by Bromlei between the 1960s and 80s, held that 'a conscious or unconscious attachment to one's primary group is formed on the basis of blood relations, language, religion, cultural traits, and other characteristics that make for highly durable, if not permanent groups'.[415] In other words, the Soviet approach is 'primordialist'. Western anthropology, by contrast, tends to assume more fluid groups whose membership and character are subject to change. It is the Soviet version of durable ethnoses that is evident in the thinking of Gumilev and Fomenko.

Gumilev's popularity partly lay in the fact that he found history's motor not in the official Soviet ideology of classes but in a quasi-scientific biology, a new element of the historical narrative for the Soviet historical imagination. Researchers have found it hard to pin down exactly what Gumilev meant by ethnos.[416] Every known cultural, political and religious group from history seems to have had its own ethnos, although the categories of super-ethnos, sub-ethnos and ethnic chimeras suggest a hierarchy of collectivities striving to survive and flourish in the world. For some reason these ethnoses survive for approximately twelve hundred to fifteen hundred years and spring to life because of a mysterious *passionarnost*, literally bursts of energy, caused by the arrival of a charismatic figure or external pressures like climate change or war. The ethnos exhausts its energy at some point and once vibrant ethnoses decay and die.

Gumilev had no time for the conventional story of Russian history. For Gumilev, Kiev Rus is misunderstood and the Mongols are wrongly demonized. Russia was not a by-product of the European West but a symbiosis of many peoples who enjoyed a special relationship with the Russian land, a territory that extended over the vast area of Eurasia. Ancient Russia was not a handmaiden to Byzantium but grew together with its more celebrated twin.[417] Nestor, the chronicler responsible for the tale about Viking rulers of Kiev Rus was plainly mistaken.[418] The Westernizer tradition among Russian historians, fuelled by a fanatical Christianity and hostility to the non-Christian world, repressed the ancient and glorious history of the Russian

---

[415] Viktor Shnirelman, *Who Gets the Past?*, p. 8.
[416] Shnirelman and Panarin, 'Lev Gumilev', pp. 6–7.
[417] Gumilev, *Drevniaia Rus' i velikaia step'*, p. 175.
[418] Gumilev, *Drevniaia Rus' i velikaia step'*, p. 175.

Kaganate, the first state on Russian lands and the forerunner of Kiev Rus, Muscovy, the Russian Empire and the Soviet Union.[419]

For many Russian readers, Gumilev represented a breath of fresh air and clarity in his withering attacks upon the Soviet and Romanov view of the past. At the same time, he rode the boundary between conventional and pseudo-history, speculating wildly but always trying to ground his work in accepted sources and paying close attention to the work of other experts in the field. For Fomenko, there would be no such constraints. Gumilev claimed that Mongols, Polovtsy, Slavs and Turks coexisted and intermingled for centuries before and after 1223. In this context it is not so fantastic a leap for Fomenko to claim that Russia seemed little changed by the allegedly catastrophic and unprecedented Mongol invasion.

Fomenko makes the reasonable claim that chronicle sources are obviously written to a formula, are full of obvious errors and fantastic detail, and were most likely composed or altered after the Tatars came to be associated with Islam in the fifteenth century. Certainly, the reader needs to be armed with considerable skepticism when reading the chronicle accounts of the Mongols. The Novgorod chronicler, for example, seemed confused about who the Mongols were or at least found it convenient to use stock phrases to describe them. The chronicler quoted the Revelation of Methodius of Patara that described the sudden appearance of a strange people put to flight by Gideon, but had used exactly these Biblical words to describe the Polovtsi in years past.[420] The chroniclers are amazingly unforthcoming about why, once the ferocious Mongols left in 1223, no precautions were taken against their return a decade later. That the war affected different areas differently is attested to by the Vladimir chronicler who, amid the apparent carnage of the era, reported that between March 1238 and February 1239, 'there was peace'.[421]

Riazan fell in December 1237 after resisting for a mere five days. Fennell notes that the principal source we have is the fragmentary *Povest o razorenii Riazani Batuem* or 'Tale of the Destruction of Riazan by Batu'. As a Russian historian has put it: 'for a description of the Mongol invasion of

---

419 Gumilev, *Drevniaia Rus' i velikaia step'*, p. 200; See also Christian, *A History Russia, Central Asia and Mongolia*, pp. 282–303.
420 Fennell, *The Crisis of Medieval Russia*, p. 68.
421 Fennell, *The Crisis of Medieval Russia*, p. 81.

Russia, researchers, teachers and artists rely upon the *Povest*.[422] Yet it is not clear when this document was written and how reliable it is. *Povest* resembles other chronicle accounts and, in place of credible information, simply lists the usual litany of princes murdered, nuns raped and all manner of barbaric acts perpetrated by the Mongols.[423] We are asked to believe that Batu Khan was possessed by lust and beheaded the city's prince for refusing to present his wife. The servant of the prince, who lived to tell the tale, not only saw the execution, but also succeeded in smuggling the beheaded prince's body out of Batu Khan's camp to bury it nearby.

According to the chroniclers, Vladimir was taken in just four days in February 1238 after the use of siege guns to breach the walls. Here the unfortunate inhabitants were, it seems, burned to death after they took refuge in the Cathedral of the Assumption. This story of Christian martyrdom is for Fomenko just another staged piece of latter-day chronicle writing. Fomenko notes that the much smaller town of Kozelsk took two months to subdue, no siege guns were used and the siege cost thousands of Tatar lives, if the chronicles are to be believed. It is not only Fomenko who is puzzled as to why and how Kozelsk resisted, why casualties were so high and why the Mongols even bothered with this seemingly unimportant town when they chose not to ride to Novgorod.[424] Whereas the professionally trained historian might accept as typical the puzzling nature of these events, the lack of logic is, Fomenko claims, damning evidence that the chronicles in the form that they have reached us cannot be taken literally.

Part Five: Western Fantasies

Much of our knowledge about the Mongols comes from Western travelers, papal envoys and merchants, who visited the Mongol heartland. They reported seeing fantastic things. According to the testimony of William of Rubruck, the Franciscan monk who claimed to have traveled to Khan Mongke's headquarters in Karakorum in 1253–55, there was even a Parisian goldsmith named Buchier who created a magnificent mechanical silver fountain, which spurted different alcoholic beverages from each pipe.[425]

---

422 Andrei Amel'kin, 'Kogda rodilsiia Ievpatii Kolovrat', *Rodina* 3–4 (1997): p. 48
423 Andrei Amel'kin, 'Kogda rodilsiia Ievpatii Kolovrat', p. 79.
424 Fennell, *The Crisis of Medieval Russia*, p. 81.
425 Peter Jackson, 'From Ulus to Khanate', *The Mongol Empire and its Legacy*, p. 20.

Plano Carpini, whose travels among the Mongols preceded William of Rubruck, commented that the Mongols exterminated everyone in the conquered Russian lands except for the artisans and that this explains the wonders of Karakorum.[426] According to the testimony of Carpini, in Karakorum the supreme khan sat upon an ivory throne that was carved for him by the Russian master Kozma.[427]

Yet Plano Carpini contradicted himself when he wrote that Kiev, which had just been ravaged by Batu Khan, was under the control of the Kievan commander, Vladimir Eikovich, who continued to carry out his duties as he did prior to the Mongol attack.[428] According to Rubruck, 'the Russians lived with the Tatars...they mixed with them...borrowed Tatar customs, traditions, clothes...all the river crossing are manned by Russians, all the transportation systems are served by Russians'.[429] Fomenko comments ironically that it took only twenty years for the Tatars and the Russians to blend into a homogenous ethnic entity.[430] Fomenko insists that Rubruck and Carpini saw the riches of the cities of the Volga River, the capital of the Golden Horde, where archaeologists have discovered numerous and ornate eastern Slavonic artefacts, enamel and amber Orthodox crosses. Carpini wrote that Russian clergy lived 'in the horde with the emperor', evidence for Fomenko that Carpini had visited the court of a Russian tsar-khan on the Volga.

Fomenko is especially interested in Carpini's geography. Fomenko asks how it could be that Carpini does not describe in detail the countries lying to the east of the Volga.[431] Geographically, Carpini indicated that China was to the east of the Mongol lands, whereas Fomenko points out that it is to the

---

426 Marina Poluboiarinova, 'Russkie v Zolotoi Orde', *Rodina* 3–4 (1997): p. 53.
427 Vernadsky, *A History of Russia*, III, p. 63; Poluboiarinova, 'Russkie v Zolotoi Orde', p. 54.
428 Christopher Dawson (ed), *The Mission to Asia: narratives and letters of the Franciscan missionaries in Mongolia and China in the thirteenth and fourteenth centuries*, translated by a Nun of Stanbrook Abbey, ed. by Sheed and Ward (London: 1955); Dawson, Plano Carpini, *Istoriia Mongalov/Rubruck, Puteshestvia v vostochnye strany/kniga Marko Polo* (Moscow: Mysl', 1997); The analysis of his journeys is in Nosovskii and Fomenko, *Bibleiskaia Rus'* II, pp. 287–295; Poliakovskii, *Tatary-Mongoly, Evraziia, Mnogovariatnost'*, p. 83; Bushkov, *Rossiia kotoroi ne bylo* I, pp. 178–190.
429 Nosovskii and Fomenko, *Novaia khronologiia Rusi*, p. 71.
430 Nosovskii and Fomenko, *Novaia khronologiia Rusi*, p. 71.
431 Nosovskii and Fomenko, *Bibleiskaia Rus'* II, pp. 288–89.

east only from the Volga, and that it has to be south of the real Mongolia. Carpini instead has the Saracens located to the south of Mongolia. Fomenko points to the fact that the medieval Saracens lived to the south of the Volga and Caspian, whereas south of Mongolia there is present day China. Carpini wrote that to the west of Karakorum there were tribes of Naiman. Most probably, Fomenko concludes, implausibly, the Naiman was a reference to the Normans who lived to the west of Russia. Carpini wrote that to the north of the lands of the Tatars there are oceans and seas, while Fomenko points out that it is common knowledge that there are thousands of kilometres of dense forests and tundra to the north of present-day Mongolia. On the other hand, north-eastern Russia is indeed located very close to the Arctic Ocean, having cities and villages running almost all the way up to the northern coast.[432]

There is widespread scepticism among experts about much of this travel literature. The historian, Denis Sinor has pointed out that Carpini was often wrong in factual matters. Carpini claimed to have come across peoples called *parossites* with 'small stomachs and tiny mouths' that feed simply by smelling their cooked meat. Later he met peoples who had a human shape in every respect except for their ox-like hooves and dog-like heads, who barked after every two or three words.[433] It seems unlikely that Carpini was an eyewitness to all that he reported. In the West, there has long been a debate over whether Marco Polo saw the Far East. Frances Wood, for example, has argued that Marco Polo never reached China, in part, because Polo did not describe the Great Wall, tea drinking, or foot binding. On the other hand, Marco Polo did report witnessing banquets for forty thousand people. For schoalrs, such claims reflect 'the Western cultural imaginary with its Orientalist phantasms and its fascination with the marvels of foreign worlds'.[434] Fomenko insists that observers like Polo really did witness such marvels but they did so while travelling among Slavs and Turks who settled the Volga River, an area that was certainly more accessible to travellers from Western Europe than Beijing.

---

432 Nosovskii and Fomenko, *Bibleiskaia Rus'* II, pp. 289–290.
433 See Dawson (ed), *The Mission to Asia*, pp. 30–31.
434 Gabriele Schwab, 'Traveling literature, traveling theory: literature and cultural contrast between East and West', *Studies in the Humanities* 29:1 (June 2002): p. 5.

Part Six: Selecting the Evidence

Fomenko finds evidence of the plot against Russian history almost everywhere he looks. *Slovo o pogibeli Russkoi zemli* is a famous medieval document less than a page in length that describes how successful Kiev Rus was before misfortune came upon it. Conventional historians believe that its gloomy prognosis was simply a reflection of the level of disintegration in Kiev Rus on the eve of its wars against the Mongols.[435] For alternative writers, *Slovo* is clearly a reference to the Mongol invasion. The reason it is so brief is that Romanov historians edited it in order to hide the truth about the Russian nature of the Mongols. For alternative history, the reason that we have only fragmentary information about pagan priests in Novgorod, medieval maps displaying the conquests of the Russian horde and clear proof that Vikings and Mongols served Russian princes and tsar/khans and not the other way round is that this inconvenient information has been excised from the historical record by Romanov propagandists.

Alternative historians cherry pick the historical record in search of evidence that suits their purposes Rashid Ad Din, the Persian writer who knew the Mongols best, seemed to suggest that the first people to suffer from the Mongol invasion were Christian Bulgars, neighbors of the Franks.[436] For Morozov it was obvious that the Mongol invasion was in fact an invasion of Western Europeans who attacked the Bulgarian lands north of Greece. Reading the remainder of Rashid Ad Din's account it becomes obvious that this first observation was simply an error. Elsewhere, Rashid Ad Din discusses Bulgars whose neighbors are the Bashkirs, in other words, clearly the Bulgars who live on the middle Volga who were indeed attacked and overrun by Batu Khan's horde before the invasion of Russia. Nonetheless, alternative writers, including Fomenko, Bushkov and Poliakovsky, invariably mention this initial mistake by Rashid Ad Din as confirmation that the early writers were at best confused about what happened at the time of the Mongol invasion.

Fomenko lays great importance upon the testimony of ibn-Hawqal who wrote that 'Rus consisted of three tribes, one is the closest to the kingdom of Bulgar. The tsar of this tribe lives in Kuiaba [an Arabic name for Kiev]...

---

[435] Gumilev, *Drevniaia Rus' i velikaia step'*, p. 376.
[436] I have used Rashid Ad Din, *Sbornik letopisei*, translated from Persian by Iurii P. Verkhovskii, (Moscow: Izdatel'stvo akademii nauk SSSR, 1960), p. 37.

the second tribe is located above the first and is called Slaviia...the third tribe is called Artaniia, and its tsar lives in Arta'.[437] For Fomenko, Arab writers understood, correctly, that ancient Russia was divided into three parts. One part of Russia was based around Kiev and a second was found farther north and known as *Slaviia* (Novogorod or Iaroslavl). The third tribe of Slavs lived in *Arta* (thus *Orda* or Horde in Russian), obviously (for Fomenko) a reference to a horde present on the Volga river hundreds of years before the Mongols.[438] For conventional scholars like Pritsak, there are far too many possible translations for the Arabic word Fomenko wants to translate as Arta to make any conclusion at all.[439] For Fomenko, this perceptive ancient source has made reference to the three constituent territorial pieces of ancient Russia whose modern footprints confront us to this day. Kuiaba, Slaviia and Artaniia became the White, Blue and Golden Horde of the medieval period, White Russia, Russia Minor and Great Russia of the Imperial period, and Belarus, Ukraine, and Russia of the twentieth and twenty first centuries.[440]

Alternative history is not opposed to fudging the truth. Fomenko extensively cites Herberstein, the Holy Roman Empire's ambassador to Russia in 1517 and 1526 who is generally regarded as an acute observer of Russian life and meticulous recorder of Russian words and pronunciations. Fomenko claims that Herberstein noted that Muscovites were very proud of Attila the Hun, boasting that he, a Russian Muscovite, devastated Europe. However,

---

437 Nosovskii and Fomenko, *Novaia khronologiia Rusi,* pp. 13–14.
438 Nosovskii and Fomenko, *Novaia khronologiia Rusi,* pp. 13–14. Conventional Russian historians disagree, arguing that this Arta is a reference to a southern Russian principality situated at the Azov Sea that was cut off from the rest of Russia by the nomadic raids—famous Tmutorakan' princedom. See Alexander Novosel'tsev, 'Vostochnye istochniki o vostochnykh slavianakh i Rusi VI-IX vekov,' *Drevnerusskoe Gosydarstvo i ego mezhdunarodnoe* znachenie (Moscow: Nauka, 1965), pp. 355–420, and Mishin, *Sakaliba (slaviane) v islamskom mire v rannee srednevekov'e* (Moscow: In-t Vostokovedeniia RAN, Kraft+, 2002).
439 Omeljan Pritsak, 'The Name of the Third Kind of Rus and their City', *Studies in medieval Eurasian history* XII (London: Variorum Reprints, 1981), pp. 2–9.
440 Pritsak, points out that there are many views on this issue. He examined the works of Ibn Hawqal and Al-Istakhri and notes that it is possible to find affinities with many semi-legendary places including Arkona, Biarma, and Varton. See Pritsak, 'The Name of the Third Kind of Rus and their City', 12, pp. 2–9; also see Alexander Novosel'tsev, 'Vostochnye istochniki o vostochnykh slavianakh i Rusi VI–IX vekov', *Drevnerusskoe Gosydarstvo i ego mezhdunarodnoe znachenie* (Moscow: Nauka, 1965), pp. 355–420.

in the Latin edition of Herberstein's work published in 1549 and cited by Fomenko, Attilla is referred to as a Hungarian chieftain, a detail that Fomenko preferred not to share with his Russian readers.[441]

Fomenko claims to have discovered sources uncontaminated by the lies of the chroniclers and Romanov historians. Fomenko's favourite source is Andrei Lyzlov's *Skifiiskaia Istoriia*.[442] Before his death in 1697, Lyzlov wrote accounts of Russia's war against the Mongols, translated Polish historical works and studied the Turkish court. For Lyzlov, the peoples of Eurasia—Slav and Turk alike—were descendants of the Scyths, the invincible warriors memorably described in Herodotus. Whatever its merits, Lyzlov's book was not reprinted for more than two hundred years in Russia after printings in 1776 and 1787. For Fomenko, Lyzlov's account was suppressed because it told the inconvenient truth about the origins of Russia. Lyzlov identified the Tatar-Mongols with the Scyths, who fought in Morgol fashion to overcome such famous Persian rulers as Cyrus and Darius. For Lyzlov, the Tatars lived on the territory of modern Russia but were divided into European and Asian Tatars.[443] For Fomenko, this is evidence that Russians and Turks were respectively European and Asian Tatars. Unlike the Arab writer cited above, Lyzlov seemed to consider that Russia was divided into two and not three parts. This is not a difficulty for Fomenko who claims that Russia was ethnically two halves (Slav and Turk) but geographically located in three different strongholds.

Thus the nomadic invaders of Russia, whom the West called the Mongols, came not from far-away Mongolia, but, like the Scyths, emerged from the northern Black Sea steppe and the Caucasus.[444] Lyzlov guessed about the origins of other peoples of the steppe in ways that appeal to Fomenko. The Pechenegs and Polovts according to Lyzlov were the descendants of the Goths, Lithuanians and old Prussians. That their language was a peculiar mixture of Russian and Polish, according to Lyzlov, is further evidence for Fomenko that the Pechenegs, Polovtsi and the Goths were all Slavs.[445]

---

441 See Anna Khoroshkevich, 'Novoe neizdannoe poslanie 'Sigizmuda Gerbershteina'', *Istoriia i antiistoriia: Kritika 'novooi khronologii' akademika Fomenko* (Moscow: Iazyky russkoi kultury, 2000), pp. 274–290.
442 Andrei Lyzlov, *Istoriia skifiiskaia* (Moscow: Nauka, 1990).
443 Lyzlov, *Istoriia skifiiskaia*, p. 9.
444 Lyzlov, *Istoriia skifiiskaia*, pp. 14, 18–19.
445 Lyzlov, *Istoriia skifiiskaia*, pp. 20, 21.

Fomenko finds further support for his theory in the relatively obscure account of the eighteenth-century religious cleric Koniskii.[446] Fomenko, who normally condenses history has in this case extended it in order to transform Koniskii into an important medieval source. The archbishop, commenting on the wars between the Slavs, Pechenegs, Polovtsi and Khazars, came to the conclusion that their wars were nothing but transient disputes between otherwise fraternal tribes. Koniskii wrote that the eastern Slavs were the Scyths. The southern ones were Sarmatians. Northern Slavs living along the Baltic were Varangians. In the middle between the three lived Roxolans, or Russes, named after the Biblical prince Rus, and Muscovites, who named themselves after their prince Meshekh who used to migrate along the Moscow River with his tribe, and thus gave the future Russian capital its current name. Ultimately, all Slavic warriors came to be called Khazars or Cossacks who were chosen from the general population for permanent war service. They supplied their own ammunition and armour, and migrated with entire families, if necessary. During times of war the civilian population was obliged to help these troops with the tax that was called with indignation 'the Khazar tax'. Koniskii was convinced that these warriors were renamed by the Byzanine Tsar Constantine Monomachus as Cossacks, and since then kept this name.[447]

This is a statement of a huge significance for Fomenko. First of all, Khazars are clearly not simply steppe people whose ruling class mysteriously adopted Judaism as conventional history alleged, but Cossacks. The alleged massacre of the Khazars by the Russians is an invention of the Romanovs whose aim was to separate Russia from its eastern steppe heritage.[448] Khazars, Pechenegs and Polovtsi were all ethnic Slavs in this account. Koniskii also described the ancient Russian state exactly as Fomenko does—the separation of the society into two distinct parts, one purely military, the Cossack Hordes, and the second purely civilian, which had to pay a tithe in order to guarantee its protection. The infamous Tatar yoke was in fact nothing more dramatic than the continuation of tithe payments to the Cossacks.

---

446 George Koniskii, *Istoriia Russov ili maloi Rusi* (Moscow: Universiteskaia tipografia, 1846).
447 Koniskii, *Istoriia Russov ili maloi Rusi*, p. 2.
448 Nosovskii and Fomenko, *Bibleiskaia Rus'* I, pp. 149–150.

Part Seven: How could the Mongols have succeeded when Napoleon and Hitler failed?

The opponents of the conventional story of the Tatar-Mongol invasion claim that nomads would have had great difficulty in establishing an empire of any sort. Alternative historians argue that sedentary peoples were more likely to accumulate sufficient wealth to wage prolonged wars of conquest than a nomadic people, whose scarce resources would limit military capacity, as much they would provide a motive for aggression.[449] For alternative historians, their conventional rivals do not have a clue about why barbarian invasions get under way in the first place. Khazanov has written the best-known recent account of nomads and their periodic irruptions into the histories of sedentary societies. His explanation entailed cycles of power and weakness that depended upon such factors as climate or the relative strength of sedentary neighbours. A number of writers cite changing weather patterns as important to the sudden irruptions of nomad societies. Toynbee emphasized desertification[450] while Gumilev argued that increased precipitation prompted nomadic restlessness.[451] Some historians suggest that the nomads were naturally aggressive and were perhaps motivated by periodic overpopulation. Marxists fought to find evidence of class struggle between nomadic and sedentary societies or an economic contest driven by nomads who attack sedentary populations in order to replenish their livestock. Nomads may have resented the rejection of their goods for trade or have been inspired by a charismatic leader.

Gumilev was sufficiently disappointed in existing explanations that he offered the suggestion that it was the *passionarnost* or vibrant exuberance of a new conquering people.[452] But this seems one of the weaker arguments put forward by Gumlev, not endorsed by either professional of amateur historians of Russia. For Fomenko, the fact that conventional historians drastically disagree about why nomadic invasions take place is not evidence of a healthy scholarly debate but the futility of present explanations.

---

449 See, for example, Poliakovskii, *Tatary-Mongoly, Evraziia, Mnogovariatnost'* (Moscow: 2002), p. 122.
450 Arnold Toynbee, *A Study of History* (Oxford: Oxford University Press, 1934; 1935; 1945), pp. 3, 393, 395, 399–402, 431.
451 Gumilev, *Drevniaia Rus' i velikaia step'*, pp. 514–15.
452 Gumilev, *Konets i vnov' nachalo* (Moscow: 1992).

The conventional account claims that in the short space of a few years Ghengiz Khan created the strongest army in the world out of dispersed nomadic clans. The distance from Mongolia to European Russia is approximately 5000 kilometres. If the distance covered by the Mongols in their European expedition is added, the Mongols travelled 6500 kilometres. They defeated and secured not just cities but entire civilisations along the way. Meanwhile, the Mongols tried to assail Japan twice and fought in Korea, Vietnam, Indonesia and Burma.

Impossible, claim alternative historians. Russian and American pioneers took approximately thirty to forty years in order to reach the eastern and western shores of the Pacific respectively. Russian and American forces enjoyed the backing of government finances and military institutions with sophisticated weapons in their possession. They fought against enemies that were technologically inferior and geographically dispersed. In both cases the expansion was accompanied by the gradual erection of forts and towns used as protection against the indigenous population.[453]

Russian explorers in their march eastwards, travelling across the Urals in the sixteenth century, found no staging posts of the once glorious Mongolian Empire. There were only technologically primitive tribes living in small numbers in the wilderness. The Mongols left behind no military, or civilian, infrastructure to remind future generations of their deeds. Not surprisingly, alternative writers ignore the reverse of this argument that if, as they claim, there were Russians who acted as powerful political and military figures at the court of the khans in Beijing, how did they cover these mighty distances and do so without leaving a trace of their presence? Nor does alternative history wish to take into account the fact that the Mongols, unlike colonial settlers, were often able to move along established trade routes on their way to Russia, replenishing their strength as they moved westwards.

The Tatar-Mongols displayed outstanding military capabilities fighting in unexpected conditions and ambushing, encircling and fully eradicating Russian military expeditions at Kalka in the summer of 1223 and returned, a decade later, to defeat Grand Prince Iurii of Vladimir on the river Sit'. The second battle took place on unknown land for the Mongols, in wintertime.[454] How did the nomadic Mongols live and travel, let alone fight, in the Russian winter? Although the first military encounter between the Russians and

---

453 Bushkov, *Rossiia I*, p. 170–73.
454 Bushkov, *Rossiia I*, p. 116.

Mongols occurred in summer, the subsequent invasions took place in winter. It is true that the Kazan Tatars were known to conduct their raids against Muscovy throughout all seasons, including winter. But Kazan is much closer to Moscow than Mongolia and its Turkic inhabitants were intimately familiar with the geography of what would later be known as European Russia.[455] The more distant Crimean Tatars preferred to attack Moscow in early spring, summer, or late autumn, but not winter.

Vernadsky explained the fact that 'general winter' did not work for the Russians because of the Mongols' toughness. They, like their Russian opponent, were used to extreme weather conditions in Mongolia, wore well-insulated fur coats and knew how to use the frozen rivers as roads.[456] Halperin points out that Kiev Rus' was too close to the steppe for its own good, so that even the most remote Russian cities were within easy striking distance of mobile punitive expeditions, while armies of horses could feed on the vast pastures in the land bridge between the Volga and Don, and on the Caspian steppe.[457]

Fomenko is unimpressed with this type of argument, claiming that even the sturdy and compact Mongolian horse, born in an area of continental climate similar to Russia, would not have been able to find sufficient sustenance in an unknown land covered with thick snow cover, deeper than that usually encountered in Mongolia. It seems likely that the invaders also had to supplement their cavalry with non-Mongolian horse breeds, which are likely to have been even more sensitive to subzero temperatures.[458]

Many historians, dealing with the reasons why Russia was defeated so easily and swiftly, claimed that the Russians were not inferior to the Mongols from a military point of view but were simply inferior in numbers. Contemporaries and early histories described a huge invasion force. It has been claimed that there may have been one million Mongols on the march, about as many as could have been found in Mongolia itself.[459] Chronicles esti-

---

[455] William Pokhlebkin, *Tatary i Rus', 360 let otnoshenii 1238–1598* (Moscow: Mezhdunarodnye otnosheniia, 2001), 179–180; Pokhlebkin notes that on the frequent occasions when the winters were harsh, entire military expeditions launched by the Kazan Tatars against Moscow froze to death.
[456] Vernadsky, *A History of Russia* III, p. 50.
[457] Halperin, *Russia and the Golden Horde*, p. 31.
[458] Vernadsky, *A History of Russia* III, 112; Bushkov, *Rossiia I*, p. 115.
[459] Ed. by Morgan and Amitai-Preiss, Udo Barkmann, 'Decline of the Mongol Empire', *The Mongol Empire and its Legacy*, p. 275.

mated that Mongol forces comprised 300–400 thousand horsemen for the invasion of Russia alone,[460] while Lyzlov estimated the force of Batu Khan as 600,000 strong.[461] According to Carpini, Batu's army consisted of six hundred thousand men, one hundred and fifty thousand of whom were Tatars, alongside four hundred and fifty thousand foreigners, Christians and infidels.[462] Rashid Ad Din thought that the Mongols had a surprisingly exact 129,000 troops at the time of Genghis Khan's death in 1227. Among nineteenth-century Western historians Rambaud, for example, repeats the legend that Batu Khan probably had with him five hundred thousand warriors.[463] Other sources tell us how in 1256, reinforcements increased the Mongol presence in the Middle East to 150,000 troops, accompanied by half a million women and children and fifteen million animals. Yet we are told that simultaneously an even larger Mongol contingent attacked southern China.[464]

Fennell endorses the figure arrived at by the Soviet historian Kargalov who estimated the invasion force at 120,000–140,000 troops when Batu Khan's scouts first approached Russia in 1237.[465] Soloviev too considered that when the Mongols struck in the thirteenth century, the Russian princes had a potential army of one hundred thousand fighters. Fennell has pointed out that this figure assumes that the fifteen or so large Russian cities provided between three thousand and five thousand soldiers. The Polovtsi, then in alliance with the Kievan princes, may have numbered around forty thousand soldiers.[466] This, however, was only a potential figure if all the princedoms united. This was not the case at any of the battles in which Russian princes fought the Mongols.

Alternative writers doubt that such extraordinary movements of people happened at all. In the case of Russia they like to point out that the invading Mongols travelled with three horses, thus hundreds of thousands of warriors

---

460 *Drevnerusskaia Literatura*, p. 170.
461 Lyzlov, *Skifiiskaia Istoriia*, p. 22.
462 In Carpini's testimony, he mentions that he had his letters of introduction translated into 'Ruthenian' or Russian as well as 'Saracen'. See Dawson, *Mission to Asia*, 56.
463 Rambaud, *History of Russia*, p. 156.
464 John Masson Smith Jr., 'Nomads on Ponies vs. Slavs on Horses', *The Journal of the American Oriental Society* 118:1 (January–March 1998): 54; 'Mongol Nomadism and Middle Eastern Geography', *The Mongol Empire and its Legacy*, ed. by Morgan and Amitai-Preiss, pp. 39–40.
465 Fennell, *The Crisis of Medieval Russia*, p. 84.
466 Fennell, *The Crisis of Medieval Russia*, p. 85.

required an implausibly large herd of horses. Eyewitnesses confirm that each Mongol brought three or four horses with him. The Western historian, Denis Sinor, used data collected from nineteenth century Chinese Turkestan to argue that 100,000 horses meant 1,500 camel loads of fodder per day, a figure Sinor regarded as staggeringly large.[467] The invasions of 1237–38 and 1239–1240 took place in winter, allowing the Mongols to use the rivers as roads but making it extremely difficult for them to secure food and pasture. According to Rubruck and Carpin, Mongols relied upon mare's milk and were understandably reluctant to slaughter the animals needed for war and transportation. The conditions were obviously difficult even for the best of soldiers. Moreover, a frequent complaint from the alternative writers is that Russia's hardy steppe mares do not give milk in winter. Morozov could not imagine how nomads could obtain sufficient mass to defeat much larger sedentary empires. The essence of a nomadic existence amounted to living in separate patriarchal groups scattered over a vast territory requiring plentiful food for herds of cows, sheep and horses. If the tribes united, they would have had to join their livestock together. The greatly increased number of cattle would force the entire nomadic population to relocate constantly in search of new pastures. A prolonged and successful conquest conducted by a combination of nomadic tribes feeding off their livestock was impossible, claimed Morozov.[468] For Morozov, it was clear that the Mongol invasion must have come from the West, that is, the Hungarian plain.

It is often thought that the Mongols sent raiding parties into the forests of Russia, using the steppe as a base. On the other hand, the Russian chronicles reported how at the siege of Kiev 'the grinding of the wooden chariots, the bellowing of the buffaloes, the cries of the camels, the neighing of the horses, the howling of the Tatars rendered it impossible to hear your own voice in the town'.[469] The depiction of this huge supply train creates an impression that apart from warriors, many civilian Mongols travelled with the army.

---

[467] See Greg S. Rogers, 'An examination of historians' explanations for the Mongol withdrawal from East Central Europe', *East European Quarterly* 30:1 (Spring 1996): 3.
[468] Bushkov, *Rossiia I*, p. 123.
[469] *Rasskazy Russkikh Letopisei XII–XIV vekov*, p. 84.

If the Mongols did take their families, as the above-mentioned passages might suggest, then how are we to accept the thesis that the Mongols' lightning speed was integral to their victory? Some sources suggest that because of the huge size of the migration, Mongol troops were capable of covering only three to four miles a day.[470] Thus, there is no, or little academic agreement in the field of Russian history on the numbers of the invading Mongol armies, on their policies of drafting alien nations in their military units, or on whether the Mongols travelled alone or together with their families, cattle and belongings.

The major striking forces in the Tatar army comprised mobile groups of cavalry archers. Each warrior carried two types of bow. The first was light and designed to be fired rapidly from horseback, while its heavier companion was for dismounted action. Vernadsky has claimed that the heavy bow's average draw weight of 166 pounds was more powerful than the British longbow.[471] Each rider used a sharpening stone for keeping the arrows in good shape. Gumilev described how the Mongols allegedly made use of poisoned arrows.[472] But how, Fomenko asks, and where could the Mongols have replenished their supplies of ammunition, especially arrows, under the stress of continuous warfare and severe cold in a hostile foreign country?

Part Eight: Benevolent Invaders

The initial picture that the chroniclers paint of Russia does seem to be of a land under foreign domination. They describe the subservience of Russian princes called to visit the Horde, raids and occupations, the increasingly large numbers of Tatars involved in military operations and Tatar involvement in inter-princely wars among the Russians.[473] At the same time, this was a very different invasion to the experience of the Napoleonic or Nazi invaders of later centuries. Modern readers often take the 'Tatar yoke' to imply a system of extortion carried out over nearly three hundred years by the Mongol overlords of Kievan Rus', a model that has parallels with the experience of the Nazis in World War Two.[474] Russian folklore suggests this

---

470 John Masson Smith Jr, 'Mongol Nomadism and Middle Eastern geography', *The Mongol Empire and its Legacy*, p. 40.
471 Vernadsky, *History of Russia* III, pp. 112, 125.
472 Gumilev, *Searches for an Imaginary Kingdom*, pp. 294–296.
473 Fennell, *The Crisis of Medieval Russia*, p. 140.
474 *Rasskazy Russkikh Letopisei XII–XIV vekov*, pp. 75–76, 78–79.

type of analogy when it proclaims: 'if there is no money, the Tatar will take your property, if there is no property, the Tatar will take your wife, if there is no wife, the Tatar will take you as a slave'.[475]

None of this makes sense, according to Fomenko. For example, the cooperation between the Russian Orthodox Church and supposedly brutal foreign invaders is difficult to explain if it really were a foreign conquest. Batu Khan issued an order according to which the plunder of Orthodox churches was to be punished by court martial, and the church itself was granted the right to prosecute Tatar soldiers and civilians for crimes against church property. The Churches and monasteries were declared exempt of any form of taxation in 1257.[476] In 1261, Khan Berke established an Episcopal See in Sarai.[477] The Church did not split into regional centres under the Mongol conquerors but remained united, powerful and wealthy.

On the surface at least, the Mongols appear to be among the most reasonable tax collectors in Russian history, taking as their booty a mere ten per cent of everything—crops, goods and people, just like the ethnic Russians princes did before them. While Soloviev compared the Mongols to petty bandits, more recent historians describe the Golden Horde as embracing the sophisticated bureaucratic practices of sedentary populations. Halperin described the Mongol taxation system as complex suggesting that the Mongols must have made excellent use of captive sedentary peoples to act as bureaucrats.[478] Halperin has found it strange that the devastated and allegedly subsistence-level Russian villages paid tribute to the Mongols in silver, and concludes that if Russia were able to sustain such taxation then the resilience of the medieval Russian economy has been so far underestimated.[479] It is certainly likely that the degree of plundering of Kiev Rus has been exaggerated by church accounts with a vested interest in demonising the Mongols.[480]

---

[475] Bushkov, *Rossiia I*, p. 200.
[476] Halperin, *Russia and the Golden Horde*, p. 9; Rambaud, *The History of Russia*, pp. 172–173.
[477] Ostrowski, *Muscovy and the Mongols*, p. 18.
[478] Halperin, *Russia and the Golden Horde*, pp. 26–27.
[479] Halperin, *Russia and the Golden Horde*, p. 84.
[480] Ostrowski, *Muscovy and the Mongols*, p. 123.

Besieging Riazan' in 1238 the Mongols asked only for a tithe and the city would be spared.[481] As Halperin has put it, the tithe was 'improbable'.[482] Why would ruthless invaders make this very reasonable offer to defenceless foreigners who were now at their mercy? To Fomenko, it seems too great a coincidence that ten per cent was the size of the tax levied on the subjugated peoples first by the Khazar Kagan, then by the princes of Kiev, and later by the Grand Prince of Vladimir. Thus, for Fomenko, the tithe of the Khans was simply the existing method of taxation well known to the citizens of Kiev Rus.

Fomenko finds the establishment of the tribute system in Russia difficult to reconcile with a genuine invasion. There is no evidence that Tatar tax collectors appeared in Russia before 1257. Why did the Tatar/Mongols wait more than a decade in order to impose taxation, failing to act when the population was first brought to heel? A break from taxation should have provided the Russians with a splendid opportunity to recuperate and to raise armies against the Mongols. Conventional historians suggest that there was no need as Russia had been terrorized into submission and a census would take time to organize. Fomenko noted that during Novgorod's rebellion against the tax collectors in 1262, the Russian princes openly expressed their approval. A wave of repression might have been anticipated but none occurred. The rebellious provinces even declared the abolition of conscription for the Tatar army. The Tatars did not retaliate. In the case of Novgorod, Prince Alexander Nevsky (1220–63) did not take stern action against his subjects when they rejected Tatar tax collectors. Vernadsky explains the benevolence of the khans toward the Russians by reference to the direct involvement of the Russian princes who begged the Khan not to punish the population.[483] For Fomenko, begging is not something that comes easily to Russian princes. It is more likely, he claims that this was routine politics. Russians taxed fellow Russians and only occasionally employed Tatars as hired thugs much as their predecessors hired Vikings for raiding parties. These were punitive and tax-collecting operations carried

---

481 'Povest' o razorenii Riazani Batyem,' *Drevnerusskaia literatura* (Moscow: Prosveshchenie, 1973), p. 153; Vernadsky, *A History of Russia* III, p. 216; Hosking, *Russia and the Russians*, p. 52.
482 Halperin, *Tatar Yoke*, p. 38.
483 Vernadsky, *History of Russia* 3, p. 161.

out periodically by warrior bands against co-ethnics, not a sudden and spectacular invasion by unknown hordes from the Far East.

Such a benign and reasonable attitude suggests that this was not an issue of invasion and resistance but more likely the bungled introduction of a new tax, different to custom, and it was this, not its foreign origins, that provoked the citizens of Novgorod to rebellion. Thus, the pragmatic Alexander Nevsky and his Tatar entourage backed down and chose not to punish the citizens too severely.[484] Fomenko is also attracted to the identity of Mongol tax collectors. In the Iaroslavl' region in 1261, the Mongol tax collector was a Russian Orthodox monk named Izosim, and, in the city of Ustuyg, a Russian Christian named Ioann.[485] These Russian tax collectors were clearly unpopular among some of their countrymen, and identified as 'vicious Muslims'.[486] One chronicler recalls with obvious relish how 'Izosim was killed in Iaroslavl, his body was eaten by the crows while his legs, (that) were so quick to do evil, were dragged by dogs through the streets to the amazement of the citizenry'.[487] Vernadsky suggests that the hostility of the local population was caused by the conversion of the monk to Islam.[488] But for Fomenko, it is simpler to envisage a war of Russian and Turk against Russian and Turk, with Orthodox and Muslim to be found on both sides. There were Christian Turks and Islamic Russians in an era when religious differences were less important than they were in the era of religious wars that was to follow. The more advanced Russians of course dominated these partnerships with the Turks but it was a partnership of peoples already living on Russian land and not a war against foreign invaders.

Could the Mongols really have been that exploitative, asks Fomenko? Where are the gold, silver, diamonds and priceless artifacts that the invaders supposedly extracted from the conquered Russian territories? If the Mongols did extract massive treasures from the enslaved lands, why are these treasures yet to be found in Mongolia? Somewhere in the mysterious Mongolian capital, Karakorum, mountains of gold and silver are waiting to be found. So far the location of the Mongol capital remains a matter of dis-

---

484 Bushkov, *Rossiia*, pp. 204–207.
485 Vernadsky, *A History of Russia* III, pp. 158–60.
486 Vernadsky, *A History of Russia* III, p. 159.
487 *Rasskazy Russkikh Letopisei XII–XVI vekov*, p. 98.
488 Vernadsky, *History of Russia* 3, p. 159.

pute while the treasures are unaccounted for.[489] This is because, in Fomenko's opinion, the magnificent Mongol capital and its treasures were just another Western fantasm.

According to Vernadsky, the tribute paid by eastern Russia to the Mongols only in 1384, without Novgorod, amounted to 145,000 silver rubles.[490] This tribute, conventional and pseudo historians agree, certainly found its way to the Volga, where archaeological digs have yielded evidence of substantial cities. Lyzlov, writing in the seventeenth century, has described the splendid homes, towns and structures erected by Russian builders and masters along the Volga and Ural rivers where the regional centres of the Golden Horde were situated. It was because of the riches of the Volga region that, according to Lyzlov, the Russians gave this area its golden name.[491]

In modern-day European Russia, many objects of eastern origin, presumably created in or acquired by the Golden Horde, have been uncovered.[492] Alternative historians argue that this is proof that the so-called Mongol invasion began from the shores of the Volga, not farther east, and that the alleged treasures of the khans in fact circulated mainly within the present-day bounds of European Russia. The Mongols certainly seem to treat the Volga as home from a very early date. Following the invasion of Europe in 1241–42, Batu Khan was expected to return to Karakorum to settle a succession crisis but he did not do so. According to Sinor, the Mongol troops who had ridden as far west as Hungary now happily made a new home in the Russian steppes.[493] Conventional accounts suggest that no tribute was paid to the Great Khan in Karakorum after the 1260s.

The Russian prince who dealt with Mongol invasion best was Alexander Nevsky, a controversial figure in Russian historiography.[494] For many Russian patriots, Alexander Nevsky seems an ambiguous figure, a patriot who saved Novgorod from German invaders, but at the same time did more than anyone else to ensure Russian servitude to the Tatar yoke. For Eurasianists, Alexander Nevsky is the embodiment of Russian virtues, an enemy

---

489 Nosovskii and Fomenko, *Bibleiskaia Rus'* II, p. 289.
490 Vernadsky, *History of Russia* III, p. 231.
491 Lyzlov, *Istoriia skifiiskaia*, p. 29.
492 Poluboiarinova, 'Russkie v Zolotoi Orde', *Rodina* 3–4 (1997): pp. 56–57.
493 Denis Sinor, 'Horse and Pasture in inner Asian history', *Oriens Extremis* 19 (1972): p. 181.
494 See Fennell, *The Crisis of Medieval Russia*, pp. 120–21.

of the west and friend of the east, a warrior elected by the people and a successful unifier of Russian territory.

Later acclaimed a saint of the Orthodox Church, Alexander Nevsky was the son of the Grand Prince of Vladimir, the most powerful individual in Russia at this time, and was elected prince of Novgorod, the Russian principality where the democratic traditions of the *veche* or popular assembly were strongest, in 1236. In 1240 Alexander Nevsky won a victory over the Swedes on the Neva River and in 1242 he defeated the Teutonic Knights at Lake Peipus. At the same time, Alexander Nevsky actively collaborated with the Mongols, who made him Grand Prince.

Alexander Nevsky was, according to Gumilev, the adopted son of Batu Khan.[495] This is a surprising relationship between conquerors and the defeated peoples, in the opinion of Fomenko. Alexander Nevsky not only ensured that Suzdalia became an obedient subject of the Tatars and put up with repeated raids and incursions, but visited the Great Khan in Karakorum and clearly profited from his cooperation with the Mongols even when his own family made efforts to defy the invaders.[496] Fomenko and his allies speculate that Alexander Nevsky was in fact a so-called Mongol khan. Rather than Batu Khan's adopted son, it was more likely that Alexander Nevsky was Batu Khan himself.

Alexander Nevsky was not alone in adapting quickly to the new reality of the Mongol invasion. In 1249, the soldiers of Daniil of Galich astounded the Poles and Hungarians with their oriental style of dress and equipment–short stirrups, very high saddles, long caftans, turbans surmounted by an *aigret*, sabres and poniards in the belt.[497] Daniil's adoption of Mongol customs came barely a dozen years after the initial Mongolian onslaught. Conventional historians argue that it would have been surprising if Kiev Rus' did not borrow from the superior strategies, tactics, and weaponry of the Mongols.[498] Fomenko insists that Daniil of Galich was not adopting, spontaneously and remarkably adroitly, the tactics of his enemy but expressing the military customs long typical of the Russian Horde.

---

495 Gumilev, *Drevniaia Rus' i velikaia step'*, p. 534.
496 Fennell, *The Crisis of Medieval Russia*, p. 141.
497 Rambaud, *History of Russia*, pp. 169–170.
498 Ostrowski, *Muscovy and the Mongols*, p. 7.

Part Nine: Russian Eurasia?

There is much continuity between Kiev Rus and the Mongol era. The Mongols prided themselves on their military organization. There were units of one thousand that broke down into hundreds and then to tens. All of this was surprisingly familiar to pre-Mongol Kiev Rus, claims Fomenko. It is well known that the basic unit of the *opolchenie* or city militia of Kiev Rus was the hundred or *sotnia*, and in the cities, there were thousands commanded by a *tysiatskii*, often an elected warlord.[499] The sotnia was also the basic tactical unit of Cossack cavalry.

European travellers thought that Muscovite soldiers fought in the style of Ottoman Turks. Halperin writes that pictures show them in a Mongol saddle with Mongols stirrups, helmet and compound bow and quiver.[500] At the same time, the khan was often depicted in medieval pictures in the robes of a Byzantine emperor. Genghis khan was known in Russia as Genghis Tsar.[501] The Russians still enjoyed great power as elite soldiers in the so-called Mongol army.[502] Russians often took command and led Tatar troops into battle. Thus we have descriptions of punitive expeditions led by *voevoda* Fedorchuk.[503] Fedorchuk is clearly a Slavic name and *voevoda* (rather than *murza*) a Russian term that the chronicler has found appropriate. Alexander Nevsky's son, Andrei Gorodetskii, and Ivan Kalita, are other examples of Russians at the head of Tatar/Mongol troops. Various sources show a significant degree of participation of Russian troops in the feudal squabbles among Tatar nobility, while the same degree of participation of Tatar troops on behalf of Russian princes fighting each other is just as evident.[504]

World history, Fomenko claims, offers few examples where the representatives of the defeated side, supposedly totally different in language, appearance, culture and religion from the victors, have found themselves in charge of running the victorious invading army in a short space of time after the initial bloody encounter. Moreover, the victors, Tatar nobles who became subordinate to the defeated opponents, seemed surprisingly content with

---

499 Hosking, *Russia and the Russians*, p. 36.
500 Halperin, *Russia and the Golden Horde*, p. 91.
501 Halperin, *Russia and the Golden Horde*, p. 98.
502 Vernadsky, *A History of Russia* III, vi, pp. 88–89.
503 Halperin, *The Tatar Yoke*, p. 86; Guts, *Mnogovariantnaia istoriia Rossii*, p. 242.
504 Nikolai Polevoi, *Istoriia Russkogo naroda* II (Moscow: Veche, 2006), p. 293; Bushkov, *Rossiia I*, p. 142; Guts, *Mnogovariantnaia istoriia Rossii*, pp. 174, 180.

that position. Just like the Varangians in service to the princes of Kiev Russ, is it not likely that these Tatars were a part of the Muscovite army.

Proud of the multi-racial composition of Russia, Russian patriots emphasise that racism is foreign to the Russian character. Nonetheless, race figures prominently in the discourse of alternative writers. The lineage of Genghis Khan is not surprisingly a murky matter even for conventional historians. We have no precise date for the birth of Temuchin, who later became Genghis Khan. The Mongols lived among other tribes including Tartars, Keraits, Naiman and Uighurs and incorporated into their armies the peoples that they conquered. Fomenko draws upon Gumilev to argue that Genghis Khan did not in appearance resemble modern Mongols. Genghis Khan, suggested Gumilev, was most likely a tall, blue-eyed individual with a long white beard given that ancient Mongols, judging by the statements of the chroniclers, and the image depicted in frescoes found in Manchuria. Gumilev explains the appearance of modern Mongols as the result of mixed marriage with a variety of neighbouring indigenous peoples.[505]

There were contemporaries who saw stereotypic Asiatic features in the Mongols. According to the striking description of the Persian Amir Khuzru:

> Their eyes so narrow and piecing that they might have bored a hole in a brazen vessel. Their stench was more horrible than their color. Their heads were set on their bodies as if they had no necks, and their cheeks resembled leather bottles, full of wrinkles and knots. Their noses extended from cheekbone to cheekbone. Their nostrils are rotting graves, and from them the hair descended as far as the lips. Their chests were covered with lice, which looked like sesame growing in bad soil.[506]

Fomenko argues that the only ethnic group of European Russia that might meet this type of description was the Kalmyk host that reached the Volga-Don steppe only after the Mongol period. Otherwise, in Fomenko's view, European Russia is remarkably free of Asiatic physical features.

This last claim seems absurd. On the other hand, conventional historians do not doubt that at least part of the Golden Horde's population was ethnically Russian.[507] The tax collectors, who worked as *baskaki* for the Mongols,

---

505 Gumilev, *Drevniaia Rus' i velikaia step'*, pp. 389, 395
506 Francis Carr, *Ivan the Terrible* (Totowa, New Jersey: Barnes and Nobles Books, 1981), p. 32.
507 Poluboiarinova, 'Russkie v Zolotoi Orde', p. 53.

boasted names with Slavic, Armenian and Turkic origins.[508] Mongol aristocrats made use of the imperial post or *yam* to as *posoly* or envoys but the chronicles make no mention of their need for interpreters.[509]

Vernadsky noted that there was a wide variety of tribes and clans involved in the Mongol conquests and suggests an admixture of Alanic, that is, Ossetian, blood in the clan of Genghis Khan.[510] Alternative writers look hard for evidence of Mongols who had blue eyes on the grounds that they were obviously related to their nearest blue-eyed neighbours, the Russians. Fennell records how the Mongols tricked the Polovtsi into abandoning their Ossetian allies with the claim that Mongols and Polovtsi were of the same blood.[511] For Fomenko, this was no trick and the Polovtsi did indeed recognize their kin.

Fomenko notes that the Arab historian Abdu-l-Fida in his 'Geography of the Lands' claimed that the Russians were of Turkic blood, and lived next to the Oghuz (*Torki* of the Russian chronicles).[512] Polish and Belarus historians including Martin Stryikovskii and George Koniskii, the archbishop of Byelorussia, considered the semi-nomadic tribes of Polovtsi-Qipchaq and Pechenegs as ethnic Slavs, related to Muscovite Russians, an opinion that was shared by Lyzlov.[513]

Vernadsky has pointed out that most of the Mongols of the Golden Horde were descendants of the four thousand troops assigned to Juchi by Chingiz-khan,[514] a number too small to produce a visible and lasting effect on the European population of Russia. The Mongols migrated primarily toward southern China, southern Central Asia and Middle East, while few Mongol warriors stayed with the ulus on the mid Volga river. The local Turkic population rapidly assimilated this relatively small reservoir of Mongol warriors.[515]

Following Gumilev, Fomenko maintains that a mixed Turkic and Slavonic speaking semi-sedentary host populated medieval Russia. It echoes obser-

---

508 Halperin, *Russia and the Golden Horde*, p. 37.
509 Halperin, *Russia and the Golden Horde*, p. 40.
510 Vernadsky, *History of Russia* III, p. 17.
511 Fennell, *The Crisis of Medieval Russia*, p. 63.
512 Nosovskii and Fomenko, *Novaia khronologiia Rusi*, p. 15.
513 See Lyzlov, Skifiiskaia *istoriia*, pp. 10–13; George Konisskii, *Istoriia rusov, ili Maloi Rossii* (Moscow: Universitetskaia tipographia, 1846).
514 Vernadsky, History *of Russia* III, pp. 208–209.
515 Vernadsky, History *of Russia* III, pp. 208–209.

vations made by Western historians, who accept the hypothesis of an ethnically mixed Russia, created under successive waves of nomadic invaders. The only difference is that the Russian element, for Fomenko, was predominant.

According to Halperin, 'it is one of the ironies of the Mongol period that Russian culture flourished under infidel domination'.[516] The relationship between Russians and the steppe was certainly diverse and pragmatic. Culturally Muscovite rulers had always resembled Eastern, rather than Western rulers until the time of Peter the Great. The eastern aspect in Russian culture and polity was very strong partly due to the proximity of the Byzantine Empire. Although geographically Constantinople lay further west than Moscow, or Kiev, nevertheless it was firmly considered as the East by Western historians who drew lines of division along religious, rather than geographical boundaries.

Western travelers who visited Muscovite Russia pointed to the Asiatic luxuries, wealth, military organization that surrounded the Muscovite ruler and the upper class.[517] Russia had always traded in eastern goods. Halperin explains the eastern customs of the Russian princes partly in terms of their background, since by the late twelfth century some Russian princes were seven-eighths Turkic by blood and could hardly have been unaware of their heritage.[518]

This steppe influence was evident long before the Mongols. Archaeological digs have revealed a society that accumulated eastern style glass beads, shells and boxwood combs.[519] Historians have emphasized the 'Asiatic cast' of Kievan politics, arguing that competing princes employed rival contingents of Turkic nomads, where steppe ornaments, dress, and modes of fashion prevailed.[520] In general, Muscovy was described as 'a rude and

---

[516] Halperin, *Tatar Yoke*, p. 25.
[517] Marshall Poe, *A People Born to Slavery, Russia in early modern European ethnography, 1476–1748* (Cornell University Press, 2000); Basil Dmytryshin, *Medieval Russia, a source book 900–1700* (Holt, Rinehart and Winston, 1973); *Moskovskoe Gosudarstvo XV–XVII vekov po skazaniiam sovremennikov-inostrantsev* (Moscow: Kraft +, 2000).
[518] Halperin, *Russia and the Golden Horde*, p. 18.
[519] Halperin, *Russia and the Golden Horde*, p. 81.
[520] D. Rasovskii, 'O roli Chernykh Klobukov v istorii drevnei Rusi', *Seminarum Kondakovianum* I (1927): pp. 93–109; also D. Rasovskii, Polovtsy', *Seminarium Kondakovianum* 7:11 (Prague: 1935–40); K. Kudriashov, *Polovetskaia step'* (Moscow 1948).

barbarous' kingdom by the European visitors of the sixteenth and seventeenth centuries, and it was omitted from the published register of Christian powers maintained by the Vatican.[521] European dress and behavior codes were rejected and despised.

In the case of the Normanist debate, anti-Normanists argued that if the Vikings left virtually no traces in terms of language or political institutions, then it stands to reason that Vikings were not important to the history of Kiev Rus. In the case of the Mongols, there is ample evidence of a substantial 'eastern' legacy. The alternative writers find no difficulty here because what Western Europeans called an Asiatic mode of dress or Eastern despotism was simply Russia in its pure form. Nomads like the Tatars cross-fertilized Russia and its customs but emerged far more changed than the Russians themselves. Underlying the flexibility of the alternative logic is that Russia is a vast sponge soaking up peoples, ideas and institutions but somehow clinging to a core identity. This identity is expressed in its greatness and the respect that other peoples felt obliged to show Russia. Therefore, alternative writers are happy to admit the connectedness of the peoples of Eurasia and then advance arguments as to why it was clearly the Russians who were first among equals.

Halperin acknowledges that looking at names is suggestive but that we cannot infer ethnicity from names with any assurance.[522] Concerning the Tatar-Mongol issue, proper names of peoples and persons are often a matter of dispute. The names of Polovtsi listed by the Kievan Prince Monomakh contain what are for, the modern Russian ear, apparently Russian and Turkic names.[523] According to Keenan, out of almost three thousand names in the Muscovite court rolls of the sixteenth century there are no persons with Kievan names such as Igor, Sviatoslav, or Mstislav and relatively few Vladimirs and Glebs; a Muscovite courtier of Ivan's time was more likely to be called Bulgak, or Temir.[524] Ostrowski, on the other hand, warns against the narrow use of the names of sixteenth century courtiers as reflecting a break with Kiev and its past.[525]

---

[521] Hosking, *Russia and the Russians*, p. 5.
[522] Halperin, *Russia and the Golden Horde*, p. 37.
[523] Halperin, *Russia and the Golden Horde*, p. 16.
[524] Edward Keenan, 'On Certain Mythical Beliefs and Russian Behaviors', in *The Legacy of History in Russia and the New States of Eurasia*, ed. S. Frederick Starr (New York: Armonk, M.E. Sharpe, 1994): p. 23.
[525] Ostrowski, *Muscovy and the Mongols*, p. 170.

Nicknames were given to children but the same could apply to adults as well.[526] In the *Razriadnaia Kniga* where the names of all Muscovite military commanders were stored for 150 years, the Russian voevoda Pronski is also identified under a Turkic name as 'Turuntai'. The celebrated Tamerlane was also known as Timur, Temir-Aksak, Temir-Kutlu, and Timurleng. The Russian military commander of the pre-Petrine era, Nogavitsa-Pestry, was known as Zasekin-Sosun, Solntsev, and Cherny-Sovka. The Turkic armies knew the Russian field marshal Suvorov as Topal-pasha.[527]

Fomenko cites the work of Karnovich, where the author argued that Tatar-sounding nicknames such as Bulat, Akhmat, Murat were used by ethnic Russians so often that they eventually acquired the status of proper names.[528] Morozov claimed that in the medieval archival Russian law acts there were not a single Greek name and only one Slavonic name (Iaroslav). Among the remaining names, 'Tatar' etymology predominates in names such as Tatarinko, Saltyr', Saltanko, Sunbul, Shaban, Tenbiak, Tursulok, Sumgur.[529]

Fomenko's favourite example is the story of the Tatar noble Solokhmir Miroslavov, who was invited to Riazan in 1371 by its prince, Oleg. Solokhmir adopted Christianity, became Ivan Miroslavovich, married the daughter of the Grand Prince and thus seeded the famous boyar clan of Verderevskikh in Russia. His son was named Grigorii, his grandsons Mikhail, nicknamed Abumailo, Ivan nicknamed Kanchei, and Konstantin nicknamed Divnoi. As Fomenko describes it, this was a typical of medieval Russia. Thus, a pagan Tatar bearing a Slavic name Solokhmir was baptized with Christian names. His children and grandchildren bore Christian names, but Tatar-sounding nicknames.[530]

Bogdan Khitrovo, an arms master under Tsar Alexis had the Christian name Iov that became known only after his death. The medieval Russian law acts contain personal names that seem to be numbers or animals such as Pervyi, Vtoroi, Volk, and Zaiats; or, they bear Tatar etymology–such as Mansur, Bulat, Uriupa, Urzan, Suleisha, Temir, Murza, Ermak, Kudiar,

---

526 Halperin, *Russia and the Golden Horde*, p. 111.
527 Bushkov, *Rossiia I*, pp. 105–107.
528 Nosovskii and Fomenko, *Novaia khronologiia Rusi*, p. 78.
529 Nosovskii and Fomenko, *Novaia khronologiia Rusi*, p 78.
530 Nosovskii and Fomenko, *Novaia khronologiia Rusi*, p 80.

Khazarin, Bakhmet, Tork, and Mamai.[531] It is often noted that there were well-connected Mongol families in Russian history, including at least one hundred and thirty Mongol families that became Christian and served the Russian state.[532] Among them were the Turgenevs, Glinskiis, Naryshkins and Yusupovs, and even the kingmaker and tsar, Boris Godunov.[533] Fomenko is happy to describe Godunov as a Tatar, a Tsar/Khan descended from Juchi's ulus.[534] Natalia Naryshkin, Peter the Great's mother, is described as descended from Mongols. Yet contemporary drawings suggest the face of a Slavic woman.[535] Fomenko argues that the misunderstanding originated due to the fact that ethnic Russians were very often described as Tatars in Western Europe.[536] Some Europeans made a distinction between the 'white' or European Tatars and 'yellow' or Asiatic Tatars,[537] a point that according to Fomenko reinforces his reconstruction about a Slavic/Turkic union where the two halves were sometimes recognisable and sometimes obscured.

Part Ten: Russia's Medieval Civil War

The Russian chronicles described medieval Russia as an era of war and violence. Sometimes the violence was inflicted upon Russia by waves of barbarian nomads but just as often seemed to revolve around internal feuds and civil wars. Gumilev noted that relations between the forest farmers and the steppe nomads appear peaceful compared to the brutal civil wars that the Russian princes constantly waged with one another. From the fall of the Khazar Kaganate in 965 to the founding of the Golden Horde in 1241, there was no unity among the people of the steppe, and therefore no danger to the Russian land from the east.[538] Kiev Rus was however a place of great internal strife. For Fomenko, this tradition of civil war continued into the period known erroneously to history as the Mongol era.

---

531 Nosovskii and Fomenko, *Novaia khronologiia Rusi*, p. 16.
532 Carr, *Ivan the Terrible*, p. 38.
533 Carr, *Ivan the Terrible*, p. 38.
534 Nosovskii and Fomenko, *Bibleiskaia rus'* 1, pp. 1232–23.
535 Robert Massie, *Peter the Great* (London: Victor Gollancz, Ltd, 1981), p. 211.
536 Nosovskii and Fomenko, *Novaia khronologiia Rusi*, pp. 12–16.
537 Poluboiarinova, 'Russkie v zolotoi orde', p. 55.
538 Gumilev, *Searches for an Imaginary Kingdom*, p. 292.

As conventional history describes the medieval period, there was constant war and successive waves of barbarian invasions. The chronicles claimed that the Rus destroyed the Khazar kingdom in consecutive blows that began with Sviatoslav's raid on Itel in 965. Meanwhile, the Polovtsi, who were also known as Kipchak in Turkic and Cuman in Latin, swept the Pechenegs from the steppe. The same fate awaited the Kipchak when the Mongols arrived. The image of waves of invaders—Pechenegs overrun by Polovtsi who are then overrun by Mongols strikes the alternative writers as a key fantasy of conventional history. Pritsak for example has estimated the Pecheneg population at 800,000 in 1048 yet the conventional literature gives the reader the impression that they were washed away or exterminated by a wave of Kipchak/Polovtsi who in turn fell victim to the Mongols.[539]

Gumilev argued that the Pechenegs and Polovtsi resembled each other so closely that they were in fact part of a single entity that together made up the semi-nomadic populations of the Caucasian, Caspian and Black Sea territories. According to Kluichevski, the Pechenegi lived along the lower Dnieper in eight clans, each of which was further divided into five tribes. Such a substantial host could not have vanished overnight giving way to newcomers, the Polovtsi. These peoples were not purely nomadic or insignificant in number. The Polovtsi were a settled agricultural people; the Primary Chronicle provides details about the villages and towns of Polovtsi that were burned by the Tatars.[540] For some Soviet writers, Polovtsi were in a sense the 'Russian' steppe peoples while the Mongols, more Asian in appearance, were clearly foreign invaders. Because of their continuous presence and familiarity with the geography, language and culture of the Rus, the Polovtsi became in effect a part of the social fabric of Kiev Rus'.[541] For Fomenko, this seems to have been true of all the steppe peoples.

In any case, having described the demise of the Pechengs, the chronicles continued to invoke their name hundreds of years after they should have left the historical stage. The Pechenegs made their final appearance in the Battle of Kulikovo Field in 1380, when the Tatar champion, reportedly a Pecheneg, challenged the army of Moscow to single combat. The chronicler, describing the aftermath of this duel when both combatants suffered mortal

---

539 Pritsak, 'The Pechenegs: A case of Social and Economic Transformation', *Studies in Medieval Eurasian history* 10 (Variorum reprints, 1981), p. 25.
540 Ostrowski, *Muscovy and the Mongols*, pp. 63, 91.
541 Halperin, *Russia and the Golden Horde*, p. 16.

wounds, referred to the 'infidel Pecheneg, the evil Tatar, lying like a mountain' on the battlefield.[542] For alternative historians, this is clear evidence that if the Pechenegs were an ethnic group, then Tatar refers to something else, such as the cavalryman status of this Pecheneg soldier.[543] For Fomenko the battle of Kulikovo Field was part of the horde's civil war and took place in Moscow and not on the lower Don as conventional accounts suggest. This seems unlikely although it must be admitted that serious historians share Fomenko's doubts about the location of the battle; one recent account suggests that the battle took place on the upper Don and not at Kulikovo on the lower Don.[544]

Many Soviet writers were happy to accept that trade and not war was the dominant mode of intercourse in relations between Russians and Polovtsi.[545] Recent accounts published in the West tend to agree, arguing that trade was the dominant form of interaction on the steppe frontier, that there were special trading posts and markets along the border with the steppe where Russian merchants exchanged goods with their nomadic counterparts.[546] There is evidence too of familiarity between nomads and Kievan Rus. The Primary Chronicle records under the year 968 the story of a Kievan escapee who deceived his Pecheneg captors by waving a bridle as he ran through the camp, calling for his missing horse. Halperin points out that the story shows that readers of the Primary Chronicle were evidently unsurprised to learn that a Kievan knew the Pecheneg language and that his appearance was not especially strange to the enemy.[547] Other stories in the Primary Chronicle seem to confirm that Russians, Pechenegi, Polovtsi, and Tatars did not need interpreters to communicate with one another.[548]

---

542 See *Kulikovskaia bitva v literature i iskusstve* (Moscow: Nauka, 1980), pp. 46–48.
543 Guts, *Mnogovariantnaia istoriia Rossii*, p. 203.
544 Iu. Zviagin, *Zagadki polia kulikova* (Moscow: Veche, 2010)
545 See, for example, Alexander Iakubovskii, 'Feodal'noe obshchestvo Srednei Azii i ee torgovlia s vostochnoi evropoi v X–XV', in *Materialy po istorii Uzbekskoi, Tadzhikskoi i Turkmenskoi SSR*, III and I (Leningrad: 1932), p. 24; Vasilii Parkhomenko, 'Sledy polovetskogo etnosa v letopisiakh', *Problemy istochnikovedeniia* III (Moscow-Leningrad: 1940): p. 39. For further evidence of this view, see Irina Konovalova, 'Stepnoi biznes', *Rodina* 3:4 (1997): pp. 36–37.
546 T. Noonan, 'Rus', 'Pechenegs and Polovtsi: Economic Interaction along the Steppe Frontier in the pre-Mongol Era', *Russian History* 19 (1992, 1–4): pp. 313–314.
547 Halperin, *Russia and the Golden Horde*, p. 13.
548 Ellen Hurwitz, *Prince Andrey Bogoliubsky: the man and the myth* (Firenze: Licosa editrice, 1980), p. 44.

Several Russian princes were executed at Sarai but often it was Russians and not Mongols who carried out these murderous deeds. Thus, we are told that Prince Mikhail of Chernigov was tried in Sarai, and then was stabbed to death by ex-Christians.[549]

For the alternative writers, the Mongol domination of a mixed host in Asia was no more than a reflection of Russia as it was at the time of Kiev Rus' with the Slavs interacting freely with neighbouring khanates. This was a military society where membership depended not upon blood or citizenship but loyalty to the horde, host or state. Its modern remnant is the Cossack model of a warrior society geared permanently to war and accepting warriors from any region or ethnicity so long as they were prepared to serve the ataman, the elected chief of the host.

Fomenko transformed Gumilev's concept of two halves of the one whole, a settled agricultural Russia living alongside a semi-nomadic deeply multiethnic steppe stretching from the Volga across the Don to the Dnieper, into a single Slav-Turk ethnos. This invasion was the process of internal unification as Slav-Turkic Russia transformed itself during the period between the disintegration of the Kievan state and the rise of Moscow.

As for the present state of play in this debate within Russia, it would seem that the Mongol invasion is a thing of the past. Putin himself has turned out to be something of a self-taught expert on this aspect of Russian history. Commenting on Russian television on Dmitrii Donskoi's victory over the Mongols in the Kulikovo battle of 1380, Putin noted that the Russians won because of their superior cavalry tactics. Putin surprised some viewers when he noted that these 'Russian' cavalrymen were baptized Tatars. Putin suggested that:

> We need to look at reality of those days in such a way that will help us in our development today and tomorrow. What is interesting and curious about this battle is that there were Russian regiments on both sides, and the Tatar cavalry was on both sides of the engagement. The Russians used this Tatar Cavalry as their main striking force. This battle is a curious page in our history that we can look upon today without any ideological prejudices.[550]

In the new Russian history that Putin is advocating, it sems that the Mongol-Tatar yoke will disappear altogether. New generations of Russian school

---

549 *Rasskazy Russkikh Letopisei XII–XIV vekov*, pp. 85–89.
550 http://www.youtube.com/watch?v=rwfALHO3rW8&list=PL-I_by33m-TRYdGOMjJTvc1osHQkg7rHw

children will learn about the complex interactions of the Russian horde. This is not exactly Fomenko's version of events, but it is an important step in his direction.

Part Eleven: The Russian Columbus

Fomenko, unsurprisingly, has claimed the new world as part of the old. The Slav-Turks were allegedly behind the discovery of the Americas in 1492. In that year, Christopher Columbus claimed the new world in the name of his imperial backers. These backers were not Ferdinand and Isabella of Spain, but the Russian Horde. How does Fomenko justify this amazing claim? Firstly, Fomenko alerts his readers to the fact that there is much that is not known about Christopher Columbus and his journeys. Fomenko notes that there are conflicting versions of Columbus's name—Colombo, Peter Columbus, Christobal Colom, Xpoual de Colon, Xpo Ferens. Most likely his real name was nothing like Columbus and 'colon' or 'column' merely designated 'a person who colonized in the name of God'. Columbus's place of birth is unknown; Corsica, Majorca, Aragon, France, Portugal, Greece, Galicia and Poland are some of the suggestions that have been made. Even conventional accounts do not accept Columbus's own vague assertions of coming from Genoa or Italy. There is much speculation that Columbus was a *converso* given that Spanish Jews were the map-making specialists in early modern Spain.[551]

Most likely, Fomenko claims, Columbus was a Cossack. A miniature from the book *De Insulis inventis* published in Basel in 1493 depicts, at least to Fomenko's satisfaction, a bearded Columbus in a boat and typically Cossack or traditional Turkic dress as he approaches the native peoples of the New World.[552] This image is identical, Fomenko believes, to one that depicts the siege of Vienna by the Turks in 1529. Thus Columbus was most likely one of these Cossack Turks. Only later did Columbus come to be dressed as a noble Spanish knight in armour once the chronology of Scaliger tightened its grip on the writing of history in the 17th century.

---

551 See, for example, Ralph De Toledano, 'The 'Mystery' of Christopher Columbus', *Midstream* 47 (February 2001): 17.
552 Nosovskii and Fomenko, *Bibleiskaia Rus'* II, p. 156.

HISTORY AS THERAPY 177

Figure Three: A drawing that Fomenko claims represents a contemporary view of Columbus dressed as a Horde Cossack making an offering to the newly discovered peoples of the New World.
Source: Fomenko, Nosovski, Bibleiskaia Rus'

The original diary of Columbus's travels did not survive. Columbus's son Ferdinand published his first biography decades after Columbus's travels. While the details of Columbus's journey were suppressed, Fomenko has still succeeded in finding clues that hint at the truth. Fomenko notes that the date of Columbus's journey coincided with considerable political and military activity in Russia itself. Conventional historians have noted the coincidence that just as the Spanish were driving out Muslims towards the end of the fifteenth century, a similar process was happening in the east under Ivan the Third, whose victory at the Ugra River in 1480 over the Muslim Khan Ahmad signalled Moscow's victory over the 'Tatar yoke'.[553] Alternative historians doubt that these simultaneous campaigns of Christian expansion were a coincidence.

Fomenko found inspiration in Morozov regarding the connection between the old and new worlds. Morozov's painstaking investigation of the Bible led him to the conclusion that the names Israel and Judea did not designate separate Biblical places or peoples but separate castes within the one state. Israelis were the 'fighters for God' or *bogobortsy*, while Judeans were the 'glorifiers of God', or *bogoslavtsy*. Israelis fought for God on the battlefield as professional soldiers while Judeans were the monks and the bishops who glorified God through their prayers. This is a key finding for Fomenko, for it reflects a principal feature of Russian politics with its division into secular and church authority. The books of the Bible are reflections of the political and religious history of Russia from the tenth to the sixteenth centuries. In each case, the state was divided into political/military and religious/educational wings. The Jews living in Spain in the fifteenth century were not Jews in any religious sense but *bogobortsy* who served the Slav-Turk Tsar or Great Khan. The khans themselves were the generals or tsars (Caesars) of the Russian Horde, that is, its military wing. The civilian wing of the Russian Horde was under the sway of the princes led by a Grand Prince.

According to Fomenko's reconstruction, in the fourteenth and fifteenth centuries, columns of the Russian Horde moved out across the globe. This same episode is retold differently in different lands. The Bible narrates this piece of history as the exodus of the Israeli tribes and the travels of Noah's Ark. It is no coincidence for Fomenko that at the beginning of August 1492, one day prior to the commencement of Columbus's first journey, tens of thousands of Jews were banished from their homes by the Spanish authorities. As Fomenko speculates, this was not anti-Semitism because the Spanish Jews were in reality the *bogobortsy* of the Russian Horde. They

---

[553] See Davies, *Europe*, 453–54.

were not banished because of an Inquisition, but were soldiers temporarily based in Spain as they prepared for a long and arduous military mission on behalf of the Russian tsar-khan.

Fomenko claims that in official documents relating to Columbus, there is not a word about a mission to look for an alternative route to India or China, the mission described in school textbooks. According to Scaliger's chronology, China was already under the suzerainty of the Great Khan when Columbus undertook his journeys. Therefore Columbus, who was to assume the position of Viceroy of all newly discovered lands, was not heading for the East since he and everyone else knew that there were no new lands waiting to be discovered there. Departing on his travels, Columbus did not take with him any precious gifts for the Great Khan that might have been expected if he were intending merely to visit these established states. The might and power of the Great Khan were already well known worldwide. In reality, Columbus's task, which is stated at least nine different times in official documents signed by Columbus and the Spanish monarchs, was in discovery and exploration of the islands and continents still hidden in the western ocean.

Why then did Columbus carry letters from the Spanish monarchs addressed to the Great Khan? Columbus was a general of the Ottoman Cossacks and, like the Spanish monarchs, was ultimately a subject of the Great Khan, military ruler of the Russian Horde. Columbus knew that the lands ahead had not yet been settled. The letter from the Spanish monarchs was in effect Columbus's *iarlyk* or imprimatur, an official sign of Imperial recognition that Columbus was not a pirate but deserving of assistance from all the lands and governors of the Empire. Columbus was going to claim the New World, and the letter would guarantee his safe passage to the Great Khan to report about the new conquests.

There is, it seems, ample evidence of the global reach of Russia in this period of history. The myth of Prester John, the mysterious ruler of a lost Christian kingdom in the East, is a source of fascination to historians and alternative historians alike. Gumilev devoted a study to explaining why Crusaders in the Holy Land considered they had an ally ruling this imaginary kingdom. He believed that he found the starting point of the myth in Kuchlug, the last Gur Khan and a Nestorian Christian.[554] The well-known letter from the mythical Prester John to the Byzantine Emperor Manuil is regarded as a forgery. For alternative history, it was unlikely to have been a forgery. There is no original of this letter, but there is a translation in Latin from the original Arabic. It starts with the following introduction – 'Prester John, by the might of our Lord Jesus Christ the Tsar of the Tsars, and the ruler of all rulers, wishes his friend, the prince of Constantinople Manuil good health and prosperity'.[555] About Prester John's address to Manuil, Gumilev noted that Prester John addressed a sovereign ruler of Constantinople as a mere prince.[556] As Fomenko insists, this is not the only example of Russian rulers displaying staggering arrogance towards lesser rulers. One of the few documents we have from the reign of Ivan the Terrible was addressed to the English queen. In this letter, Ivan described himself respectfully as *my* or 'we' in English, while Elizabeth the First is referred to with the Russian *ty*, you in the familiar form, as compared to the much more polite *vy*.

Fomenko's history ultimately is the story of the rise and fall of a great civilization. Fomenko notes that in 1771, the the first edition of the Encyclopaedia Brittanica described Russia's Siberian and North American possessions as 'Moscow Tartary', one of the last expressions of the Russian horde. Fomenko argues that the capital of what the British called Moscow Tartary at this time was in Tobolsk in Siberia.[557] Its days were numbered. Moscow Tartary finally succumbed to the West in the great war of 1773–1775, known in Russian history as the 'Peasant Wars', or 'Pugachev Uprising'. As a consequence of this war, the horde's lands were divided between Russia under the pro-Western Romanov clan and what would soon become the United States of America. After this war, Moscow Tartary disappeared from European maps, and Siberia became a part of Romanov's Russia. All that remains today of Moscow Tartary are the remnants of the amazing cities that we are now uncovering in the Urals, including the famous Arkaim.

As for the Napoleonic invasion of Russia in 1812, Fomenko believes that he can explain why the French emperor chose not to attack the capital of Saint

---

554 Lev Gumilev, *Searches for an imaginary kingdom: the legend of the kingdom of Prester John* translated by R.E.F. Smith (Cambridge: Cambridge University Press, 1987), pp. 166–67.
555 Lev Gumilev, *Poiski vymyshlennogo tsarstva* (Moscow: Tanais, 1994), p. 83.
556 Gumilev, *Poiski vymyshlennogo tsarstva*, p. 83.
557 See A. Fomenko and G. Nosovskii, G, *Pugachev i Suvorov. Taina Sibirsko-amerikanskoi istorii* (Moscow, Vladimir: Astrel', VKT, 2012).

Petersburg and instead turned his sight on the more difficult and peripheral task of capturing Moscow. It turns out that Napoleon hoped to find in Moscow representatives of the Horde dynasty that had survived the so-called Pugachev rebellion. Having allied with the Horde, Napoleon intended to conquer not only Russia, but also the whole world. However, Napoleon did not realise the degree of the Romanov's tyranny, which had mercilessly destroyed the entire elite of the now extinct Horde. To understand the complexity of the internal politics that led to the destruction of the Horde, we need to turn to the hopelessly confused history of Ivan the Terrible.

Chapter Seven: Terrible History: the Four Ivans

'Let me tell you an old tale
About the tsar named Ivan Vasil'evich
He, our white tsar, cunning and wise
He was cunning and wise,
Wiser than him, there is no-one in the whole wide world'.

Sixteenth century Russian folk song

Part One: Good and Bad Ivans

The 'Time of Troubles' (1598–1613) is a relatively obscure moment in the West but is well known to every student of Russian history, especially those who grew up in Soviet times. It was a time of great weakness and change when Russia, just as it would in 1917, literally collapsed, suffered foreign invasion and remerged under the Romanov dynasty. In conventional history it was a tragic period made good by its legacy of brilliant Romanov triumphs culminating in Peter the Great. Fomenko believes that he has identified the moment in Russian history when the West began to get the upper hand in its struggle with Russia. It was the era of Ivan the Terrible. Fomenko pursues the dual aim of pinpointing the wrong turn in Russia's history and to restoring the good reputation of Ivan the Terrible, a loyal servant of the Slav-Turk Empire. The alleged atrocities that took place in that era were not the deeds of the 'real' Ivan the Terrible but of a pretender to the Russian throne put forward by the pro-Western faction among the restless and competing nobility. The bloodbath of the boyars known to history as the *oprichnina* actually took place after the death of Ivan the Terrible.

In reality, Ivan the Terrible has not experienced a particularly bad press in Russia, except among the liberal minority who saw continuity between this tsar and Stalin. State school historians like Soloviev in the nineteenth century tended to exonerate Ivan the Terrible for his bloodthirsty deeds on the grounds that his war against the nobles was essential for the task of building a Russian state in an era when the state was vital to the survival of a people. In the Stalin era, Vipper's book and Eisenstein's film idealized this people's tsar who accumulated power only because ordinary people wanted it to be so. The real issue for Fomenko is that Ivan the Terrible's significance as a representative of the leadership of the Russian Horde has been overlooked, having fallen victim, like so much else in Russian history, to the Romanov conspiracy against history that got under way in the eighteenth century.

Since the nineteenth century, historians have tended to divide Ivan the Terrible's reign into two halves, the 'good' and 'bad' Ivans. In the first part of his reign, 1547–1560, the 'good' Ivan listened to his able advisors, Aleksei Adashev and the priest Sylvester. He reformed Russian government, encouraged the use of the printing press, extolled the virtues of piety and moderation, and dedicated his conquest of the Tatar khanate of Kazan to the Orthodox Church. The 'bad Ivan' pretended to abdicate in 1565, but instead unleashed the *oprichnina*, in effect a reign of terror, in which the tsar encouraged his bloodthirsty and servile supporters to repress rival clans and confiscate their lands. The 'bad Ivan' murdered his own son in a fit of rage, suffered military defeat in the West, and left a legacy of division that culminated in Russia's dismemberment during the Time of Troubles.[558]

The period when Ivan the Terrible ruled Russia is well studied but poorly documented.[559] Historians tend to agree that the second half of the sixteenth century is one of the most interesting periods of Russian history, separating old, medieval Russia and its Golden Horde heritage from the early modern period when the Romanov dynasty transformed and Westernized Russia. Fomenko sees parallels between the Time of Troubles, 1917 and 1991. In the twentieth century, Lenin and the Communists published documents from the Tsarist archives that seemed to prove the imperialistic and generally evil nature of Tsarist government. Later, in the era of Glasnost a flood of documents appeared that claimed to tell the truth about the first socialist revolution, concealed and twisted by Lenin and his propagandists. In history when there is a drastic change of power, the newcomers try to portray themselves as the progressive and rightful claimants, while the losers are usually depicted as darkly as possible. Given that the Tsarist past was declared as a totally negative experience by the Bolsheviks, it is

---

[558] See Charles Halperin, 'False Identity and Multiple Indentities in Russian History: The Mongol Empire and Ivan the Terrible', *The Carl Beck Papers in Russian and East European Studies* [Online], (2011).

[559] The early testaments of Ivan the Terrible (1553 and 1554) have not been preserved and the same is true of a testament written in 1582. We do have a copy of the testament of 1572 copied inexpertly in the early nineteenth century. Robert Howes, *The testaments of the Grand Princes of Moscow*, Translated and edited with commentary by Robert Craig Howes (Ithaca: Cornell University Press, 1967), p. 306.

likely, argues Fomenko, that the same, or similar processes took place at the beginning of the seventeenth century when the Romanov clan came to power after the Times of Troubles.

Ivan the Terrible reached the throne as a child in 1533. Grand Prince Ivan Vassilievich the Fourth was crowned as tsar on January 16, 1547 and in the same year married Anastasia Romanovna. By giving himself the title 'tsar', Ivan was supposed to have asserted Russia's independence from the Golden Horde and its rightful claim to be the latter's successor. Popular accounts describe Ivan the Terrible as a forceful ruler but a deranged personality who as a child threw animals off roofs and who would eventually murder his own son.[560] On the other hand, his supporters note that Ivan the Terrible showed no lack of reason when he fought religious and territorial wars both against the West in the name of recovering the lost Orthodox lands of Ukraine and Belarus from Polish and Lithuanian Catholic oppressors, and against the East, conducting a crusade against Islamic Kazan on the Volga river in 1552–1553. Ivan the Terrible personally took part in the campaign against Kazan. Upon the completion of his crusade Ivan ordered an impressive Orthodox cathedral to be erected in Red Square, to symbolize the religious significance of his victory. By 1560, the army of the Catholic Livonian order was completely routed, and the Order itself ceased to exist.

Thereafter, Ivan the Terrible's military record was more mixed. From 1565, Russia was racked by civil war, the era of the *oprichinina*. The Crimean Khan sacked Moscow in 1571 and defeats at the hands of the Poles and Swedes would follow. When Ivan the Terrible died in 1584 the so-called Livonian War had only just come to an end and Russia's ambitions in the West had not been realized. After the death, by poisoning, of Anastasia, Ivan the Terrible seemed to lose both his humanity and his mind. He eventually found solace in a religious rebirth that culminated in his burial in the robes of a monk.

Ivan's family life was, to say the least, complicated. After a bride show of fifteen hundred eligible women, Ivan the Terrible chose Anastasia Romanovna whose father Roman Iurevich-Zakharin was head of the hitherto undistinguished clan that would be known to history as the Romanovs. Anastasia gave birth to three sons. The first, Dmitrii, drowned while still an infant. The

---

560 See, for example, Andrei Yurganov 'The father of Tsarism', *Russian Life* 40:1 (January 1997): p. 12.

second, Ivan Ivanovich lived from 1554 until 1581 when his father murdered him. The third son, Fedor, became tsar in 1584 upon the death of Ivan the Terrible but ruled under the influence of Boris Godunov. When Fedor died childless in 1598, the Riurikid dynasty was extinct and the Time of Troubles ensued.

Ivan fell out with almost all of his close associates during his long reign. Prince Andrei Kurbskii, for example, had to flee abroad in 1564 to save his life. During the *oprichnina*, much of the Muscovite state was placed under the control of the Boyar Duma, whose members were responsible for the torture and murder of at least four thousand victims.[561]

Predictably, Fomenko has dismissed as open to doubt and speculation, the documents that are left to us from the times of Ivan the Terrible. The most authoritative specialist in Russia on the era of Ivan the Terrible, Skrynnikov, wrote a number of works on this subject. According to Skrynnikov, the major problem that any student of that era will encounter is the lack of sources for 'the state of the Russian archives and libraries in the sixteenth century was the worst in Europe'.[562] Moreover, even those documents that have reached us are clearly edited.[563] Historians have noted that the paucity of documents from the era of Ivan the Terrible is surprising given that testaments from other Muscovite princes have survived in their original form. Prince Vasilii I (1389–1425) wrote three different testaments at different periods of time, and they have survived although Vasilii lived 150 years earlier than Ivan.[564] Even the original of Ivan Kalita's will has survived although it is 250 years older than Ivan the Terrible's documents.[565] Ivan the Terrible's will has reached us only in the form of a damaged copy with no exact date on it.[566] Even when historians hope to rely upon the original, as is the case with the letter of Ivan the Terrible to Queen Elizabeth received in London in 1570, parts of this letter were scratched and damaged.[567] How could there be almost forty original decrees dated to the times of Ivan the Third, but

---

561 Martin, *Medieval Russia*, p. 349.
562 Ruslan Skrynnikov, *Ivan Groznyi* (Moscow: Nauka, 1975), p. 23.
563 Skrynnikov, *Ivan Groznyi*, p. 81.
564 Nadezhda Soboleva, *Russkie pechati* (Moscow: Nauka, 1991), pp. 149–150; also see Soboleva, *Ocherki istorii rossiiskoi simvoliki: Ot tamgi do simvolov gosudarstvennogo suvereniteta* (Moscow: Iazyki slavianskikh kul´tur, 2006).
565 Soboleva, *Russkie pechati*, pp. 149–150.
566 Ruslan Skrynnikov, *Tsarstvo Terrora* (St-Petersburg: Nauka, 1992), p. 51.
567 *Pamiatniki literatuty drevnei Rusi, vtoraia polovina 16 veka*, pp. 115, 587.

none from Ivan the Fourth. Fomenko asks rhetorically. Destroyed as part of a plot against the reputation of Ivan the Terrible and the Tatars, is his answer. The era of Ivan the Terrible has reached us in the descriptions, documents and forgeries of the seventeenth and eighteenth centuries.[568]
Analyzing Skrynnikov's works Fomenko has come across glaring inconsistencies. Thus, according to Skrynnikov, in 1553 Ivan the Terrible instituted Council of Trustees to look after his young son Dmitrii since Ivan himself was very sick and his supporters feared an early death. The Tsar recovered from illness, but the Council of Trustees continued its work. Fomenko asks why this awesome and almighty tsar needed an obsolete council after he was restored to health?[569]
Ivan's subjects had to take numerous oaths of loyalty to the Tsar, even though according to a regular practice it should have needed to be done only once. Moreover, a second coronation took place in 1572, repeating the procedure of 1547. Why did Ivan the Terrible need a second coronation after twenty-five years in power?[570] The explanation usually given is that Ivan the Terrible was so deranged that he needed constant reassurance as to his status. This seems to be the only example in Russian history when a monarch was crowned twice and received an oath on more than one occasion.[571]
In 1575 Ivan the Terrible decided to abdicate in favor of the former khan of the Kasimov Khanate, Semen Bekbulatovich, who became the Tsar of all Russia.[572] Bekbulatovich boasted royal blood and traced his ancestry to Genghis Khan. Conventional accounts explain this once more in terms of the erratic Tsar's behavior, or that it was some shrewd calculated maneuver in order to rule the Boyar Duma more efficiently.[573] Ivan the Terrible sacked and burned Novgorod in 1569–70, and then allegedly moved there with his entire court and treasury.[574] Why had the Russian monarch moved from Moscow to a smoldering and devastated hotbed of his enemies?
Ivan the Terrible's behavior and motives are so difficult to explain that generations of researchers found it easier to find answers in psychology and

---

568 Nosovskii and Fomenko, *Bibleiskaia Rus'*, I, p. 107.
569 Nosovskii and Fomenko, *Bibleiskaia Rus'*, I, p. 107.
570 Nosovskii and Fomenko, *Bibleiskaia Rus'*, I, p. 107.
571 Nosovskii and Fomenko, *Bibleiskaia Rus'*, I, p. 107.
572 Halperin, *Russia and the Golden Horde*, p. 101.
573 Halperin, *Russia and the Golden Horde*, p. 101.
574 Skrynnikov, *Tsarstvo Terrora*, p. 498.

found echoes of his behavior in the twentieth century in Stalin. Kovalevski's diagnosis insisted that Ivan the Terrible was a neurotic, and his paranoiac psychology combined with the complex of megalomania were the foundation for the creation of his repressive state, the *oprichnina*.[575] Shcherbatov noted that Ivan the Terrible was represented in so many different ways that he 'does not appear to be one person' while Billington considered the schizophrenia of Ivan the Terrible to be so acute that he was in effect 'two people'.[576]

Fomenko tackles the puzzling events of Ivan's reign in typical fashion when he suggests that the above-mentioned events are parts of the biographies of several tsars, not one, and that Ivan the Terrible in the singular is a latter-day composite created by the propagandists of the Romanovs.[577] Ivan the Terrible did not have a multiple or dysfunctional personality: he was literally four different tsars.

According to Fomenko's reconstruction, the period from 1547 to 1584, the reign of Ivan the Terrible, breaks naturally into four consecutive parts. The Romanovs subsequently created the composite Ivan the Terrible in the seventeenth century in order to justify their claims and the legitimacy of Mikhail, the first Romanov to the Russian throne. Simultaneously they achieved the equally important goal or reorienting the Russian state towards the West and away from its Turkic/Tatar associations. The Romanovs won what was in fact a civil war and having achieved a military takeover of power, blamed the bloodshed of the terror period known as the *oprichnina* upon the invented personality of Ivan the Terrible.

In order to disguise the beneficial character of Slavic-Turkic friendship and cooperation during the time of the Russian Horde, Romanov historians presented this part of Russia's history as a bitter struggle for survival between Slavic and Turkic-nomadic ethnic groups. The Romanovs presented themselves as the true Russian dynasty, which had consolidated Russian rule over the lands that would become the Russian Empire. Boris Godunov, the last legitimate Slav/Turk Tsar-Khan was declared an evil impostor, a usurper, and his descendants' rights to the Russian throne were denied. As Fomenko imagines it, the justification for Mikhail Romanov as the only rightful

---

575 Skrynnikov, *Tsarstvo Terrora*, pp. 500–501.
576 Ostrowski, *Muscovy and the Mongols*, pp. 88–89.
577 Nosovskii and Fomenko, *Bibleiskaia Rus'*, I, p. 107.

contender for the Russian throne was one of the primary reasons behind the merging of the reigns of several Tsars into one.

The Romanovs presented the eight wives of four different tsars as the wives of a single depraved ruler.[578] According to Fomenko, this could not have been so. The strict church rules in Russia stipulated that the third marriage must be the last legal one. All other marriages were considered as illegal and children born from these marriages were illegitimate. According to Romanov history, Tsar Fedor Ivanovich, the last son of Ivan the Terrible, was childless. According to Fomenko, he did have a son, Boris Fedorovich Godunov whom the Romanovs later declared a usurper of the throne.[579]

According to the hypothesis put forward by Fomenko, in 1547, the future Ivan the Terrible, then 16 years old, was crowned as a Tsar; he was married only once, and his first and last wife was Anastasia Romanov.[580] Her father was Roman Zahar'in, the patriarch of the future Romanov clan.[581] Ivan the Terrible ruled until 1553 and his most outstanding accomplishment was the siege and capture of Kazan in 1552.[582] In 1553 tsar Ivan IV became seriously ill. By that time he already had a son Dmitrii, and soon a second son, Ivan, was born.[583]

Conventional historians believe that Dmitrii died soon after Ivan's illness, but there is confusion surrounding Dmitrii's death in Russian historiography. One version of his death suggests that he died in 1553 from drowning; his nanny was crossing an unstable bridge and because of her carelessness the infant heir fell into the river.[584] Fomenko has described events differently. In the early 1550s, it was Ivan the Terrible who was dying. Ivan failed to recognize people he knew and was consumed by fever to the point where his death was anticipated. On 11 March 1553 the boyars swore an oath of loyalty to little Dmitrii.[585] As Fomenko described it, Ivan's illness was nearly terminal, and although he did not die, he nevertheless abandoned his royal duties. As Skrynnikov pointed out, the premature oath of loyalty of 1553 is

---

578 Nosovskii and Fomenko, *Bibleiskaia Rus'*, I, p. 107.
579 Nosovskii and Fomenko, *Bibleiskaia Rus'*, I, p. 109.
580 Skrynnikov, *Ivan Groznyi*, p. 23.
581 Skrynnikov, *Tsarstvo Terrora*, p. 94.
582 Nosovskii and Fomenko, *Bibleiskaia Rus'*, I, p. 109.
583 Skrynnikov, *Tsarstvo Terrora*, p. 109.
584 Skrynnikov, *Tsarstvo Terrora*, p. 117.
585 Skrynnikov, *Ivan Groznyi*, p. 48.

clear proof that there was a widespread belief that the Tsar was on the brink of death.[586]

Before his death, Ivan became increasingly pious, greatly influenced by the preaching of Sylvester, the tsar's priest. According to Skrynnikov, it was Sylvester who inspired the religious fanaticism in the Tsar. According to the testimonies of his English visitors, the Tsar no longer liked hunting and rude jokes but instead found solace in religious services. In 1552, Ivan saw his first visions.[587] This was an era of holy fools or *iurodivye*, whose strange actions included wearing chains, renouncing comforts and working miracles.[588]

The most famous was Vasilii Blazhennyi, the holy fool whom, despite or perhaps because he roamed Moscow naked even in winter, was especially respected and revered. Vasilii, was, it seems, so beloved by Ivan the Terrible, that when he died in 1552, he was accorded the unusual honor of having his death registered in official papers and was buried in the Troitse-Sergiev Monastery.[589] Crowds of people attended the funeral.[590]

Fomenko's reconstruction suggests that Vasilii the Holy Fool and Ivan the Terrible were one person.[591] In 1553 Ivan the Terrible, recovered in body but not in mind from his illness, abandoned the throne and became a holy fool; his early piety and religiously-inspired visions only contributed to his new spiritual awareness, or alternatively, mental breakdown. For Fomenko, this is the only possible explanation of Vasilii the Holy Fool and his enormous popularity in Moscow. That his funeral was well attended is not surprising given that he was an ex-Tsar.[592] The name 'Vasilii', Greek in origin, means 'tsar' in Russian. Therefore 'Vasilii Blazhennyi' should be read in Russian as 'tsar–holy fool'. Another indirect evidence that Fomenko believes identifies these two personalities is the fact that the Cathedral of the Deposition of the Robe on the Moat in Red Square, which was built in order to commemorate the victory of Ivan the Terrible over the Kazan khanate, is

---

[586] Skrynnikov, *Tsarstvo Terrora*, p. 114.
[587] Skrynnikov, *Tsarstvo Terrora*, p. 125.
[588] Geoffrey Hosking, *Russia and the Russians* (Massachusetts: Harvard University press, 2001), p. 25.
[589] See, for example, Robert Payne and Nikita Romanoff, *Ivan the Terrible* (New York: Cooper Square Press, 2002), pp. 177–178.
[590] Skrynnikov, *Tsarstvo Terrora*, p. 126.
[591] Skrynnikov, *Tsarstvo Terrora*, p. 126.
[592] Nosovskii and Fomenko, *Bibleiskaia Rus'*, I, pp. 110–111.

still popularly known as the Cathedral of Vasilii the Holy Fool, or *Sobor Vasiliia Blazhennogo*.[593]

Finally, according to Fomenko, the earliest and most reliable picture of Ivan the Terrible is the so-called Copenhagen portrait, preserved in the Danish royal archive. This portrait resembles, for Fomenko, a typical Russian icon, and was clearly painted with the idea in mind that the conqueror of Kazan had died a holy fool.[594] Ivan the Terrible, who was dressed in a monk's robe after his death to emulate the model of taking holy orders set by his father, was, according to Fomenko, an object of religious veneration. Portraits are of course often a matter of opinion. Payne saw in the Copenhagen portrait not a saintly, iconic image, but a rakish warrior with sensual lips and brooding countenance weighed down by the troubles of the world.[595]

According to Fomenko, when Ivan the Terrible believed that he was dying, he established Council of Trustees or *Izbrannaia Rada* so that it would be responsible for watching over young Dmitrii, his first son whose mother was his beloved Anastasia. This council functioned till 1563. Conventional history maintains that little Dmitrii died in 1553 after the oath of loyalty to him was taken by the boyars.[596] Ivan the Terrible, having miraculously recovered, continued his rule, but still shared his power with the Council of Trustees. The presence of such a Council makes more sense according to Fomenko if it is admitted that little Dmitrii did not die in 1553 but continued to rule as a child sovereign, while Ivan the Terrible degenerated into his holy dementia.[597] Representatives from the future Romanov clan were appointed as Trustees.[598] However, their influence at court soon came under pressure from rival nobles who resented the Romanov regency over the infant Tsar.[599] Conventional history offers another explanation, whereby Ivan was still a somewhat progressive state ruler, who wanted to rule the country benefiting from the close advice of his associates. Only later, after Anastasia's death did he lapse into his famed hatred of the world, and of his former allies and friends.

---

593 Nosovskii and Fomenko, *Bibleiskaia Rus'*, I, pp. 110–111.
594 Nosovskii and Fomenko, *Bibleiskaia Rus'*, I, pp. 110–111.
595 Payne, *Ivan the Terrible*, p. 331.
596 Skrynnikov, *Tsarstvo Terrora*, p. 109.
597 Nosovskii and Fomenko, *Bibleiskaia Rus'*, I, p. 111.
598 Skrynnikov, *Tsarstvo Terrora*, p. 111.
599 Skrynnikov, *Tsarstvo Terrora*, pp. 111, 115.

Janet Martin has described this era as one of competing clans, although whether it represented a battle between established and newly elevated families is unclear.[600] The Glinskii family, of Lithuanian descent and relatives of Ivan the Terrible's mother replaced the Romanov clan as the principal guardian. There was a long-standing history of hostilities between the Glinskii and Romanov clans. According to Skrynnikov, when Russian troops marched into Livonia under the leadership of Glinskii, his soldiers treated the Romanov's northwestern estates as enemy's lands.[601]

In 1563 Dmitrii died, probably as a result of accidental drowning. Now the Romanovs seized their opportunity, according to Fomenko. Ivan Ivanovich, the second son of Ivan the Terrible became tsar, and again the court and the boyars had to take an oath of loyalty. What evidence is there of a change of tsar at this time? The same year, according to Skrynnikov, 'fifteen years after the Tsar's coronation, messengers from Constantinople's patriarch arrived to Moscow bringing confirmation of the Muscovite (Ivan's) rights to Tsar's title...the splendid services were designed to strengthen his power'.[602] There is a problem here, Fomenko claims, since it is doubtful that such an endorsement would have occurred fifteen years after the original coronation of Ivan the Terrible. Instead this event signified the coming to power of young Ivan, now recognized in Constantinople.[603] According to Skrynnikov, this year saw the third oath given to the same sovereign Ivan the Terrible.[604] Since the Romanov family brought up the ten-year old Tsar Ivan, they were effectively now in power. They disbanded the Council of Trustees, prevented Adashev, the trusted advisor of the deceased Ivan the Terrible, from entering the capital, and began the terror of the *oprichnina* that the reign of Ivan the Terrible is famous for.

Having abandoned Adashev and Sylvester, young Ivan Ivanovich started to rule with the help of his family and at the same time abolished century old traditions, offending ordinary people in the process. The traditional nobility's anger was directed at the Romanov clan whom they held responsible for Adashev's untimely death and the style of rule of the new tsar.[605] By means

---

600 Martin, *Medieval Russia*, p. 331.
601 Skrynnikov, *Tsarstvo Terrora*, p. 147.
602 See Ruslan Skrynnikov, *Ivan the Terrible*, edited and translated by Hugh F. Graham, Gulf Breeze (FL: Academic International Press, 1981), p. 55.
603 Nosovskii and Fomenko, *Bibleiskaia Rus'*, I, p. 112.
604 Nosovskii and Fomenko, *Bibleiskaia Rus'*, I, p. 171.
605 Skrynnikov, *Tsarstvo Terrora*, p. 171.

of the *oprichnina*, the Romanov clan acted brutally against their political opponents.[606] These opponents were the rightful rulers of Russia, friends and family of the first Ivan the Terrible and representatives of the old Tatar dynasties.

This is how the civil war known as the Times of Troubles began. It was not simply a matter of clans but of political and geographic orientation.[607] According to Fomenko, the Romanovs oriented themselves toward the West, hoping for assistance in their royal ambitions. This was in stark contrast to Ivan the Terrible, a typical Russian tsar-khan.

According to Fomenko's reconstruction, Ivan Ivanovich ruled from 1562 to 1571. Fomenko quotes Skrynnikov to the effect that; 'The Tsar was alarmed at the discovery of boyar traitors and set out to fix the history of his rule in 1563–1564.'[608] Fomenko is especially proud of his apparent discovery that government orders from this period were printed on paper bought in Europe.[609] For Fomenko, this connection to Western printers was added proof that the Romanovs were in league with the West. Skrynnikov noted that: 'The rise in the book printing in the end of 1550s and beginning of 1560s and its sudden termination in 1568 came about because of the tragic fate of those people who were in charge of chronicle-writing.'[610] As Fomenko would have it, the chronicle writers fulfilled their duties by presenting the history of this civil war in a pro-Romanov light and were then dispatched by the ruling group to hide the evidence of this forging of the historical record.[611]

The destruction of Novgorod in 1569–1570 is considered as the culmination of the terror of the *oprichnina*. Forces opposing the *oprichnina*, and therefore the Romanovs, started a rebellion. Conventional accounts present this military episode as an invasion of Moscow by the Crimean Khan, when, 'in 1571, the Tatars burned Moscow while Ivan, having abandoned his troops, escaped to Rostov.'[612] Not long before, in 1569, Ivan the Terrible negotiated with English ambassadors, asking for political asylum in Britain, perhaps fearing that his purges may end badly. For Fomenko, this was the cowardly

---

606 Nosovskii and Fomenko, *Bibleiskaia Rus'*, I, p. 112.
607 Nosovskii and Fomenko, *Bibleiskaia Rus'*, I, p. 113.
608 Skrynnikov, *Tsarstvo Terrora*, p. 172.
609 Skrynnikov, *Tsarstvo Terrora*, p. 20.
610 Skrynnikov, *Tsarstvo Terrora*, p. 22.
611 Nosovskii and Fomenko, *Bibleiskaia Rus'*, I, p. 113.
612 Skrynnikov, *Ivan Groznyi*, p. 162.

young Ivan negotiating with Elizabeth the First, one of the Western backers of the Romanov clan.

As a result of the Crimean Khan's invasion, the Romanov party suffered heavy losses in men and their power declined. According to the conventional accounts, Maliuta Skuratov then weeded out the ranks of the old *oprichnina* executing its members on behalf of Ivan the Terrible.[613] Skuratov made his dramatic appearance only after the siege of Novgorod, so he did not participate in the first wave of terror.[614] According to Fomenko, Skuratov was part of the opposition to the Romanov clan.[615] In conventional accounts, Skuratov is always portrayed as a bloodthirsty executioner. For Fomenko, Skuratov is portrayed in such negative terms because the nucleus of the prosecuted *oprichnina* boyars belonged to the temporarily defeated Romanov clan.

With the end of *oprichnina*, sweeping changes took place in governmental institutions. Representatives of the oldest families, that had formerly been victims of the *oprichnina*, formed a new Boyar Duma.[616] The English ambassador was notified that political asylum for a Russian Tsar was unnecessary.[617] In 1572, the Tsar prohibited the very use of the word *oprichnina* on pain of death.[618] For Fomenko, the tsar's behavior was very strange if the conventional accounts are to be believed. Strangest of all, in 1572 the Tsar even moved to Novgorod, which he had recently destroyed,[619] with his court and treasury.[620]

The conventional account continues in its strange way when it describes Ivan the Terrible as having abdicated the throne once more in 1575 in order

---

613 Skrynnikov, *Ivan Groznyi*, p. 175.
614 Skrynnikov, *Ivan Groznyi*, p. 169.
615 Nosovskii and Fomenko, *Bibleiskaia Rus'*, I, p. 114.
616 Skrynnikov, *Ivan Groznyi*, pp. 174–175.
617 Skrynnikov, *Ivan Groznyi*, p. 189.
618 Skrynnikov, *Ivan Groznyi*, p. 190.
619 According to Nosovskii and Fomenko, old Novgorod was the name of modern Yaroslavl' that used to be the capital of the northeastern Russia. The Romanovs later renamed the city leaving only one Novgorod in the northwest in order to tie their dynasty regionally to Riurik, since originally Romanovs were from Pskov. Therefore it was Iaroslavl that was burned by Ivan; according to his orders Novgorod's walls were erased, and Yarsolavl today is the only city with powerful towers surrounding the city and no walls.
620 Skrynnikov, *Ivan Groznyi*, p. 181.

to allow the Tatar khan Semen Bekbulatovich to rule Russia.[621] Semen Bekbulatovich moved to the Tsar's chambers while Ivan the Terrible resided in the Arbat district of Moscow. The Khan gave orders while Ivan the Terrible, now adopting the name of Ivan Vasilievich Moscovskii or Ivan of Moscow, listened obediently.[622] Historians have struggled to explain the actions of Ivan the Terrible, blaming it on schizophrenia, or arguing that his actions were political ploys aimed at giving him a better chance to rule his restive nobles. Ostrowski has endorsed the view that Ivan the Terrible was acting out a parody of steppe custom according to which 'powerful non-Chingizid emirs (beks), such as Nogai, Tamerlane, Edige, and Mamai... set up Chingizid puppet khans on the throne.'[623] Because Ivan the Terrible was hailed by Church chroniclers as a descendant of the brother of Rome's Augustus Caesar and was therefore non-Chingizid, he may have suddenly felt the need to appoint the Chingizid Bekbulatovich as his puppet. Ivan the Terrible told the English ambassador that Semen Bekbulatovich reigned only at his pleasure and that the situation could quickly change.[624] The next year, 1576, Ivan the Terrible resumed his title of Grand Prince and appointed Semen Bekbulatovich Grand Prince of Tver.[625] History would never hear from Semen Bekbulatovich again. Ostrowski acknowledges that, however the matter is examined, it can only be described as 'bizarre'.[626]

Part Two: 'How it really was' according to Fomenko

For Fomenko, the whole episode makes more sense if it is assumed that Semen Bekbulatovich really was in control from 1575 and that it was he who ordered the young Ivan Ivanovich, the Romanov favorite, into exile. The strange events of 1576 were not a case of Ivan the Terrible taking up the reins once more but of Semen Bekbulatovich officially consolidating his position as tsar. As a result of the civil war of 1571–1572 the 'Muscovite' party of Romanovs was defeated and its leaders executed.[627] A new *oprichnina* was created headed by representatives of the old dynastical

---

621 Skrynnikov, *Ivan Groznyi*, p. 195.
622 Skrynnikov, *Ivan Groznyi*, p. 195.
623 Ostrowski, *Muscovy and the Mongols*, p. 188.
624 Payne, *Ivan the Terrible*, p. 360.
625 Payne, *Ivan the Terrible*, p. 362.
626 Ostrowski, *Muscovy and the Mongols*, p. 188.
627 Skrynnikov, *Tsarstvo Terrora*, p. 163.

families who were the victims of the original *oprichnina*. As Skrynnikov put it, 'the *oprichnina* achieved its greatest increase in size when five hundred Novgorodian nobles joined.[628] The Novgorodians under Skuratov were the means by which Semen Bekbulatovich achieved his victory over Ivan Ivanovich.

Semen Bekbulatovich was probably the youngest son of Ivan the Third, Fomenko speculates, and uncle of the deceased Ivan the Terrible. In 1575, young Ivan Ivanovich was forced to abdicate but Semen Bekbulatovich could not yet seal his victory by taking the title of tsar. In 1576 Semen Bekbulatovich was crowned as Tsar of Russia, after adopting the name Ivan and ruling until 1584. As Fomenko tells the story, the change of a royal name was common practice in medieval Russia. Otherwise it is difficult to explain why for one hundred and fifty years there were no names other than Ivan or Vasilii among Russia's rulers.[629] Vasilii the Third was known as Gavriil before he became tsar. The custom of changing female royal names survived until the early seventeenth century when Mikhail Romanov's future wife Maria was renamed Anastasia.[630]

For Fomenko, the conventional account indirectly supports the claim that a Tatar khan did become Russian tsar. Skrynnikov wrote, 'in the following years (after 1575), the Tsar, who had always enjoyed excellent health, started to look for expert doctors abroad and overseas.'[631] The Tsar seemed to have become fifty years older, his decline attributed to his poor mental and health state.[632] The 'original' Ivan the Terrible was only forty-four years old when he allegedly resumed the throne in 1576 and should not have appeared old and in poor health in the years that followed. Semen Bekbulatovich was about eighty years old and therefore a more likely candidate to have become this suddenly wizened and senile tsar so unkindly commented upon by the observers quoted above.

For Fomenko, it was not Ivan the Terrible who mysteriously relocated to Novgorod but Semen Bekbulatovich who abandoned Moscow, the nest of the Romanov conspiracy against him. Semen Bekbulatovich first settled in ancient Novgorod where he began the construction of a powerful fortress,

---

[628] Skrynnikov, *Ivan Groznyi*, p. 169.
[629] Nosovskii and Fomenko, *Bibleiskaia Rus'*, I, p. 116.
[630] Ivan Zabelin, *Domashnii byt Russkikh Tsarits v 16–17 stoletiyakh* (Novosibirsk: Nauka, 1992), p. 114.
[631] Skrynnikov, *Ivan Groznyi*, p. 178.
[632] Payne, Romanoff, *Ivan the Terrible*, p. 227.

and then moved to Tver where he took the title of Grand Prince.[633] The young ex-tsar, Ivan Ivanovich, following his abdication, escaped punishment for the crimes committed during the *oprichnina*. For Fomenko the Tatar Semen Bekbulatovich proved an excellent ruler because there is no record of terror or domestic disturbances in Russia in the period of 1572–1584, only foreign wars.

Conventional accounts suggest that Ivan the Terrible had five, six, seven or eight wives, the single example in Christian Russia of a tsar who married so often. In Fomenko's reconstruction, while none of these four tsars had more than three wives as prescribed by Church laws, the person of Ivan the Terrible created by Romanov history was saddled with them all.[634] Russian sources do not contain evidence of a conflict between the Tsar and the church on the issue of Ivan the Terrible's marriages. Therefore, it seems probable to Fomenko that Ivan the Terrible's only wife was Anastasia Romanov. The son Ivan Ivanovich had three wives and Tsar Fedor one. There were one or two wives for Semen Bekbulatovich.[635] The third and last wife of Ivan Ivanovich, Maria Nagaya, was the mother of Dmitrii, the future False Pretender from the Time of Troubles. He was crucial to the next phase of Russia's history.

Part Three: The True Boris Godunov and the False Dmitrii

According to the conventional accounts, Ivan the Terrible died in 1584. According to Fomenko it was Semen Bekbulatovich who died in this year. Conventonal accounts suggest that Ivan the Terrible's son Fedor Ivanovich became Tsar in that year. For Fomenko, Fedor was Semen Bekbulatovich's son. In the last years of his rule, the boyar Boris Godunov suddenly became very influential if the conventional accounts are to be believed. Although conventional history stipulates that Tsar Fedor died childless, Fomenko insists that he had a son, named Boris, who is known to us under his mother's last name Godunov.[636] Meanwhile, Ivan Ivanovich's son Dmitrii, known to history as False Dmitrii, represented a second dynastical branch and a rival for Boris Godunov.[637]

---

633 Skrynnikov, *Ivan Groznyi*, pp. 169, 205.
634 Nosovskii and Fomenko, *Bibleiskaia Rus'*, I, p. 118.
635 Nosovskii and Fomenko, *Bibleiskaia Rus'*, I, p. 118.
636 Nosovskii and Fomenko, *Bibleiskaia Rus'*, I, p. 119.
637 Nosovskii and Fomenko, *Bibleiskaia Rus'*, I, p. 119.

According to Fomenko, there are a number of sources that confirm the royal lineage of Boris Godunov. In 1591 during the rule of Tsar Fedor Ivanovich, the Crimean khan Gazi-Girey sent a letter to Moscow to Boris Godunov.[638] Although the message is entitled 'Crimean Khan's letter to Muscovite Boyar Boris Godunov', the reverse side bears an inscription from the Tsar's chancellery: 'Translated in summer 7099...that which is written to Tsar Boris Fedorovich by the Crimean Tsar's confidante.' Fomenko notes that in 1591, Boris Godunov was referred to as 'a Tsar', that is, seven years before the conventional date for the death of Tsar Fedor and the crowning as tsar of Boris Godunov. They assert further that Godunov's infant son Fedor was also referred to as a Tsar in certain unspecified official papers.[639]

The Crimean khan's letter is not the only evidence that has reached us confirming Boris Godunov's affiliation with the tsars of Russia. When Fedor was still alive, Boris attended a meeting with the Austrian ambassador. The protocol, according to Skrynnikov, was arranged and handled as if Boris Godunov were a Tsar.[640] It was usual practice that an elder son would deputize for his father and received full royal honors. With their fondness for historical parallels, Fomenko point out that this honor was bestowed upon Ivan the Third when his father Vasilii the Second was still alive.[641] Skrynnikov confirmed that Boris Godunov used many titles, dealing not only with the Russian court but also with foreign countries and ambassadors long before conventional history recognized him as tsar.[642] His messages to the English Queen were signed, 'Boris, by God's will the sovereign of all Russia.'[643] In her replies the English queen referred to Boris as 'cousin', another proof, Fomenko argues, that Boris Godunov was a legitimate tsar.[644]

Boris Godunov became 'the hated usurper' only after the Romanovs came to power, because, under Boris Godunov, the family of Romanovs was the most persecuted. Boris Godunov exiled Fedor Romanov to a remote northern monastery and destroyed the Romanov party in the Boyar Duma. After the Romanovs came to power, the chroniclers painted Boris Godunov as

---

638 Nosovskii and Fomenko, *Bibleiskaia Rus'*, I, p. 120.
639 Nosovskii and Fomenko, *Bibleiskaia Rus'*, I, p. 120.
640 Ruslan Skrynnikov, *Boris Godunov* (Moscow: Nauka, 1983), p. 38.
641 Nosovskii and Fomenko, *Bibleiskaia Rus'*, I, p. 120.
642 Skrynnikov, *Boris Godunov*, p. 85.
643 Skrynnikov, *Boris Godunov*, p. 86.
644 Nosovskii and Fomenko, *Bibleiskaia Rus'*, I, p. 121.

darkly as possible while the Romanov clan was depicted as comprising holy martyrs.[645]

According to conventional accounts, Boris was born in 1552, and became a sovereign at the age of forty-seven years, in 1599.[646] Yet portraits portray him as a young person according to Fomenko. Because of his youth, he encountered opposition in the Duma from powerful boyar clans, especially the Shuisky clan. According to Skrynnikov, the tensions in the Duma ran so high that Boris had to abandon his Kremlin residence and move to a well-protected Novodevichii monastery.[647] The conventional account insists that as an experienced and cunning populist Boris Godunov left Moscow's Kremlin for a monastery in order to force his rule upon the Russian populace in a manner reminiscent of Ivan the Terrible's abdication and departure for Alexandrovskaya sloboda. After a period of turmoil Boris Gudonov won this struggle for power, and his supporters came to the monastery in order to transport Boris back from exile.[648] When Boris Godunov died in 1605 he was 53 years old, yet his heir was still an infant. Fomenko claims that this is further proof that Boris Godunov was in reality the son of Fedor Ivanovich and only 20–25 years old when he inherited the throne in 1599.[649]

Boris Godunov's death ushered in the era known to conventional history as the Times of Troubles. The Times of Troubles revolves in part around False Dmitrii who was according to popular legend Ivan the Terrible's son. The mystery surrounding Prince Dmitrii, the False Pretender, has not yet been resolved. As some historians have put it, how could Prince Dmitrii challenge Boris Godunov, a clever, energetic, charismatic powerful supreme ruler?'[650] Fomenko argues that the reconstructed version of events logically explains what happened. False Dmitrii was in fact a prince, but his father was Ivan Ivanovich who ruled in 1563–1572, not Ivan the Terrible. The Romanov family not only brought up Ivan Ivanovich but also his young son Dmitrii. He was initially sent to a monastery in order to avoid any dispute between the young Dmitrii and his father's conqueror, Semen Bekbulatovich or his de-

---

645 Skrynnikov, *Boris Godunov*, pp. 134–136.
646 Skrynnikov, *Boris Godunov*, p. 5.
647 Skrynnikov, *Boris Godunov*, pp. 110–111.
648 Skrynnikov, *Boris Godunov*, pp. 112–120.
649 Nosovskii and Fomenko, *Bibleiskaia Rus'*, I, p. 124.
650 A. Gordeev, *Istoriia Kazakov* II (Moscow: Strastnoi bul'var), p. 97.

scendant, Boris Godunov. According to Russian law, a person of royal descent who became a monk or a cleric could not be crowned as tsar.[651]

We have differing accounts of the deaths of two princely children during the reign of Ivan the Terrible, both named Dmitrii Ivanovich. Fomenko insists that there was most likely only one death, in 1563, when young Tsar Dmitrii Ivanovich, son of Ivan the Terrible, died at the age of ten or twelve. Fomenko believes that Prince Shuisky who fought against Godunov invented the story about the second Dmitrii's death in 1591 to undermine the rival to his preferred candidate as Tsar.[652] According to conventional accounts, after Ivan the Terrible's death, the new Tsar Fedor exiled Dmitrii and his mother to Uglich. Dmitrii had his throat cut in 1591. The investigation by Shuiski first found that the death was the result of a lack of supervision and youthful exuberance playing with knives. Later Shuiskii changed his story, allowing suspicion to fall on Boris Godunov. Skrynnikov noted that there has been a long-standing suspicion in academic circles that the so-called Uglich affair was falsified. Skrynnikov points out that even a superficial analysis of the documents demonstrates traces of censorship given that the lists are in the wrong order. It seems certain that the originals of the Uglich interrogation have disappeared.[653] To Fomenko it is obvious that when Prince Dmitrii became the False Pretender, a story about the Uglich tragedy was invented. The grave of the first Dmitrii, the first son of Ivan the Terrible who died, seemingly by drowning, in 1563, was declared to be the grave of Dmitrii, son of Ivan Ivanovich.[654]

Conventional accounts claim that the False Dmitrii was really the vagabond Gregory Otrep'ev. This seems incredible to Fomenko given that False Dmitrii received considerable acknowledgement as the genuine heir. Indeed, from the very beginning of Dmitrii's struggle for the throne, eyewitnesses asserted their confidence that he was a prince. The Polish king and nobility, Russian boyars, crowds of ordinary people in Putivl' and other cities, and even his own mother, Maria Nagaya, recognized Dmitrii.[655] In Putivl', Dmitrii displayed the real Gregory Otrep'ev to the crowd.[656] Meanwhile, events in Moscow developed rapidly. On 13 April 1605 tsar Boris Godunov died not

---

651 Nosovskii and Fomenko, *Bibleiskaia Rus'*, I, p. 125.
652 Nosovskii and Fomenko, *Bibleiskaia Rus'*, I, p. 126.
653 Skrynnikov, *Boris Godunov*, pp. 70–72.
654 Nosovskii and Fomenko, *Bibleiskaia Rus'*, I, p. 126.
655 Skrynnikov, *Boris Godunov*, p. 49.
656 Gordeev, *Istoriia Kazakov*, II, p. 113.

of old age as the conventional account implies but poisoned by the rival boyars clans of Shuisky, Romanov and Golitsyn.[657]

Fomenko acknowledges that there is at least one major problem with his theory. What motive did the Romanovs have for portraying Dmitrii as a False Pretender when he was brought up in their family? False Dmitrii was also an enemy of Boris Godunov who was enemy number one for the Romanovs. Fomenko answers his own question by claiming that Dmitrii was simply a tool for the Romanovs to achieve power. Dmitrii was still a Riurikid, although related to the Romanovs through his grandmother Anastasia Romanov.

When Dmitrii became tsar in 1605, he too had a son. Consequently the election of Mikhail Romanov as tsar in 1613 was not legitimate since there was a child of the royal line still alive. The Romanovs unsurprisingly declared Dmitrii to be a False Pretender, and Dmitrii's son was slandered as the 'little thief'. The problem of an unwanted heir was solved very rapidly and efficiently, as the 'little thief' was soon dispatched on the Spassky gates of the Kremlin. Thus the Romanovs and the Shuisky clan supported one another in the struggle against Dmitrii for their own self-interested reasons.[658]

As Fomenko tells it, neither the Russian people, nor Russia's neighbors, readily accepted the lies perpetrated by the Romanovs. In seventeenth century Poland, Mikhail Fedorovich Romanov was not recognized as the rightful ruler of Russia. The second Romanov, Tsar Alexis Mikhailovich sent an envoy to Poland in 1650 who demanded that 'all dishonest books be confiscated and burnt in the presence of ambassadors, while their authors, as well as the printers, owners of print houses, and landlords on whose territories the print houses were situated, were to be executed.' According to Fomenko, this process had already taken place in Russia.

Part Four: Traces of the Horde: the Cossacks

For conventional historians, the Golden Horde passed out of history in the fifteenth century. For the alternative writers it lived on through Ivan the Third, Ivan the Terrible and Boris Godunov. It survives to this day in the shape of the Cossacks. For Fomenko and other alternative historians, the Cossacks

---

657 Nosovskii and Fomenko, *Bibleiskaia Rus'*, I, p. 126.
658 Nosovskii and Fomenko, *Bibleiskaia Rus'*, I, p. 128.

of the Don and Volga are much older than conventional historians think and date back to the twelfth century. This, of course, contradicts the conventional axiom of Russian history, that the Cossacks were runaway serfs of the seventeenth century.[659]

The alternative historians dismiss as fantasy the contention that a runaway serf, whose life revolved around his plough, was miraculously transformed into a merciless warrior trained in the art of mounted combat. According to Fomenko, Cossack troops were living on the steppe at the time of the Mongols, and they were an integral part of the Russian Horde's army.[660] Fomenko notes that Cossack troops assisted Dmitrii Donskoi at Kulikovo Field and Ivan the Terrible at the siege of Kazan', at a time when serfdom was only in the process of formation. Only in 1649 under the Romanovs did serfdom take its final, repressive form. Fomenko points out that Russian textbooks tended to date the Cossacks only from the seventeenth century.[661] Another convenient fact invented by Romanov propagandists.

Fomenko notes that Cossack communities are presently scattered all over Russia's territory. There are Don, Volga, Yaik (Urals), Dnieper, Terek, Pskov, Riazan', Zaporozhie, Meschera, Nogai and Azov Cossacks, as well as the 'town' Cossacks situated in regional strongholds.[662] Fomenko cites the usual array of modern and ancient sources, including the highly dubious *Dictionary of the Cossacks*, which notes that the first of the conventionally recognized Cossack Hosts, the Zaporozhie, based in Ukraine, were known as 'Horde Cossacks'. For Fomenko, the geographic dispersion of the Cossacks suspiciously resembles the geography of the former Golden Horde.[663] According to Fomenko, Cossack troops were living on the steppe at the time of the Mongols, and they were an integral part of the so-called Tatar-Mongol army. In the first half of the twelfth century, Cossack hordes populated all eastern and Central Asia.[664] Romanov historians later disguised

---

[659] Imperial and Soviet historians often treated the Cossacks with either hatred or suspicion. See Gerasim Vdovenko and Alexei Gryzov et al, *Kazachestvo* (Moscow: Sobranie, 2007), p. 135.

[660] Nosovskii and Fomenko, *Novaia khronologiia Rusi,* p. 11.

[661] Nosovskii and Fomenko, *Novaia khronologiia Rusi,* p. 14.

[662] Skrylov and Gubarenko, *Kazachii slovar'-spravochnik* (Cleveland: Ohio, USA, 1966), 254; also *Kazachii slovar'-spravochnik* II volumes (San Anselmo: California, USA, 1968).

[663] Nosovskii and Fomenko, *Novaia khronologiia Rusi,* p. 14.

[664] Nosovskii and Fomenko, *Novaia khronologiia Rusi,* p 14.

and twisted the Cossack heritage. Cossacks were elite warriors, not runaway peasants.

Sixty years after the Romanov's ascension to power the most serious Cossack revolt occurred in Russia, the uprising of Stepan Timofeevich Razin in 1667–71. Conventional accounts portray Stenka Razin's Cossacks as rebellious peasants who wanted to sail to Moscow to reveal to their 'little father', the Tsar of Russia, the wrongdoings of his boyars. Fomenko argues that there is no evidence that the Cossacks wanted to side with the Tsar against his own advisers. Moreover, the extant copies of documents put out by the rebels ask the peasants to rise up and fight 'for the house of the Holy Mother (Russia), for the Great Sovereign, for our little father Stepan Timofeevich and all the Orthodox Christian faith'.[665]

Fomenko claims that the Romanovs at that time only controlled one part of Russia, that is, its central princedoms and the northeast. Meanwhile, the middle and lower Volga remained independent. There were other tsars there, including those who belonged to the Tatar dynasties. This is why the Cossacks insisted that they were fighting for the Tsar against the boyars. They were opposed to the Romanov-boyars and supported their own Russian Horde Tsar, not Alexis Romanov. Fomenko notes that the war lasted four years, a long war by any standards. In Europe it was looked upon as a fight for the throne. Razin's uprising became known as the 'Tatar rebellion'. The Romanovs won the war with the aid of foreign mercenaries, having failed to find reliable troops inside Russia.[666] The era of the Slav-Turks was nearing its end, its energy spent and the Romanovs triumphant. Fomenko's hope is that once Rusians learn the truth about the greatness of the Russian Horde, this victory of the West will be reversed.

---

665 Nosovskii and Fomenko, *Bibleiskaia Rus'*, I, p. 131.
666 Nosovskii and Fomenko, *Bibleiskaia Rus'*, I p. 133.

Chapter Eight: Icebreakers

'A confusing and contradictory jumble, ranging from pseudohistory to occultism and from astrology to racism, these views have reflected in their own way the collapse of the established intellectual framework and the disarray, even chaos of the time... Writers such as A.T. Fomenko have redrawn the entire course of human history along lines perhaps acceptable in science fiction but nowhere else. Some of these wild ideas have located themselves at the margins of the academic world and even occasionally entered that world.'[667]

'Suvorov is much worse. In addition to everything he has betrayed his Motherland. At least Fomenko has never attacked our Holy Victory...'[668]

One of the most successful recent contributions to the patriotic retelling of the past is a series of publications attributed to the pen of Vladimir Medinskii, a close ally of President Putin. Medinskii is not an 'alternative historian'. Rather, Medinskii is a typical representative of the post-Communist elite, an advocate of capitalism, and a critic of ethnic nationalism and Communism. His re-writing of Russian history may well contain portents of the official version of history that Putin intends for Russia's schools.

Medinskii is classically 'Western' in terms of his education, occupation, and lifestyle, but nevertheless portrays the West and its historians as alien, subversive, and cynically hypocritical when it comes to propaganda directed against Russia. The influential newspaper *Kommersant* described Medinskii's *Mify o Rossii* as the bestselling book in the history of modern Russia. It begins with a famous quote from Catherine the Great to the effect that there is no nation on earth that has had so many falsehoods directed against it as Russia. According to Medinskii, foreign observers wrote mainly about Russia's drunkenness, thievery, cruelty, and masochistic love for tyrant rulers. Indeed, Medinskii hopes that foreigners will read his book, if only to learn that 'Russians do not drink vodka in the morning straight from their *samovar*, and that they do brush their teeth'. The Russian is a hard worker and builder of a unique civilization, and not a perpetually drunken monster.

---

667 Nicholas Riasanovsky, *Russian Identities: A Historical Survey* (Oxford: Oxford University Press, 2005).
668 Igor Nastenko et al., eds., *Istoriia i antiistoriia: Kritika "novoi khronologii" akademika A. Fomenko* (Moscow: Iazyki russkoi kultury, 2000).

Medinskii's historical examples are designed to demonstrate that Russian history was not more bloodthirsty than European history and that it was decidedly less bloodthirsty than Asian or African history. According to Medinskii, Western ideological smears against Russia are far more dangerous even than their military invasions. These Western myths 'stand between Russia and its civilized future'. Medinskii singles out Western historians such as Richard Pipes, who has argued that Russia has never known freedom. For Medinskii, Russia has always been a home of freedom. He cites the example of the Cossacks who were 'fully autonomous' and whose sense of duty, state service, spirituality, and religiosity coupled with the individual initiative represents the real Russian 'ideal type'.

Critics from both the left and right have pointed out that Medinskii is prone to exaggeration and myth. He suggests, for example, that Russians were responsible for such amazing inventions as light bulbs, rifles and submarines. The West later claimed all these discoveries as its own.[669] Unlike Medinskii, conventional historians tend to see Russian contributions to these fields of endeavor rather than ownership of the invention. Like many other Russian critics of the West, Medinskii sees the West as a place of excessive violence, decadence, inequality, and self-interested expansion. The Russian Empire, by contrast, was a multi-ethnic model of tolerance with mutual benefits to all sides. Russian leadership was aimed at the collective good.

Medinskii's views are in the mainstream of Russian patriotism. He considers ancient Aryans as 'our' people, since they were inhabitants of the southern steppe. He rejects the view that Russia was some sort of by-product of superior Byzantine and Scandinavians civilizations. As for the Normanist controversy, Medinskii positions himself as a moderate, but is clearly in the anti-Normanist camp. Medinskii endorses the version put forward by Sergei Platonov in the early twentieth century. Platonov considered that the Varangians of the Chronicle were merely the inhabitants of the modern-day Kievan region and its surrounding towns. The Rus that gave Russia its name were quite different. Medinskii sees the positive in Peter the Great, but like many critics of the Petrine reforms, assesses the human

---

[669] For a sample of the many scholarly criticisms of Medinskii's offerings, see *Anti-Medinskii, Oproverzhenie, Kak Partiia Vlasti "pravit" istoriiu* (Moscow: Iauza-Press, 2012) and *Anti-Medinskii, Psevdo-Istoriya Vtoroi Mirovoi, Novye Mify Kremlia* (Moscow: Iauza-Press, 2012).

costs as far too high. For Medinskii, the early Romanovs, especially Tsar Aleksei Mikhailovich had already built a great and prosperous empire. Peter only needed to reform and not so dramatically westernize this remarkable civilizational achievement.

Medinskii trawled through the history of Kiev Rus to show how important image management has been in the past to the reputation of particular princes and other historic figures. The inference to be drawn is that Russia needs to improve its own image making. He notes with pleasure that Tor Heyerdahl, the adventurer and amateur archaeologist, came to the conclusion that Odin, the principal Scandinavian god, was both a real historical figure and once lived on the lower Don River. Scandinavia, like the West in general, clearly owed a great deal to Russia and the debt will one day be recognized. It was the Russians, after all, who invented an alphabet for the Komi people of Siberia as far back as the fourteenth century. Medinskii acknowledges that the Russian campaigns in the Caucasus in the nineteenth century were often brutal military affairs, but sees this as the exception rather than then rule. If Russians really were too brutal, why have the Volga and Siberian ethnic groups continued to thrive under Russian and Soviet rule?

Medinskii is especially keen to put an end to myths about the 'Great Patriotic War'. It would be difficult to exaggerate the importance of the victory over the Nazis in the thinking of ordinary Russians. Laruelle summed up the sense not just of pride, but also of purpose and coherence generated by the victory when she noted that:

> Russian society is fragmented in terms of living standards, contact with the external world, access to information, and political and identity-based perceptions. It has very few elements with which to create a social bond or an ideological unity. In this context, the memory of World War II plays a key role as a driver of historical consensus. Polls conducted about this question are very revealing: in 1998, 70 percent of Russian citizens considered the victory of 1945 to be the most important event of the 20th century, and today that figure has reached 90 percent.[670]

The standard accounts now suggest that the Soviet Union lost thirty million of its approximately 190 million people, 1700 towns, 70,000 villages, and

---

670 Marlene Laruelle, 'Negotiating history: memory wars in the near abroad and pro-Kremlin youth movements', *Demokratizatsiya* 19.3 (2011): p. 233.

thousands of factories.[671] Much of the loss took place in the Slavic heartland of Ukraine, Belarus, and European Russia. One-quarter of the population of Belarus and one third of the inhabitants of Leningrad perished.[672]

In the Gorbachev and Yeltsin eras, there was a brief flourishing of what might be described as the Western version of World War Two. While sympathetic to the achievements of the Red Army and the sacrifices of the Soviet people, the Western view tended to rely upon German rather than Soviet sources for its account of military developments and highlighted Stalin's joint responsibility with Hitler for the war and the dictator's cynical, bloodthirsty methods. The Eastern Front was a power play between two dictators and the totalitarian systems that they led, rather than a great patriotic war. Soviet readers learned during the Gorbachev and Yeltsin eras that Stalin made horrendous errors; he foolishly encouraged German tankists and aircraft specialists to train in Russia; shot half his command corps in the military purge; cynically signed up to a pact with Hitler to divide Eastern Europe in August 1939; suffered a humiliating defeat in the war against Finland in the Winter War of 1939–40; criminally misread the signs of an imminent German invasion in June 1941. The invasion was such a shock that according to Khrushchev, Stalin had a nervous breakdown and hid himself away. Stalin's inhumane treatment of the Soviet population was best seen in Leningrad where half the population died in the siege. Leningrad and Moscow were saved not by the efforts of the defeated Red Army but by strategic errors committed by Hitler, lack of cooperation between the Germans and the Finns, and of course the muddy roads and freezing weather. The mass surrender of Red Army soldiers and the collaboration of captives such as Vlasov came to be described as a heroic anti-Stalin protest. The war was eventually won only because of the huge resources at Russia's disposal and Stalin's willingness to resort to measures like blocking detachments. The latter executed those retreating without orders and an army of penal battalions made up of those incarcerated by the regime. The Red Army's most famous generals, Zhukov included, turned out to be brutal butchers who told lies to cover their tracks after the war. Many of these claims turned out to be wrong or exaggerated, a point not missed by an avalanche of pro-Stalin histories of the war that have appeared over the last decade.

---

671 Tumarkin, 'The Great Patriotic War', p. 597.
672 Tumarkin, 'The Great Patriotic War', p. 596.

The most startling publication to appear in Russia in the 1990s can reasonably be described as a work of alternative history. This was Viktor Suvorov's *Icebreaker. Who Started the Second World War?*, which Russian readers were able to buy from 1992.[673] According to Suvorov, Stalin was planning to attack Hitler in July 1941. Hitler got wind of Stalin's plans and launched a successful preemptive attack on 22 June 1941. Hitler himself had used exactly this justification for his invasion; historians of the Nazi period are almost unanimous in making the point that in reality Hitler had no concerns about an imminent Soviet attack.[674]

Suvorov's arguments revolved around an interpretation of Stalin's speeches, various military plans and the commentary of observers on Stalin's motives. There is for example the speech that Stalin gave on 19 August 1939. Four days before signing the Nazi-Soviet pact, Stalin told the fellow leaders of the Communist Party that it was in the interests of the Soviet state for the coming war to last as long as possible and to exhaust the belligerents. In a speech to the Military Academy on 5 May 1941, Stalin demanded that the Red Army fight an 'offensive war'. Suvorov pointed to plans drawn up by Zhukov to fight just such an offensive war with an array of new weapons such as a flying tank and a wheeled tank for fast movement along the autobahns. The Red Army's emphasis upon paratroopers, according to Suvorov, was a sure sign of aggressive intent. Suvovov was not especially pro-Hitler who is described as manipulated and incompetent. The sub text was that the Red Army was genuinely awesome: the tragedy was that Russia had become the advance guard of the world's communist movement. According to Suvorov, Stalin really was a revolutionary zealot prepared to use the war against Hitler as an icebreaker to open the way to a new sequence of revolutions across a politically frozen Europe. Most historians are skeptical, and

---

673 For the English version, see Viktor Suvorov, *The Chief Culprit; Stalin's Grand Design to Start World War Two* (USA: Naval Institute Press, 2008).
674 See, for example, Teddy J. Uldricks, 'The Icebreaker Controversy: Did Stalin Plan to Attack Hitler?', *Slavic Review*, Vol. 58, No. 3 (Autumn, 1999): 626–643; Jürgen Förster & Mawdsley, E. 'Hitler and Stalin in Perspective: Secret Speeches on the Eve of Barbarossa', *War In History*, vol. 11, no. 1, (2004): 61–103; and G. Bordiugov, (ed.), *Gotovil li Stalin nastupatel'nuiu voinu protiv Gitlera* (Moscow: AIRO-XX, 1995).

there is little support for the idea that Stalin considered himself ready or was intending to attack Hitler in July 1941, as Suvorov suggests.[675] 'Icebreaker' was a child of its time. In the 1990s, the idea of a 'stolen victory' was openly touted in the Russian press. The question was routinely asked whether it might have been better to surrender to the Nazis and remove the horrendous dictatorship of Stalin whose forced collectivisation and purges had all but destroyed Russia.[676] To this day, Suvorov remains a successful writer about World War Two, but Russians have never embraced his principal thesis. Almost immediately, there was an avalanche of criticism from academic writers. If anything, Suvorov has merely provided a pretext for the revival of pro-Stalin histories of World War Two.[677] While Russia is awash with wild conspiracy theories, a Levada poll found that only 4 percent of those surveyed considered that Stalin and not Hitler was responsible for starting World War Two.[678] Stalin's image is not easily tarnished because it will be forever bound up with the victory over the Nazi invaders.

---

675 See, for example, V. A. Nevezhin 'Stalin's 5 May 1941 addresses: The experience of interpretation', *The Journal of Slavic Military Studies*, 11:1, (1998): 116–146.
676 Tumarkin, 'The Great Patriotic War as myth and memory', pp. 602–03.
677 For some examples of the ReStalinization of World War Two, see G. Bordiugov (ed.), *Gotovil li Stalin nastupatel'nuiu voiny protiv Gitlera* (Moscow: AIRO-XX: 1995, Iurii Emel'ianov, *Stalin: na vershine vlasti* (Moscow: Iauza, 2002), Iurii Emel'ianov, *Marshal Stalin: Tvorets velikoi Pobedy* (Moscow: Iauza, Eksmo, 2007, Alexander Prokhanov, *Kreiser "Iosif Stalin"* (Moscow: Algoritm-Izdat, Eksmo, 2010), Alexander Bushkov, *Krasnyi Monarkh* (Moscow: OLMA, 2010), Vladimir Bushin, *Za Rodiny! Za Stalina!* (Moscow: Algoritm, 2007), V. Polikarpov, *Stalin velikii planirovshchik sovetskoi tsivilizatsii* (Rostov-na-Don: Vladis, Ripol-Klassik, 2007), V. Polikarpov, *Stalin – Vlastelin Istorii* (Rostov-na-Don: Vladis, Riplo-Klassik, 2007), Alexei Isaev, *Zhukov obolgannyi Marshal Pobedy* (Moscow: Iauza, Eksmo, 2012), Mikhail Tumshits, Alexander Papchinskii, *1937 Bolshaia Chistka Nkvd protiv Cheka* (Moscow: Iauza, Eksmo, 2009), A Martirosian, *200 myfof o Staline: Stalin i repressii 1920–1930 godov* (Moscow: Veche, 2008), Alexander Eliseev, *Pravda o 1937 gode. Kto razvizal "Bol'shoi Terror?"* (Moscow: Iauza, 2008), Alexander Eliseev, *1937 Stalin protiv zagovora "globalistov"* (Moscow: Iauza, Eksmo, 2009), Dmitry Lyskov, *Zapretnaia Pravda o "Stalinskikh repressiiakh" "Deti Arbata" Igut!* (Moscow: Iauza, 2012), Alexander Sever, *Stalin protiv "vyrodkov Arbata" 10 Stanskikh udarov po piatoi kolonne* (Moscow: Iauza press, 2011) and Igor Pykhalov, *Velikaia Obolgonnaia Voina*, fourh edition (Moscow: Eksmo, 2012).
678 Russian Public Opinion Research Center, Press Release No. 983, June 23, 2008 (available at http://wciom.com/news/press-rcleascs.html).

The point here is that alternative history does not succeed simply because of its capacity to astonish its readers. Suvorov and Fomenko have much in common when it comes to bold hypotheses and the selective use of evidence. Suvorov's alternative version of who was responsible for starting World War Two is likely to disappear without trace not because it is wrong, but because the message is discordant with a broader narrative about Russian greatness that has to include an uncomplicated story of good versus evil in the Great Patriotic War.

Meanwhile, Medinskii will claim both victory and the middle ground in this battle over Russian history. The point is, however, that the middle ground has moved decisively in a direction that Fomenko and other luminaries of alternative history would approve. Russia is great and autocrats, whether it is Ivan the Terrible or Stalin, will have to be defended if it is a question of defending Russian civilization. Normanism is dying, the Mongols are in danger of disappearing altogether, and Peter the Great is less great because of his Westernizing obsession. In twenty years since the collapse of the Soviet Union, the historical landscape in Russia has changed dramatically. Patriotic history, like Eurasianism, is one of the victors in Russia's post-Communist culture wars.

Conclusion

'The Sleep of Reason Produces Monsters.'

Francisco Goya

The contest presently under way for Russia's future has often taken the form of a battle over the past. For many Russian readers, the muscular approach of alternative history tackles the important questions of national identity in a more satisfying way than the offerings of better trained, but more cautious, academics. Above all, alternative history has helped to invent, or perhaps reinvent, a post-Soviet 'civilisation' imagined as great and committed to Russia's special and imperial path. Multi-ethnic, but somehow still Russian, it is this mythical, timeless Russia that is now attracting the close attention of government ideologues. This narrative has proved therapeutic to those Russians seeking to come to terms with or struggle against the loss of empire that accompanied the Soviet collapse.

Fomenko believes that his history offers the Turks in Russia a new understanding of their past that will prepare them for a new partnership in the Russian Federation. By stressing the fact that the Slav-Turk empire occupied approximately the same territories as the former Soviet Union, Fomenko indirectly lays claim to the former Soviet lands, not in the name of the Great Russian nation as it had been done before, but rather on behalf of a multi-cultural, bilingual, mixed-ethnic empire. But this is still very much an imaginary Russian empire designed to protect an imaginary Russian civilisation and, not surprisingly, Turkic alternative historians dismiss Fomenko as just another Russian imperialist. Some of Fomenko's supporters argue that the concept of the Russian Horde is a relatively benign and harmless channel for Russian nationalism to move towards. Other commentators view the underlying message of Fomenko's version of the past as serving to stir up passions about the inseparable unity of the lands stretching from Ukraine to the Pacific and the historical role of Russia in those regions. Fomenko, though, can be pleased with the direction in which 'history' is moving in the former Soviet space. There are signs that the empire is being recreated, pro-Western reformers are under constant attack, and both the Vikings and the Mongols are in full retreat from their periods of Russian history.

Of the thirty or so alternative historians mentioned by name in this study, all grew up in the Soviet era and all but two are male. They are often highly educated, but their training is in disciplines other than history. As their critics point out, they are mostly amateur historians and propagandists who defy or are ignorant of all the basic principles of the historian's craft. Alternative history plays upon the disillusionment with the liberalism of the 1990s, nostalgia for the order and greatness of the Soviet period, and an enduring xenophobia directed towards the West. It would be easy to dismiss alternative history as the home of the now redundant *homo soveticus*, the flotsam and jetsam of the former Soviet intelligentsia cast adrift in an unfriendly capitalist and democratic sea. Yet, long before it was fashionable to do so, alternative historians were crafting their fantasies about an imperial revival and Western plots. In that sense, they were men ahead of their time.

A recent survey suggested that about three in every four Russians thought that Russia needed an 'official ideology', a view at odds with the post-Communist Russian Constitution, which requires ideological pluralism. The most popular slogan in this poll (37% in favour) was 'Law, Justice and Prosperity', a neat summation of the three things that most Russians think are still absent from their society.[679] If the present Russian government is unable to deliver law, justice, and prosperity, it may be able to deliver a new Russian Empire. If that were to happen, it would be a welcome devleopment for alternative historians, and a development for which they can claim some credit.

---

679 See Adelaida Sigida, 'Soratniki Putina vydvigaiut novuiu Konstitutsiiu', *Mir Novostei*, number 23 (962) 29.05.2012, p. 6.

Bibliography

Abrashkin, A, *Predki russkikh v drevnem mire*, (Moscow: Veche, 2001)
Abrashkin, A, *Drevnie Rossy. Mifologicheskie paralleli i puti migratsii*, (Nizhny Novgorod: NNGU, 1999)
Abrashkin, A, *Chudo-Uydo: Istoriia odnogo perevoplashchenia*, (Nizhny Novgorod: NNGU, 1999)
Abrashkin, A, *Avesta v Russkikh perevodakh*, (Nizhny Novgorod: NNGU, 1997)
Abrashkin, A, *Rus' sredizemnomorskaia i zagadki Biblii*, (Moscow: Veche, 2003)
Abrashkin, A, *Tainy troianskoi voiny i sredizemnomorskaia Rus'*, (Moscow: Veche, 2006)
Abrashkin, A, *Sredizemnomorskaia Rus': velikaia derzhava drevnosti*, (Moscow: Veche, 2006)
Abrashkin, A, *Skifskaia Rus'. Ot Troi do Kieva*, (Moscow: Veche, 2008)
Abrashkin, A, Russkii D avol. *Ot Koshcheia do Volanda*, (Moscow: Iauza, 2009)
Abrashkin, A, *Rus – Ariiskaia Kolybel. Ot Volgi do Troi i sviatoi zemli*, (Moscow: Eksmo, Iauza, 2012)
Abrashkin, A, *Drevnie Tsivilizatsii Russkoi ravniny*, (Moscow: Eksmo, Algoritm, 2012)
Adzhi, M, *My – iz roda Polovetskogo*, (Moscow: Rybinsk, 1992)
Adzhi, M, *Polyn' polovetskogo polia*, (Moscow: Pik-Kontekst, 1994)
Adzhi, M, *Evropa, Turki, velikaia step'*, (Moscow: Mysl', 1998)
Adzhi, M, *Kipchaki*, (Moscow: Novosti, 1999)
Adzhi, M, *Tiurki i mir: sokrovennaia istoriia*, (Moscow: AST, 2004)
Adzhi, M, *Aziatskaia Evropa*, (Moscow: AST, 2006)
Adzhi, M, *Dykhanie Armagedona*, (Moscow: AST, 2006)
Alekseev, A, 'Opiat' o "Velesovoi knige"', *Russkaia literatura*, 1995, No. 2
Antifomenkovskaia mozaika, 5 books, (ed.) Nastenko, I, Gorodetskii, A, (Moscow: Russkaia panorama, 2000, 2001, 2002, 2003)
Artamonov, M, *Istoriia Khazar*, (St-Petersburg: 2002)
Asov, A, *Russkie Vedy: Pesni Ptitsy Gamaiun, Velesova Kniga*, (Moscow: Nauka i religia, 1992)
Asov, A, *Velesova Kniga*, (Moscow: Menedzher, 1994)
Asov, A, *Zvezdnaia Kniga Koliady*, (Moscow: Nauka i religia, 1996)
Asov, A, *Kniga Velesa*, (St-Pteresburg: Politekhnika, 2000)

Asov, A, *Mify i legendy drevnikh slavian,* (Moscow: Nauka i religia, 1998)
Asov, A, *Slavianskie runy i "Boianov gimn",* (Moscow: Veche, 2000)
Asov, A, *Atlanty, arii, slaviane: Istoria i vera,* (Moscow: Fair-Press, 2008)
Asov, A, *Sviato-Ruskkie Vedy. Kniga Velesa,* (Moscow: Fair-Press, 2001)
Asov, A, *Atlantida i Drevniia Rus',* (Moscow: AIF Print, 2001)
Asov, A, *Mir slavianskikh bogov,* (Moscow: Veche, 2002)
Asov, A, *Sviashchennye prarodiny slavian,* (Moscow: Veche, 2003)
Asov, A, *Ruskolan': Drevniaia Rus',* (Moscow: Veche, 2004)
Asov, A, *Runy slavian i "Boianov gimn",* (Moscow: Fair-Press, 2005)
Asov, A, *Pesni Alkonosta/Isvod Zlatogora,* (Moscow: Fair-Press, 2006)
Asov, A, *Tainy russkikh volkhvov,* (Moscow: Veche, 2007)
Asov, A, *Sviato-Ruskkie Vedy. Kniga Koliady,* (Moscow: Grand-Fair, 2008)
Asov, A, *Bogi slavian i rozhdenie Rusi,* (Moscow: Veche, 2008)
Asov, A, *Mify slavian,* (Moscow: AST, 2013)
Astrologiia protiv 'novoi khronologii', (ed.) Nastenko, I, (Moscow, Russkaia panorama, 2001)
Astronomiia protiv 'novoi khronologii', (Moscow: Russkaia panorama, 2001)
Azhgikhina, N, 'Terminator mirovoi istorii', *NG-Nauka,* January 19, 2000
Begunov, Iu, *Tainye sily v istorii Rossii,* (St-Petersburg: 1998)
Begunov, Iu, *Russkaia Istoriia protiv novoi khronologii,* (Moscow: Russkaia panorama, 2001)
Beliavskii, M, *M. Lomonosov i osnovanie Moskovskogo universiteta. K 200 letiuy Moskovskogo universiteta 1755–1955,* ed. by Tikhomirov, (Moscow: MGU, 1955)
Bialko, A, 'My ves', my drevnii mir razrushim?' *Priroda,* 2, 1997
Bocharov, L, Efimov, N, Chachukh, I, Chernyshev, I, *Zagovor protiv russkoi istorii,* (Moscow: ANVIK, 2001)
Bordiugov, G, (ed.), *Gotovil li Stalin nastupatel'nuiu voinu protiv Gitlera,* (Moscow: AIRO-XX, 1995)
Borisenok, Iu, 'Fomenkiada, konets istorii?' *Izvestia,* December 24, 1999
Broshten, V, 'Velikii perebor,' *Zemlia i vselennaia,* 3, 1997
Bushin, V, *Za Rodiny! Za Stalina!* (Moscow: Algoritm, 2007)
Bushkov, A, *Rossiia kotoroi ne bylo,* vol. I, (Moscow: OLMA, 1997)
Bushkov, A, Burovskii, A, *Rossiia kotoroi ne bylo, Russkaia Atlantida,* vol. II, (Moscow: OLMA, 2001)
Bushkov, A, *Rossiia kotoroi ne bylo, mirazhi i prizraki,* vol. III, (Moscow: OLMA, 2004)
Bushkov, A, *Rossiia kotoroi ne bylo. Blesk i krov' gvardeiskogo stoletiia,* vol. IV, (Moscow: OLMA, 2005)

Bushkov, A, *Ivan Groznyi. Krovavyi poet*, (Moscow: OLMA, 2007)
Bushkov, A, *Chingiz-khan. Neizvestnaia Aziia*, (Moscow: OLMA, 2008)
Bushkov, A, *Rasputin. Vystrely iz proshlogo*, (OLMA, Moscow, 2008)
Bushkov, A, *Stalin: Krasnyi monarch*, (Moscow: OLMA, 2010)
Bushkov, A, *Stalin: Ledianoi tron*, (Moscow: OLMA, 2008)
Burovskii, A, *Nesbyvshaiasia Rossiia*, (Moscow: Eksmo, 2007)
Burovskii, A, *Ariiskaia Rus': lozh' i Pravda o vysshei rase*, (Moscow: Eksmo, 2007)
Chudinov, V, *Zagadki Slavianskoi Pis'mennosti*, (Moscow: Veche, 2002)
Chudinov, V, *Runitsa i tainy arkheologii Rusi*, (Moscow: Veche, 2003)
Chudinov, V, *Sviashchennye kamni I khramy drevnikh slavian*, (Moscow: Fair-Press, 2004)
Chudinov, V, *Tainye runy Drevnei Rusi*, (Moscow: Veche, 2005)
Chudinov, V, *Vernyom etruskov Rusi*, (Moscow: Pokolenie, 2006)
Chudinov, V, *Russkie Runy*, (Moscow: Alva-Pervaia, 2006)
Chudinov, V, *Pravda o sokrovishchakh Retry*, (Moscow: Alva-Pervaia, 2006)
Chudinov, V, *Tainopis' v risunkakh Pushkina*, (Moscow: Pokolenie, 2007)
Chudinov, V, *Tainopis' na russkikh ikonakh*, (Moscow: Alva-Pervaia, 2008)
Chudinov, V, *Tainye Znaki Drevnei Rusi*, (Moscow: Algoritm, 2009)
Chudinov, V, *Vagria. Variagi Rusi Yara: ocherk depolitizirovannoi istoriografii*, (Moscow: Grand-Fair, 2009)
Chudinov, V, *Runy-Skazy Rusi kamennogo veka*, (Moscow: Traditisia, 2012)
Chudinov, V, *Russkaia osnova kitaiskoi pismennosti*, (Moscow: Traditsia, 2012)
Chudinov, V, *Tainy Sviashchennykh kamnei Rusi*, (Moscow: Traditsia, 2012)
Chudinov, V, *Chto my znaem ob Etruskakh*, (Moscow: Traditisia, 2012)
Chudinov, V, *Alternativnaia istoriografia*, (Moscow: Traditsia, 2013)
Demidenko, M, *Po Sledam SS v Tibete*, (St-Petersburg: Olma, 2003)
Demin, V, *Otkyda ty, russkoe plemia?* (Moscow: Veche, 1996)
Demin, V, *Tainy Russkogo naroda*, (Moscow: Veche, 1997)
Demin, V, *Giperboreia – kolybel' tsivilizatsii*, (Moscow: Veche, 1997)
Demin, V, *Zagadki Russkogo severa*, (Moscow: Veche, 1999)
Demin, V, *Tainy zemli Russkoi*, (Moscow: Veche, 2000)
Demin, V, *Giperboreia: istoricheskie korni russkogo naroda*, (Moscow: Veche, 2000)
Demin, V, *Drevnee drevnosti: rossiiskaia prototsivilizatsia* (Moscow: Veche, 2003)
Demin, V, *V poiskakh kolybeli tsivilizatsii* (Moscow: Veche, 2004).
Dragunskii, D, 'Massovia kultura dlia izbrannykh', *Itogi*, March 10, 1998

Drevnerusskaia literatura, (Moscow: Shkola-press, 1993)
Eliseev, G, Stankova, I, 'Pod znamenem folk-istorii', *Chitaiushchaia Rossiia*, 2, 1998
Eliseev, A, *Pravda o 1937 gode. Kto razviazal "Bol'shoi Terror"?* (Moscow: Iauza, 2008)
Eliseev, A, *1937 Stalin protiv zagovora "globalistov"*, (Moscow: Iauza, Eksmo, 2009)
Emel'ianov, Iu, *Stalin: na vershine vlasti*, (Moscow: Iauza, 2002)
Emel'ianov, Iu, *Marshal Stalin: Tvorets velikoi Pobedy*, (Moscow: Iauza, 2007)
Fedotov, G, "*Sud'ba i grekhi Rossii*", (St.-Petersburg: 1992)
Fomenko, A, Nosovskii, G, Kalashnikov, V, *Datirovka zvezdnogo kataloga 'Almagest', geometricheskii i statisticheskii analiz*, (Moscow: Faktorial, 1995)
Fomenko, A, Nosovskii, G, Kalashnikov, V, *Astronomicheskii analiz khronologii: Almagest. Zodiaki*, (Moscow: Delovoi ekspress, 2000)
Fomenko, A, Nosovskii, G, *Novaia khronologiia i kontseptsiia drevnei Rusi, Anglii, Rima. Fakty, statistikia, gipotesy*, II volumes, (Moscow: State University press (MGU), 1995, 1996)
Fomenko, A, *Novaia khronologiia Gretsii. Antichnost' i srednevekov'e*, II volumes, (Moscow: MGU, 1996)
Fomenko, A, Nosovskii, G, *Imperiia: Rus', Turtsia, Kitai, Evropa, Egipet. Novaia matematicheskaia khronologiia drevnosti*, (Moscow: 'Faktorial press', 1996, 1997, 1998, 1999)
Nosovskii, G, Fomenko, A, *Rus' i Rim. Pravil'no li my poinimaem istoriiu Evropy i Azii?* II volumes, (Moscow: 'Olimp', 'ACT ', 1997)
Fomenko, A, Nosovskii, G, *Novaia khronologiia Rusi*, (Moscow: Faktorial press, Moscow, 1997)
Fomenko, A, Nosovskii, G, *Matematicheskaia khronologia bibleiskikh sobytii*, (Moscow: Nauka, 1997)
Fomenko, A, "Smysl russkogo dela v sokhranenii imperii," *Nezavisimaia Gazeta*, 1996, November 21.
Fomenko, A, 'Globalnaia khronologicheskaia karta', *Khimia i Zhizn'*, 9, 1983
Fomenko, A, *Metody matematicheskogo analiza istoricheskikh tekstov: prilozhenie k khronologii*, (Moscow: Nauka, 1996)
Fomenko, A, Nosovskii, G, *Bibleiskaia Rus'*, II volumes, (Moscow: 'Faktorial press', 1998, 2000)
Fomenko, A, Nosovskii, G, *Rus'-Orda na stranitsakh bibleiskikh knig*, (Moscow: 'Anvik', 1998)
Fomenko, A, Nosovskii, G, *Vvedenie v novuiu khronologiiu, kakoi seichas vek?* (Moscow: 'Kraft+Lean', 1999)

Fomenko, A, Nosovskii, G, *Rekonstruktsia vseobshchei istorii. Issledovaniia 1999–2000*, (Moscow: 'Delovoi ekspress', 1999)
Fomenko, A, Nosovskii, G, *Kakoi seichas vek?* (Moscow: Aif-Print, 2002)
Fomenko, A, Nosovskii, G, *Khronologiia*, 2002–, seven volumes.
Fomenko, A, Nosovskii, G, *Gde ty, pole Kulikovo?* (Moscow: AST, Astrel', VKT, 2010)
Fomenko, A, Nosovskii, G, *Shakhname: Iranskaia letopis Velikoi Imperii 12-17 vekov,* (Moscow: AST, Astrel', VKT, 2010)
Fomenko, A, Nosovskii, G, *Vatikan. Zodiak Astronomii. Stambul I Vatikan. Kitaiskie goroskopy* (Moscow: AST, Astrel', 2010)
Fomenko, A, Nosovskii, G, *Gospodin Velikii Novgorod. S Volkhova ili s Volgi Poshla Russkaia Zemlia?,* (Moscow: AST, Astrel', VKT, 2010)
Fomenko, A, Nosovskii, G, *Antichnost' – eto srednevekovie,* (Moscow: AST, 2011)
Fomenko, A, Nosovskii, G, *Nebesnyi Kalendar' Drevnikh,* (Moscow: AST, 2011)
Fomenko, A, *Meniaem daty, meniatsia vse,* (Moscow: AST, 2011)
Fomenko, A, Nosovskii, G, *Osnovanie Rima. Nachalo Ordynskoi Rusi. Posle Khrista. Troianskaia voina,* (Moscow: AST, Astrel', 2011)
Fomenko, A, Nosovskii, G, *Novaia Khronologiia Rusi,* (Moscow: AST, 2012)
Fomenko, A, Nosovskii, G, *Taina Russkoi Istorii,* (Moscow: Astrel', 2012)
Fomenko, A, Nosovskii, G, *Rastsvet Tsarstva. Gde na samom dele puteshestvoval Marko Polo. Kto takie italianskie Etruski. Drevnii Egipet. Skandinavia. Rus-Orda na starinnykh kartakh,* (Moscow: AST, Astrel', 2012)
Fomenko, A, Nosovskii, G, *Zvesdy svidetel'stvuiut. Datirovka zvezdnogo kataloga Al'magesta,* (Moscow: AST, 2012)
Fomenko, A, Nosovskii, G, *Kak bylo na samom dele. Rekonstruktsiia podlinnoi istorii,* (Moscow: Astrel', 2012)
Fomenko, A, Nosovskii, G, *Zapadnyi Mif. Antichnyi Rim i nemetskie Gabsburgi – eto otrazhenie Russko-Ordynskoi istorii 14–17 vekov. Nasledie Velikoi Imperii v culture Evrazii i Ameriki,* (Moscow: Astrel, 2012)
Fomenko, A, Nosovskii, G, T. Fomenko, *Russkie Korni "Drevnei" Latyni. Yazyki i Pis'mennost' Velikoi Imperii,* (Moscow: Astrel', 2012)
Fomenko, A, Nosovskii, G, *Pugachev i Suvorov. Taina Sibirsko-amerikanskoi istorii,* (Moscow, Vladimir: Astrel', VKT, 2012)
Fomenko, A, Nosovskii, G, *Chudo Sveta na Rusi pod Kazan'iu. Kak bylo na samom dele. Pervaia Kaaba byla na Rusi pod Kazan'iu,* (Moscow: AST, 2013)
Fomin, V, (ed), *Varyago-Russkii vopros v istoriografii,* (Moscow: Russkaia panorama, 2010)

Globa, P, *O chem molchit Luna*, (Moscow: 1991)
Globa, P, *Zhivoi Ogon'. Uchenie drevnikh Ariev*, (Moscow: 1996)
Golubtsova, E, Koshelenko, G, 'Istoriia drevnego mira i novye metodiki', *Voprosy istorii*, 8, 1982
Gorbachev, N, 'Mify novoi khronologii ili raskrutka na temnoi volne', *Moskovskii literator*, 5 (731), 2000
Grinevich, G, *Praslaviaskaia pis'mennost': resultaty deshifrovki*, vols one and two (Moscow: Obshchestvennaia pol'za, 1993, 1997)
Grinevich, G, *V nachale bylo slovo...Slavianskaia semantika lingvisticheskikh elementov geneticheskogo koda*, (Moscow: Obshchestvennaia Pol'za, 1997)
Grinevich, G, *Nachalo gennoi lingvistiki*, (Moscow: Letopis', 2001)
Gumilev, L, *Drevniaia Rus i velikaia step'*, (Moscow: Mysl, 1992)
Gumilev, L, *Drevnie Turki*, (Moscow: 1999)
Gumilev, L, *Poiski vymyshlennogo tsarstva*, (Moscow: Tanais, 1994)
Gumilev, L, *Chernaia legenda*, (Moscow: Ekopross, AST, 1994, 2002)
Gumilev, L, *Ot Rusi k Rossii*, (Leningrad: 1989)
Gumilev, L, *Etnogenez i biosfera zemli*, (Leningrad: 1989)
Gumilev, L, *Geografiya etnosa v istoricheskii period*, (Leningrad: 1990)
Gumilev, L, 'Biografiya nauchnoi teorii ili avtonekrolog', *Znamia*, 1988
Guseva, N, *Slaviane i Arii. Put' bogov i slov*, (Moscow: Fair-Press, 2001)
Guseva, N, *Russkii Sever – prarodina indo-slavov: iskhod predkov ariev i slavian*, (Moscow: Veche, 2003)
Guts, A, *Mnogovariantnaia Istoriia Rossii*, ACT, 2000, (Moscow: Poligon, 2001)
Guts, A, 'Mif o vosstanovlenii istoricheskoi pravdy', *Matematicheskie struktury i modelirovanie*, 6, (Omsk: OMGU, 1998)
Guts, A, *Podlinnaia Istoriia Rossii*, (Omsk: OMGU, 1999)
Guts, A, 'Modeli mnogovariantnoi istorii', *Matematicheskie struktiru i modelirovanie*, 4, (Omsk: OMGU, 1999)
Hamtsiev, V, Balaev, A, *David Soslan, Friedrich Barbarossa, Alaniia ot Palestiny to Britanii*, (Vladikavkaz: 1992)
Isaev, A, *Zhukov Obolgannyi Marshal Pobedy*, (Moscow: Iauza, Eksmo, 2012)
Istoriia otechestva: Drevniaia Rus', IX–XIII vekov; Moskovskaia Rus', XIII–XVI vekov; Moskovskoe Tsarstvo, XVI–XVII vekov, (St-Petersburg: Norint, 2000)
Iskhakov, D, 'Istoriia naroda' in *Tatary, Tatarstan: Spravochnik* ed. Mukhametshin, R, (Kazan: Tatknigizdat, 1993)
Istarkhov, V, *Udar Russkikh Bogov*, (Moscow: 1999)
Istoriia i antiIstoriia: *Kritika "novoi khronologii" akademika A. Fomenko*, (ed.), Nastenko, I, (Moscow: , Iazyki russkoi kultury, 2000)

Kandyba, V, *Istoriia ruskogo naroda*, (St-Pteresburg: Lan', 1996)
Kandyba, V, *Rigveda: religiia i ideologiia Russkogo naroda*, (Moscow: Maket, 1996)
Kandyba, V, Zolin, P, *Real'naia Istoriia Rossii*, (St-Petersburg. Lan', 1997)
Kandyba, V, Zolin, P, *Istoriia i ideologia ruskkogo naroda*, (St-Pteresburg, Lan', 1997, II volumes)
Kandyba, V, *Istoriia Russkoi Imperii*, (Moscow: Efko, 1997)
Kandyba, V, *Istoriia velikogo russkogo naroda*, (Moscow: Svetoton, 2000)
Kesler, Ia, *Russkaia tsivilizatsia*, (Moscow: Eko-press, 2000, 2002)
Kesler, Ia, *Kniga tsivilazatsii*, (Moscow: Eko-press, 2001)
Kharitonovich, D, 'Fenomen Fomenko', *Novyi Mir*, 3, 1998
Khrestomatiia po drevnerusskoi literature, (Moscow: Prosveschenie, 1973)
Khlebnikov, M, *Teoriia zagovora*, (Moscow: Kuchkovo Pole, 2012)
Khlestkov, Ui, Ura. *Smyslovoi slovar bazovykh slov ruskkogo iazyka* (Moscow, TOO Nov na: 1996)
Kifishin, A, *Drevnee Sviatilishche Kamennaia Mogila*, (Kiev: Aratta, 2001)
Klimishin, I, *Kalendar' i knronologia*, (Moscow: Nauka, 1990)
Kliuchevskii, V, *Neopublikovannye proizvedenia*, (Moscow: Nauka, 1983)
Куда идут мастера фолк-хистори?" *Novaya Gazeta*, 10-06-28 (retrieved March 11, 2013)
Kungurov, A, *Kievskoi Rusi ne bylo, ili chto skryvaiut istoriki*, (Moscow: Eksmo, Algoritm: 2011)
Kuz'min, A, *Padenie Peruna. Stanovlenie Khristianstva na Rusi*, (Moscow: 1988)
Lapenkov, Vladimir, *Istoriia Netraditsionnoi Orientatsii, Legendy i Mify Vsemirnoi Istorii*, (Moscow: Bystrov, 2006)
Laushkin, A, *Lozh' novoi khronologii*, (Moscow: Palomnik, 2002)
Lesnoi, S, *Peresmotr osnov istorii slavian*, (Melbourne: Omega-Press, 1956)
Lesnoi, S, *Istoriia Russov v neizvraschennom vide*, pts. 1–7, (Paris: 1953–1958)
Leskov, S, 'Po raschetam vyshlo: sluzhil Iisus Khristos rimskim papoi', *Izvestia*, January 29, 1997
Lomonosov, M, *Trudy po russkoi istorii, obschestvenno-ekonomicheskim voprosam i geografii 1747–1765*, (Moscow, Leningrad: 1952)
Lomonosov, M, *Polnoe sobranie sochinenii*, ed. Vavilov, S, 10 volumes, (Moscow-Leningrad: 1950–1959)
Lyskov, D, *Zapretnaia Pravada o "Stalinskikh prepressiiakh" 'Deti Arbata" Igut!* (Moscow: Iauza. 2012)
Lyzlov, A, *Istoriia Skifiiskaia*, (Moscow: Nauka, 1990)
Martirosian, A, *200 myfof o Staline: Stalin i repressii 1920–1930 godov*, (Moscow: Veche, 2008)

Medinskii, V, *Mify o Rossii: o russkom pianstve, leni i zhestokosti,* (Moscow, 2002–2006)
MGU History Department (ed.), *Kritika novoi khronologii,* (Moscow: Anvik, 2001)
Mishin, D, *Sakaliba (slaviane) v islamskom mire v rannee srednevekov'e,* (Moscow: In-t Vostokovedeniia RAN, Kraft+, 2002)
Morozov, N, Khristos, *Istoriia chelovecheskoi kultury v estestvennonauchnom osveshchenii,* 7 volumes, (Moscow, Leningrad: Gosizdat, 1924–1932)
Morozov, S, *Zagovor protiv narodov Rossii segodnia,* (Moscow: Algoritm, 1999)
Muldashev, E, *Misticheskaia Aura Rossii,* (Moscow: 2008)
Nasonov, A, 'K voprosy ob obrazovanii drevnerusskoi narodnosti,' *Vestnik AN SSSR,* 1951, 8
Nastenko, I, (ed.) *Istoriia i antiIstoriia: Kritika "novoi khronologii" akademika A. Fomenko* (Moscow: Yazyki russkoi kultury, 2000); Nastenko, I, (ed.) *Antifomenkovskaia mozaika* 5 books, (Moscow: Russkaia panorama, 2000, 2001, 2002, 2003)
Nechvolodov, A, *Skazaniia o Russkoi Zemle,* (Moscow: Belyi Gorod, 2007)
Novgorodov, N, *Sibirskii Pokhod Alexandra Makedonskogo,* (Tomsk: Agraf-Press, 2006)
Novgorodov, N, *Sibirskaia Prarodina: v poiskakh Giperborei,* (Moscow: Belye Al'vy, 2006)
Oleinikov, D, 'Globalnyi rozygrysh', *Rodina,* 6, 1997
Peredolskii, V, *Bytovye ostanki ilmentsev,* (Moscow: 1893)
Petukhov, Iu, *Kolybel' Zevsa: Istoriia Russov ot antichnosti do nashikh dnei,* (Moscow: Mysl, 1998)
Petukhov, Iu, *Gibel' Rossii,* (Moscow: Mysl, 1999)
Petukhov, Iu, *Istoria Russov: 40000 let do nashei ery,* vol. I, (Moscow: Mysl, 2000)
Petukhov, Iu, *Russkaia Khazaria,* (Moscow: Mysl, 2001)
Petukhov, Iu, *Tainy drenikh russov,* (Moscow: Veche, 2001, 2002, 2003)
Petukhov, Iu, *Rusy drevnego Vostoka,* (Moscow: Veche, 2003)
Plano Carpini, *Istoriia Mongalov/Rubruck, Puteshestvia v vostochnye strany/kniga Marko Polo,* (Moscow: Mysl', 1997)
Pogodin, M, *Kniaz Andrey Yurievich Bogoliubsky,* (Moscow: 1850)
Poliakov, Iu, *Istoricheskaia nauka: liudi i problemy,* (Moscow: Rosspen, 1999)
Polikarpov, V, *Stalin - velikii planirovshchik Sovetskoi tsivilizatsii,* (Rostov-na-Don: Vladis, Ripol-Klassik, 2007)
Polikarpov, V, *Stalin – Vlastelin Istorii,* (Rostov-na-Don: Vladis, Ripol-Klassik, 2007)

Pokhlebkin, W, *Tatary i Rus'*, (Moscow: Mezhdunarodnye otnoshenia, 2001)
Popov, I, *Rossiia i Kitai: 300 let na grani voiny*, (Moscow: Ast, Astrel', Ermak, 2004)
Poliakovskii, V, *Tataro-Mongoly, Evraziia, Mnogovariantnost'*, (Moscow: 2002)
Ponomarev, A, 'O chem svidetelstvuiut novye datirovki Ptolemeia', *Istoriia i komputer*, 22, 1998
Portnov, A, 'Iaroslav Mudry byl khanom batuem?' *Trud*, September 11, 1998
Prokhanov, A, *Kreiser "Iosif Stalin"*, (Moscow: Algoritm-Izdat, Eksmo, 2010)
Pykhalov, I, *Velikaia Obolgonnaia Voina*, fourh edition, (Moscow: Eksmo, 2012)
Rich, V, 'Byl li temnyi period?' *Khimia i Zhizn'*, 9, 1983
Platonov, O, *Russkaia tsivilizatsia*, (Moscow: Rada, 1992)
Revzin, L, *Bessmertnyi Sulakadzev*, (Moscow: Russkaia Literatura, 1979)
Rodina, Collection of articles on the Mongols, 3–4, 1997
Russkaia istoriia protiv 'novoi khronologii', (Moscow: Russkaia panorama, 2001)
Rybakov, B, *Kievskaia Rus'*, (Moscow: Progress, 1984)
Rybakov, B, 'O preodolenii samoobmana,' *Voprosy istorii*, 1971, 3
Rybakov, B, Sakharov, A, Preobrazhensky, A, Krasnobaev, B, *Istoriia otechestva*, (Moscow: Prosveshchenie, 1993)
Rybakov, B, 'Problema obrazovaniia drevnerusskoi narodnosti,' *Voprosy Istorii*, 1952, 9
Sandulov, Iu, *Istoriia Rossii, narod i vlast'*, (St-Petersburg: 1997)
Sakharov, A, and Buganov, V, *Istoriia Rossii*, (Moscow: Prosveschenie, 1995)
Sbornik Russkogo istoricheskogo obshchestva, vol. 3, (ed.) Nastenko, (Moscow: Russkaia panorama, 2000)
Scherbakov, V, *Gde zhili geroi eddicheskikh mifof*, (Moscow: 1989)
Scherbakov, V, *Gde iskat' Atlantidu*, (Moscow: 1990)
Shcherbakov, V, *Vse ob Atlantide*, M., 1990.
Scherbakov, V, *Asgard –gorod Bogov*, (Moscow: 1991)
Sever, A, *Stalin protiv "vyrodkov Arbata" 10 Stalinskikh udarov po piatoi kolonne*, (Moscow: Iauza, 2011)
Shakhmatov, A, *Razyskania o russkikh letopisyakh*, (Moscow: Kuchkovo pole, 2001)
Shilov, Ui, *Djerela*, (Kiev: Aratta, 2002)
Sedov, V, *U istokov vostochnoslavianskoi gosudarstvennosti*, 'URSS', (Moscow: 1999)
Shreider, Iu, 'Ot Kolumba – k Niutonu', *Znanie-sila*, 4, 1983

Shmidt, S, *Fenomen Fomenko* (Moscow: Nauka, 2005)
Shul'ts, P, *Tavro-skifskaia ekspeditsiia v Krymu* (Simferopol': Sovetskii Krym, 1946)
Shul'ts, P, *Mavzolei Neapolia skifskogo* (Moscow, 1953)
Соглашение "О жрецах славянских" от 23 мая 2012 года", retrieved March 11, 2013
Sorokin, P, *O Russkoi natsii: Rossiia i Amerika, teoria natsionalnogo voprosa*, (Moscow: 1994)
Skrynnikov, R, *Boris Godunov*, (Moscow-Leningrad: Academic International Press, 1982)
Skrynnikov, R, *Ivan Groznyi*, (Moscow: Nauka, 1975)
Smirnov, A, 'Globalnyi sdvig', *Rodina*, 6, 1997
Storozhev, A, Storozhev, V, *Rossiia vo vremeni*, book 1, (Moscow: ANVIK, Veche, 1997)
Tak ono i okazalos': kritika 'novoi khronologii, (ed.) Chashchikhin, U, (Moscow: ANVIK, 2001)
Tvorogov, O, Chto zhe takoe «Vlesova kniga»? *Russkaia literatura*, 1998, No 2
Tilak, B, *Arkticheskaia rodina v vedakh*, translation by Guseva, (M: Fair-Press, 2001)
Tumshits, M, Papchinskii, A, *1937 Bolshaia Chistka NKVD protiv CheKa*, (Moscow: Iauza, Eksmo, 2009)
Uliankin, N, *Antinauchnaia sensatsia (o gipotezakh Fomenko)*, (Moscow: 1999)
Valianskii, S, Kaliuznyi, D, *Put' na vostok ili bez vesti propavshie vo vremeni*, (Moscow: Kraft+Lean, 1997)
Vinskaia, L, 'Narkotik po imeni Bushkov', *Argumenty i Fakty*, 44(889), 1997
Vol'fkovich, S, 'Nikolai Aleksandrovich Morozov, ego zhizn' i trudy po khimii', *Priroda*, 1947, no. 11
Volodikhin, D, Oleinikov, D, Eliseeva, O, *Istoriia Rossii v melkii goroshek*, (Moscow: Manufactura-Edinstvo, 1998)
Volodokhin, D, 'Uchil li Khristos na Altae?' *Knizhnoe obozrenie*, 9, 1999
Volodokhin, D, 'Fenomen folk-istorii,' *Otechestvennaia Istoriia*, 4, 2000
Yanin, V, 'Byl li Novgorod Iaroslavlem, a Batyi – Ivanom Kalitoi', *Isvestia*, June 11, 1998
Yanin, V, 'Ziiaiuschie vysoty akademika Fomenko', *Rodina*, 4, 2000
Yanov, A, *Posle Eltsina*, (Moscow: 1995)
Yanov, A, *Rossiia protiv Rossii*, (Sibirskii khronograf, 1999)
Zharnikova, S, *Arkhaicheskie Korni Traditisionnoi Kultury Russkogo severa*, (Moscow: MDK, 2003)
Zharnikova, S, *Zolotaia Nit'* (Vologda: 2003)

Zlobin, E, 'Mashinochitaemye dokumenty v svete novoi khronologii', *Informatsionnyi biulletin Assotsiatsii "Istoriia i Komputer"*, 16, 1996

Sources published outside of Russia:

Aaronovich, D, *Voodoo histories. The Role of Conspiracy in Shaping Modern History*, (London: Johnathan Cape, 2009)

Abu-Lughod, Janet, L, *Before European hegemony: the world system A. D. 1250–1350*, (Oxford: Oxford University Press, 1991)

Andreev, A, 'Europe or Asia', *Herald of the Russian Academy of Sciences*, 2010, Vol. 80, No. 5

Anthony, David, The *Horse, The Wheel, and Language*, (Princeton: Princeton University Press 1995)

Arch Getty, J, *Practicing Stalinism: Bolsheviks, Boyars, and the Persistence of Tradition*, (New Haven: Yale University Press, 2013)

Arias-King, Fredo, Arlene King De Arias, and Fredo Arias De La Canal, 'Russia's Borderline Personality', *Demokratizatsiya*, 16.2, 2008

Aron, L, 'Russia's revolution', *Commentary*, Nov. 2002, v114, i4

Aron, L, 'The Problematic Pages', *New Republic*, 239 (5), 2008

Bassin, M, 'Russia between Europe and Asia: The Ideological Construction of Geographical Space', *Slavic Review*, 50, 1, 1991

Bassin, M, '*Asia*' in Nicholas Rzhevsky (ed.), *Modern Russian Culture*, (Cambridge: Cambridge University Press, 1988)

Beichelt, Timm, 'Two variants of the Russian radical right: Imperialism and social nationalism', *Communist and Post-Communist Studies*, 42, 2009

Billington, J, *Russia in Search of Itself*, (Washington: Woodrow Wilson Research Center, 2004)

Black, J, 'The State School Interpretation of Russian History: A reappraisal of its genetic origins', *Jahrbucher for Geschichte Osteuropas*, 2, 173

Black, J, *G.F. Mueller and the Imperial Russian Academy* (Kingston and Montreal: McGill Queen's University Press, 1986)

Bray, W, *Russian Frontiers from Muscovy to Khrushcev*, (Bobbs-Merrill Company, 1963)

Brandenberger, David, *National Bolshevism: Stalinist mass culture and the formation of modern Russian national identity, 1931–1956*, (Cambridge: Harvard University Press, MA, 2002)

Brandenberger, David, 'A new Short Course? A. V. Filippov and the Russian state's search for a 'usable past'', *Kritika*, 10.4, 2009

Breully, J, *Nationalism and the State*, (Manchester University Press, 1982)

Browne, E, *A History of Persian literature under Tartar Dominion*, (Cambridge: Cambridge University Press, 1920)

Brubaker, R, *Nationalism Refrained. Nationhood and the National Question in the New Europe*, (Cambridge: Cambridge University Press, 1996)

Brudny, Y, *Reinventing Russia: Russian Nationalism and the Soviet State, 1953–1991*, (Cambridge: Harvard University Press, Massachusetts, 1998)

Bryant, E, *Quest for the Origins of Vedic Culture: The Indo-Aryan Migration*, (Oxford: Oxford University Press, 2004

Byrnes, R, *V. O. Kliuchevskii. Historian of Russia*, (Bloomington: Indiana University Press, 1995)

Canovan, M, *Nationhood and Political Theory*, (Cheltenham: Edward Elgar, 1996)

Carnaghan, Ellen, 'The Difficulty of Measuring support for democracy in a changing society: evidence from Russia', *Democratisation*, 18:3

Carr, F, *Ivan the Terrible*, (Totowa, New Jersey: Barnes and Nobles, 1981)

Chinn, J, and Kaiser, R, (eds), *Russians as the new minority: ethnicity and nationalism in the Soviet successor states*, (Boulder: Westview Press, 1996)

Chulos, C, and Piirainen, T, *The Fall of an Empire, the Birth of a Nation: national identities in Russia*, (Aldershot: Ashgate, 2000)

Christian, David, *Russia, Central Asia and Mongolia*, (Malden: Blackwell Publishers, 1998)

Clark, K, *The Soviet Novel: History as Ritual*, (Bloomington: Indiana University Press, 2000)

Cleaves, Francis Woodman (ed), *The Secret History of the Mongols*, (Cambridge, Massachusetts: Harvard University Press, 1982)

Cross, S, Sherbowitz-Wetzor, O, *The Russian Primary Chronicle*, Laurentian text, (Cambridge, Massachusetts: The Medieval Academy of America, 1953)

Daniels, V, *Tatishchev: Guardian of the Petrine Revolution*, (Philadelphia: Franklin Publishing Company, 1973)

Davidson, H, *The Viking Road to Byzantium*, (London: Allen and Unwin, 1976)

Davies, N, *Europe: a history*, (Oxford: Oxford University Press, 1996)

Davies, S, *Popular Opinion in Stalin's Russia: terror, propaganda, and dissent, 1934–1941*, (Cambridge: Cambridge University Press, 1997)

Davies, R, *Soviet History in the Yeltsin Era,* (Basingstoke: Macmillan, 1997)

Devlin, J, *Slavophiles and Commissars: Enemies of democracy in modern Russia,* (Macmillan: Basingstoke, 1999; New York: St. Martin's Press, 1999)

Diacu, F, *The Lost Millennium: History's Timetables under Siege* (Baltimore: Johns Hopkins University Press, 2011)

Fennel, J, *Prince Kurbsky's History of Ivan IV*, (Cambridge: Cambridge University Press, 1965)

Finkel, E, & Brudny, Y, 'Russia and the colour revolutions', *Democratization*, 19:1, 2012

Fennel, J, *Crisis of Medieval Russia, 1200–1304*, (London: Longman, 1983)

Fomenko, A, *History: Fiction or Science*, vol. 1, (London: Delamere, 2003)

Franklin, S, and Shepard, J, *The Emergence of Rus, 750–1200*, (London: Longman, 1996)

Furedi, F, *Therapy Culture: Cultivating Vulnerability in an Uncertain Age*, (London: Routledge, 2003)

Gellner, E, *Nations and Nationalism*, (Ithaca: Cornell University Press, 1983)

Gill, G, *Symbolism and Regime Change in Russia*, (Cambridge: Cambridge University Press, 2012)

Gleeson, W, 'The course of Russian History According to an eighteenth Century layman', *Laurentian University Review*, 10, 1, 1977

Grekov, B, *Kiev Rus*, trans. by Sdobnikov, (Moscow: Foreign Languages Publishing House, 1959)

Gumilev, L, *Searches for an imaginary kingdom: the legend of the kingdom of Prester John*, translated by R.E.F. Smith, (Cambridge: Cambridge University Press, 1987)

Halperin, C, *Russia and the Golden Horde: the Mongol impact on modern medieval history*, (Bloomington: Indiana University Press, 1985)

Halperin, C, 'False Identity and Multiple Indentities in Russian History: The Mongol Empire and Ivan the Terrible', *The Carl Beck Papers in Russian and East European Studies* [Online], (2011)

Hastings, A, *The construction of nationhood: ethnicity, religion, and nationalism*, (Cambridge: Cambridge University Press, 1997)

Hedlund, Stefan, *Russia's 'Market' Economy: A Bad Case of Predatory Capitalism*, (London: UCL Press, 1999)

Hedlund, Stefan, 'Vladimir the Great, Grand Prince of Muscovy: Resurrecting the Russian Service State', *Europe-Asia Studies*

Hellie, R, 'The Structure of Russian Imperial History. Toward a Dynamic Model', *History and Theory*, 44, December 2005

Hobsbawn, E, *Nations and Nationalism since 1780: Program, Myth, Reality*, (Cambridge University Press, 1990)

Hobsbawn, E, and Ranger, T, (eds), *The Invention of tradition*, (Cambridge: Cambridge University Press, 1983)

Hoffman, D, and Kotsonis, Y (eds), *Russian Modernity: Politics, Knowledge, Practices*, (New York: St. Martin's Press, 2000)

Horvath, R, 'Apologist of Putinism? Solzhenitsyn, the Oligarchs, and the Specter of Orange Revolution', *The Russian Review*, 70, 2011

Hosking G, and Schopflin, G, *Myths and Nationhood*, (London: Hurst and Company, 1997)

Hosking, G, *Russia and the Russians*, (Cambridge, Massachusetts: Harvard University Press, 2001)
Hosking, G, *Russia. People and Empire 1552–1917*, (London, 1997)
Howe, S, *The False Dmitri*, (London: Williams and Norgate, 1916)
Katz, M, 'Primakov Redux? Putin's Pursuit of "Multipolarism" in Asia', *Democratizatsiya*, 14.1, Winter 2006
Keenan, E, 'On Certain Mythical Beliefs and Russian Behaviors', in *The Legacy of History in Russia and the New States of Eurasia*, ed. S. Frederick Starr, (NY, M.E. Sharpe, Armonk, 1994)
Kerblay, B, *Modern Soviet Society*, (London: Methuen, 1983)
Keyser, C, et al., 'Ancient DNA provides new insights into the history of south Siberian Kurgan people', *Human Genetics,* 126:3, 2009
Khazanov, A, 'Ethnic nationalism in the Russian Federation', *Daedalus*, summer 1997, v126, i3
Khazanov, A, *After the USSR: Ethnicity, Nationalism, and Politics in the Commonwealth of Independent States*, (Madison: University of Wisconsin Press, 1996)
Kuzmina, E, and Mair, V, *The Prehistory of the Silk Road*, (University of Pennsylvania press, 2007)
Laruelle, M, 'The Two Faces of Contemporary Eurasianism: An Imperial Version of Russian Nationalism', *Nationalities Papers*, 32: 1, (March 2004)
Laruelle, M, *Russian Eurasianism: An Ideology of Empire* (Washington, 2008)
Laruelle, M, 'Negotiating history: memory wars in the near abroad and pro-Kremlin youth movements', *Demokratizatsiya* 19.3 (2011)
Laruelle, M, 'Conspiracy and Alternate History in Russia: A Nationalist Equation for Success?' *The Russian Review*, 71 (2012)
Lieven, A, 'The Weakness of Russian Nationalism', *Survival*, vol. 41, no. 2, Summer 1999
Linan, Miguel Vazquez, 'History as a Propaganda Tool in Putin's Russia', *Communist and Post-Communist Studies*, 2010, Volume 43, Issue 2
Marsden, John, *Harald Hardrada*, (Sutton: Oxbow books, 2007)
Martin, Janet, *Medieval Russia 980–1584*, (Cambridge University Press, 1995)
Masson, J, Smith Jr., 'Nomads on Ponies vs. Slavs on Horses,' *The Journal of the American Oriental Society*, Jan–March 1998, v. 118, n. 1
Melvin, N, *Russians Beyond Russia. The Politics of National Identity*, (London, 1995)
McDaniel, T, *The Agony of the Russian Idea*, (Princeton: Princeton University Press, 1996)
Morgan, David, *The Mongols*, (Oxford and New York: Blackwell, 1986)

Morozova, N, 'Geopolitics, Eurasianism and Russian Foreign Policy Under Putin', *Geopolitics*, 14, 2009

Naarajarvi, T, 'China, Russia and Shanghai Cooperation Organisation: blessing or curse for new regionalism in Central Asia?' *Asia Europe Journal* 10, 2012

Neumann, I, *Russia and the Idea of Europe*, (London and New York: 1996)

Noonan, T, Rus', 'Pechenegs and Polovtsi: Economic Interaction along the Steppe Frontier in the pre-Mongol Era', *Russian History*, 1992, 19, 1–4

Ortmann, S, and Heathershaw, J, 'Conspiracy Theories in the Post-Soviet Space', *The Russian Review* 71, October 2012

Ostrowski, D, *Muscovy and the Mongols. Cross-cultural influences on the steppe frontier, 1304–1589*, (Cambridge: Cambridge University Press, 1998)

Oushakine, Serguei, *Patriotism of Despair: Nation, War, and Loss in Russia*, (New York: Cornell University Press, Ithaca, 2009)

Oushakine, S, '"Stop the Invasion!": Money, Patriotism, and Conspiracy in Russia', *Social Research*, 76.1, Spring 2009

Paul, M, 'The Military Revolution in Russia, 1550–1682' The *Journal of Military History* v. 68, no 1, January 2004

Payne R, and Romanoff, N, *Ivan the Terrible*, (Cooper Square Press, 2002)

Perrie, M, *The Cult of Ivan the Terrible in Stalin's Russia*, (New York: Palgrave, 2000)

Poe, Marshall, *A People Born to Slavery, Russia in early modern European ethnography, 1476–1748*, (Ithaca: Cornell University Press, 2000)

Poe, M, *The Russian Moment in World History*, Princeton: Princeton University Press, 2003)

Pritsak, O, *Studies in Medieval Eurasian History*, (London: Variorum Reprints, 1981)

Riasanovsky, Nicholas, *Russian Identities: A Historical Survey* (Oxford: Oxford University Press, 2005)

Rogers, G, 'An examination of historians' explanations for the Mongol withdrawal from East Central Europe', *East European Quarterly*, spring 1996, v30, n1

Rogger, H, *National Consciousness in Eighteenth Century Russia*, (Cambridge: Cambridge University Press, 1960)

Rowley, D, 'Imperial versus national discourse: the case of Russia,' *Nations and Nationalism*, 6 (1), 2000

Rosefelde, S, 'Russia: An Abnormal Country', *The East European Journal of Comparative Economics*, 2:1 (2005)

Russian Public Opinion Research Center, Press Release No. 983, June 23, 2008 (available at http://wciom.com/news/press-rcleascs.html)

Said, E, *Orientalism*, (London: Penguin, 1995)
Sakwa, R, 'Conspiracy Narratives as a Mode of Engagement in International Politics: The Case of the 2008 Russo-Georgian War', *The Russian Review*, 71, 2012
Satter, David, *Darkness at Dawn: The Rise of the Russian Criminal State*, New Haven: Yale University Press, 2003)
Schwab, G, 'Traveling literature, traveling theory: literature and cultural contact between East and West', *Studies in the Humanities*, June 2002, v29, i1
Seton-Watson, H, *Nations and States*, (London: Methuen, 1982)
Sinor, D, 'Horse and Pasture in Inner Asian History', *Oriens Extremis*, 19, 1972
Shevtsova, L, 'The Next Russian Revolution', *Current History*, 111.747 (Oct 2012)
Shlapentokh, D, 'Eurasianism: past and present,' *Communist and Post-Communist Studies*, vol. 30, No. 2, 1997
Shlapentokh, D, 'Russia on the Eve. The Illusions and Realities of Russian Nationalism', *The Washington Quarterly*, 23.1, 2000
Shlapentokh, D, 'Russian nationalism today: the views of Alexander Dugin,' *Contemporary Review*, July 2001 v. 279 i. 1626
Shlapentokh, D, 'Is the greatness Syndrome Eroding?', *The Washington Quarterly*, 25:1, January 1, 2002
Shlapentokh, D, 'Russian Nationalists as Georgian Allies',' *Iran & The Caucasus* [serial online] 16:3 (October 2012)
Shnirelman, V, *Who gets the Past? Competition for Ancestors among Non-Russian Intellectuals in Russia*, (Johns Hopkins University Press: 1996)
Shnirelman, V, Panarin, S, 'Lev Gumilev: His Pretensions as a Founder of Ethnology and his Eurasian theories', *Inner Asia*, 3, 2001
Shnirelman, V, 'Russian Response. Archaeology, Russian Nationalism, and the "Arctic Homeland"' in Philip L. Kohl et al, *Selective Remembrances: Archaeology in the Construction, Commemoration, and Consecration of National Pasts*, (Chicago: University of Chicago Press, 2007)
Shnirelman, Victor, 'Stigmatized by History or by Historians?: The Peoples of Russia in School History Textbooks', *History & Memory* 21.2 (2009): 110–149.
Skrynnikov, R, *Ivan the Terrible*, edited and translated by Hugh F. Graham, (Gulf Breeze, FL: Academic International Press, 1981)
Slezkine, Yu, 'Who Gets the Past: Competition for Ancestors Among Non-Russian Intellectuals in Russia (book review)', *The Journal of Modern History*, Sept 1998, v70, n3

Solonari, V, 'Creating a 'People': A Case Study in Post-Soviet History-Writing', *Kritika: Explorations in Russian and Eurasian History*, 4.2, 2003

Smith, A, *The Ethnic Revival*, (Cambridge: Cambridge University Press, 1981)

Szporluk, R, 'The Ukraine and Russia', in R. Conquest (ed.), *The Last Empire, Nationality and the Soviet Future*, (Stanford: Stanford University Press, 1986)

Szporluk, R, 'After Empire: What?', *Daedalus*, Summer 1994, v123, n3

Snorri, *Heimskringla*, translated with an introduction by Magnus Magnusson and Hermann Pálsson, (Harmondsworth: Penguin, 1966)

Suny, R, *The Revenge of the Past*, (Stanford: Stanford University Press, 1993)

Suvorov. V, *The Chief Culprit; Stalin's Grand Design to Start World War Two*, (Naval Institute Press: USA, 2008)

Tamir, Y, 'The enigma of nationalism', *World Politics* April 1995, v47, n3

Thaden, E, *Conservative Nationalism in Nineteenth Century Russia*, (Seattle: University of Washington Press, 1964)

Thaden, E, 'V. Tatischev, German Historians, and the St-Petersburg Academy of Sciences', *Russian History*, 13, 4, winter 1986

Tishkhov, V, *Ethnicity, Nationalism and Conflict in and after the Soviet Union. The Mind Aflame*, (London: 1997)

Tismaneanu, V, 'Discomforts of victory: democracy, liberal values and nationalism in post-communist Europe', *West European Politics*, April 2002 v25 i2

Tolz, V, *Reinventing the Nation*, (London: Arnold, 2001)

Tolz, V, 'Forging the nation: National identity and nation building in post-Communist Russia', *Europe-Asia Studies*, Abingdon, September 1998, 50, 6

Toledano, R, 'The 'Mystery' of Christopher Columbus', *Midstream*, Feb 2001, v47

Trubetskoi, N, *The Legacy of Chengiz-Khan*, (Ann Arbor: Michigan Slavic Publications, 1991)

Tumarkin, N, 'The Great Patriotic War as myth and memory', *European Review*, 11:4, 2003

Tuminez, A, 'Nationalism, Ethnic Pressures, and the Breakup of the Soviet Union', *Journal of Cold War Studies*, Sept 1, 2003, v5, I4

Verkhovskii A, and Pain, E, 'Civilizational Nationalism. The Russian Version of the "Special Path"', *Russian Politics and Law*, 50:5

Vernadsky, G, *A History of Russia: Russia and the Mongols*, vol. 3, (Yale University Press, 1952)

Vernadsky, G, *Kievan Russia*, (New Haven and London: Yale University Press, 1948)

Wohlforth, W, 'The Russian-Soviet Empire: a test of neo-realism', *Review of International Studies*, 27.5, 2001.

Yanov, A, 'Russian nationalism in Western studies: misadventures of a Moribund paradigm', *Demokratizatsiya*, autumn 2001, v9, i4

Yun, Y, and Park, K, 'An Analysis of the Multilateral Cooperation and Competitin between Russia and China in the Shanghaii Cooperation Organization: Issues and Prospects', *Pacific Focus*, XXVII: 1, April 2012

Yurganov, A, 'The Father of Tsarism', *Russian Life,* Jan 1997 v40 n1

Znamenski, A, *Red Shambhala: Magic, Prophecy, and Geopolitics in the Heart of Asia* (Wheaton: Quest Books, 2011)

SOVIET AND POST-SOVIET POLITICS AND SOCIETY

Edited by Dr. Andreas Umland

ISSN 1614-3515

1 *Андреас Умланд (ред.)*
Воплощение Европейской
конвенции по правам человека в
России
Философские, юридические и
эмпирические исследования
ISBN 3-89821-387-0

2 *Christian Wipperfürth*
Russland – ein vertrauenswürdiger
Partner?
Grundlagen, Hintergründe und Praxis
gegenwärtiger russischer Außenpolitik
Mit einem Vorwort von Heinz Timmermann
ISBN 3-89821-401-X

3 *Manja Hussner*
Die Übernahme internationalen Rechts
in die russische und deutsche
Rechtsordnung
Eine vergleichende Analyse zur
Völkerrechtsfreundlichkeit der Verfassungen
der Russländischen Föderation und der
Bundesrepublik Deutschland
Mit einem Vorwort von Rainer Arnold
ISBN 3-89821-438-9

4 *Matthew Tejada*
Bulgaria's Democratic Consolidation
and the Kozloduy Nuclear Power Plant
(KNPP)
The Unattainability of Closure
With a foreword by Richard J. Crampton
ISBN 3-89821-439-7

5 *Марк Григорьевич Меерович*
Квадратные метры, определяющие
сознание
Государственная жилищная политика в
СССР. 1921 – 1941 гг
ISBN 3-89821-474-5

6 *Andrei P. Tsygankov, Pavel
A.Tsygankov (Eds.)*
New Directions in Russian
International Studies
ISBN 3-89821-422-2

7 *Марк Григорьевич Меерович*
Как власть народ к труду приучала
Жилище в СССР – средство управления
людьми. 1917 – 1941 гг.
С предисловием Елены Осокиной
ISBN 3-89821-495-8

8 *David J. Galbreath*
Nation-Building and Minority Politics
in Post-Socialist States
Interests, Influence and Identities in Estonia
and Latvia
With a foreword by David J. Smith
ISBN 3-89821-467-2

9 *Алексей Юрьевич Безугольный*
Народы Кавказа в Вооруженных
силах СССР в годы Великой
Отечественной войны 1941-1945 гг.
С предисловием Николая Бугая
ISBN 3-89821-475-3

10 *Вячеслав Лихачев и Владимир
Прибыловский (ред.)*
Русское Национальное Единство,
1990-2000. В 2-х томах
ISBN 3-89821-523-7

11 *Николай Бугай (ред.)*
Народы стран Балтии в условиях
сталинизма (1940-е – 1950-е годы)
Документированная история
ISBN 3-89821-525-3

12 *Ingmar Bredies (Hrsg.)*
Zur Anatomie der Orange Revolution
in der Ukraine
Wechsel des Elitenregimes oder Triumph des
Parlamentarismus?
ISBN 3-89821-524-5

13 *Anastasia V. Mitrofanova*
The Politicization of Russian
Orthodoxy
Actors and Ideas
With a foreword by William C. Gay
ISBN 3-89821-481-8

14 Nathan D. Larson
Alexander Solzhenitsyn and the
Russo-Jewish Question
ISBN 3-89821-483-4

15 Guido Houben
Kulturpolitik und Ethnizität
Staatliche Kunstförderung im Russland der neunziger Jahre
Mit einem Vorwort von Gert Weisskirchen
ISBN 3-89821-542-3

16 Leonid Luks
Der russische „Sonderweg"?
Aufsätze zur neuesten Geschichte Russlands im europäischen Kontext
ISBN 3-89821-496-6

17 Евгений Мороз
История «Мёртвой воды» – от страшной сказки к большой политике
Политическое неоязычество в постсоветской России
ISBN 3-89821-551-2

18 Александр Верховский и Галина Кожевникова (ред.)
Этническая и религиозная интолерантность в российских СМИ
Результаты мониторинга 2001-2004 гг.
ISBN 3-89821-569-5

19 Christian Ganzer
Sowjetisches Erbe und ukrainische Nation
Das Museum der Geschichte des Zaporoger Kosakentums auf der Insel Chortycja
Mit einem Vorwort von Frank Golczewski
ISBN 3-89821-504-0

20 Эльза-Баир Гучинова
Помнить нельзя забыть
Антропология депортационной травмы калмыков
С предисловием Кэролайн Хамфри
ISBN 3-89821-506-7

21 Юлия Лидерман
Мотивы «проверки» и «испытания» в постсоветской культуре
Советское прошлое в российском кинематографе 1990-х годов
С предисловием Евгения Марголита
ISBN 3-89821-511-3

22 Tanya Lokshina, Ray Thomas, Mary Mayer (Eds.)
The Imposition of a Fake Political Settlement in the Northern Caucasus
The 2003 Chechen Presidential Election
ISBN 3-89821-436-2

23 Timothy McCajor Hall, Rosie Read (Eds.)
Changes in the Heart of Europe
Recent Ethnographies of Czechs, Slovaks, Roma, and Sorbs
With an afterword by Zdeněk Salzmann
ISBN 3-89821-606-3

24 Christian Autengruber
Die politischen Parteien in Bulgarien und Rumänien
Eine vergleichende Analyse seit Beginn der 90er Jahre
Mit einem Vorwort von Dorothée de Nève
ISBN 3-89821-476-1

25 Annette Freyberg-Inan with Radu Cristescu
The Ghosts in Our Classrooms, or: John Dewey Meets Ceauşescu
The Promise and the Failures of Civic Education in Romania
ISBN 3-89821-416-8

26 John B. Dunlop
The 2002 Dubrovka and 2004 Beslan Hostage Crises
A Critique of Russian Counter-Terrorism
With a foreword by Donald N. Jensen
ISBN 3-89821-608-X

27 Peter Koller
Das touristische Potenzial von Kam''janec'-Podil's'kyj
Eine fremdenverkehrsgeographische Untersuchung der Zukunftsperspektiven und Maßnahmenplanung zur Destinationsentwicklung des „ukrainischen Rothenburg"
Mit einem Vorwort von Kristiane Klemm
ISBN 3-89821-640-3

28 Françoise Daucé, Elisabeth Sieca-Kozlowski (Eds.)
Dedovshchina in the Post-Soviet Military
Hazing of Russian Army Conscripts in a Comparative Perspective
With a foreword by Dale Herspring
ISBN 3-89821-616-0

29 Florian Strasser
    Zivilgesellschaftliche Einflüsse auf die
    Orange Revolution
    Die gewaltlose Massenbewegung und die
    ukrainische Wahlkrise 2004
    Mit einem Vorwort von Egbert Jahn
    ISBN 3-89821-648-9

30 Rebecca S. Katz
    The Georgian Regime Crisis of 2003-
    2004
    A Case Study in Post-Soviet Media
    Representation of Politics, Crime and
    Corruption
    ISBN 3-89821-413-3

31 Vladimir Kantor
    Willkür oder Freiheit
    Beiträge zur russischen Geschichtsphilosophie
    Ediert von Dagmar Herrmann sowie mit
    einem Vorwort versehen von Leonid Luks
    ISBN 3-89821-589-X

32 Laura A. Victoir
    The Russian Land Estate Today
    A Case Study of Cultural Politics in Post-
    Soviet Russia
    With a foreword by Priscilla Roosevelt
    ISBN 3-89821-426-5

33 Ivan Katchanovski
    Cleft Countries
    Regional Political Divisions and Cultures in
    Post-Soviet Ukraine and Moldova
    With a foreword by Francis Fukuyama
    ISBN 3-89821-558-X

34 Florian Mühlfried
    Postsowjetische Feiern
    Das Georgische Bankett im Wandel
    Mit einem Vorwort von Kevin Tuite
    ISBN 3-89821-601-2

35 Roger Griffin, Werner Loh, Andreas
    Umland (Eds.)
    Fascism Past and Present, West and
    East
    An International Debate on Concepts and
    Cases in the Comparative Study of the
    Extreme Right
    With an afterword by Walter Laqueur
    ISBN 3-89821-674-8

36 Sebastian Schlegel
    Der „Weiße Archipel"
    Sowjetische Atomstädte 1945-1991
    Mit einem Geleitwort von Thomas Bohn
    ISBN 3-89821-679-9

37 Vyacheslav Likhachev
    Political Anti-Semitism in Post-Soviet
    Russia
    Actors and Ideas in 1991-2003
    Edited and translated from Russian by Eugene
    Veklerov
    ISBN 3-89821-529-6

38 Josette Baer (Ed.)
    Preparing Liberty in Central Europe
    Political Texts from the Spring of Nations
    1848 to the Spring of Prague 1968
    With a foreword by Zdeněk V. David
    ISBN 3-89821-546-6

39 Михаил Лукьянов
    Российский консерватизм и
    реформа, 1907-1914
    С предисловием Марка Д. Стейнберга
    ISBN 3-89821-503-2

40 Nicola Melloni
    Market Without Economy
    The 1998 Russian Financial Crisis
    With a foreword by Eiji Furukawa
    ISBN 3-89821-407-9

41 Dmitrij Chmelnizki
    Die Architektur Stalins
    Bd. 1: Studien zu Ideologie und Stil
    Bd. 2: Bilddokumentation
    Mit einem Vorwort von Bruno Flierl
    ISBN 3-89821-515-6

42 Katja Yafimava
    Post-Soviet Russian-Belarussian
    Relationships
    The Role of Gas Transit Pipelines
    With a foreword by Jonathan P. Stern
    ISBN 3-89821-655-1

43 Boris Chavkin
    Verflechtungen der deutschen und
    russischen Zeitgeschichte
    Aufsätze und Archivfunde zu den
    Beziehungen Deutschlands und der
    Sowjetunion von 1917 bis 1991
    Ediert von Markus Edlinger sowie mit einem
    Vorwort versehen von Leonid Luks
    ISBN 3-89821-756-6

44 *Anastasija Grynenko in Zusammenarbeit mit Claudia Dathe*
Die Terminologie des Gerichtswesens der Ukraine und Deutschlands im Vergleich
Eine übersetzungswissenschaftliche Analyse juristischer Fachbegriffe im Deutschen, Ukrainischen und Russischen
Mit einem Vorwort von Ulrich Hartmann
ISBN 3-89821-691-8

45 *Anton Burkov*
The Impact of the European Convention on Human Rights on Russian Law
Legislation and Application in 1996-2006
With a foreword by Françoise Hampson
ISBN 978-3-89821-639-5

46 *Stina Torjesen, Indra Overland (Eds.)*
International Election Observers in Post-Soviet Azerbaijan
Geopolitical Pawns or Agents of Change?
ISBN 978-3-89821-743-9

47 *Taras Kuzio*
Ukraine – Crimea – Russia
Triangle of Conflict
ISBN 978-3-89821-761-3

48 *Claudia Šabić*
"Ich erinnere mich nicht, aber L'viv!"
Zur Funktion kultureller Faktoren für die Institutionalisierung und Entwicklung einer ukrainischen Region
Mit einem Vorwort von Melanie Tatur
ISBN 978-3-89821-752-1

49 *Marlies Bilz*
Tatarstan in der Transformation
Nationaler Diskurs und Politische Praxis 1988-1994
Mit einem Vorwort von Frank Golczewski
ISBN 978-3-89821-722-4

50 *Марлен Ларюэль (ред.)*
Современные интерпретации русского национализма
ISBN 978-3-89821-795-8

51 *Sonja Schüler*
Die ethnische Dimension der Armut
Roma im postsozialistischen Rumänien
Mit einem Vorwort von Anton Sterbling
ISBN 978-3-89821-776-7

52 *Галина Кожевникова*
Радикальный национализм в России и противодействие ему
Сборник докладов Центра «Сова» за 2004-2007 гг.
С предисловием Александра Верховского
ISBN 978-3-89821-721-7

53 *Галина Кожевникова и Владимир Прибыловский*
Российская власть в биографиях I
Высшие должностные лица РФ в 2004 г.
ISBN 978-3-89821-796-5

54 *Галина Кожевникова и Владимир Прибыловский*
Российская власть в биографиях II
Члены Правительства РФ в 2004 г.
ISBN 978-3-89821-797-2

55 *Галина Кожевникова и Владимир Прибыловский*
Российская власть в биографиях III
Руководители федеральных служб и агентств РФ в 2004 г.
ISBN 978-3-89821-798-9

56 *Ileana Petroniu*
Privatisierung in Transformationsökonomien
Determinanten der Restrukturierungs-Bereitschaft am Beispiel Polens, Rumäniens und der Ukraine
Mit einem Vorwort von Rainer W. Schäfer
ISBN 978-3-89821-790-3

57 *Christian Wipperfürth*
Russland und seine GUS-Nachbarn
Hintergründe, aktuelle Entwicklungen und Konflikte in einer ressourcenreichen Region
ISBN 978-3-89821-801-6

58 *Togzhan Kassenova*
From Antagonism to Partnership
The Uneasy Path of the U.S.-Russian Cooperative Threat Reduction
With a foreword by Christoph Bluth
ISBN 978-3-89821-707-1

59 *Alexander Höllwerth*
Das sakrale eurasische Imperium des Aleksandr Dugin
Eine Diskursanalyse zum postsowjetischen russischen Rechtsextremismus
Mit einem Vorwort von Dirk Uffelmann
ISBN 978-3-89821-813-9

60 Олег Рябов
«Россия-Матушка»
Национализм, гендер и война в России XX века
С предисловием Елены Гощило
ISBN 978-3-89821-487-2

61 Ivan Maistrenko
Borot'bism
A Chapter in the History of the Ukrainian Revolution
With a new introduction by Chris Ford
Translated by George S. N. Luckyj with the assistance of Ivan L. Rudnytsky
ISBN 978-3-89821-697-5

62 Maryna Romanets
Anamorphosic Texts and Reconfigured Visions
Improvised Traditions in Contemporary Ukrainian and Irish Literature
ISBN 978-3-89821-576-3

63 Paul D'Anieri and Taras Kuzio (Eds.)
Aspects of the Orange Revolution I
Democratization and Elections in Post-Communist Ukraine
ISBN 978-3-89821-698-2

64 Bohdan Harasymiw in collaboration with Oleh S. Ilnytzkyj (Eds.)
Aspects of the Orange Revolution II
Information and Manipulation Strategies in the 2004 Ukrainian Presidential Elections
ISBN 978-3-89821-699-9

65 Ingmar Bredies, Andreas Umland and Valentin Yakushik (Eds.)
Aspects of the Orange Revolution III
The Context and Dynamics of the 2004 Ukrainian Presidential Elections
ISBN 978-3-89821-803-0

66 Ingmar Bredies, Andreas Umland and Valentin Yakushik (Eds.)
Aspects of the Orange Revolution IV
Foreign Assistance and Civic Action in the 2004 Ukrainian Presidential Elections
ISBN 978-3-89821-808-5

67 Ingmar Bredies, Andreas Umland and Valentin Yakushik (Eds.)
Aspects of the Orange Revolution V
Institutional Observation Reports on the 2004 Ukrainian Presidential Elections
ISBN 978-3-89821-809-2

68 Taras Kuzio (Ed.)
Aspects of the Orange Revolution VI
Post-Communist Democratic Revolutions in Comparative Perspective
ISBN 978-3-89821-820-7

69 Tim Bohse
Autoritarismus statt Selbstverwaltung
Die Transformation der kommunalen Politik in der Stadt Kaliningrad 1990-2005
Mit einem Geleitwort von Stefan Troebst
ISBN 978-3-89821-782-8

70 David Rupp
Die Rußländische Föderation und die russischsprachige Minderheit in Lettland
Eine Fallstudie zur Anwaltspolitik Moskaus gegenüber den russophonen Minderheiten im „Nahen Ausland" von 1991 bis 2002
Mit einem Vorwort von Helmut Wagner
ISBN 978-3-89821-778-1

71 Taras Kuzio
Theoretical and Comparative Perspectives on Nationalism
New Directions in Cross-Cultural and Post-Communist Studies
With a foreword by Paul Robert Magocsi
ISBN 978-3-89821-815-3

72 Christine Teichmann
Die Hochschultransformation im heutigen Osteuropa
Kontinuität und Wandel bei der Entwicklung des postkommunistischen Universitätswesens
Mit einem Vorwort von Oskar Anweiler
ISBN 978-3-89821-842-9

73 Julia Kusznir
Der politische Einfluss von Wirtschaftseliten in russischen Regionen
Eine Analyse am Beispiel der Erdöl- und Erdgasindustrie, 1992-2005
Mit einem Vorwort von Wolfgang Eichwede
ISBN 978-3-89821-821-4

74 Alena Vysotskaya
Russland, Belarus und die EU-Osterweiterung
Zur Minderheitenfrage und zum Problem der Freizügigkeit des Personenverkehrs
Mit einem Vorwort von Katlijn Malfliet
ISBN 978-3-89821-822-1

75 Heiko Pleines (Hrsg.)
Corporate Governance in postsozialistischen Volkswirtschaften
ISBN 978-3-89821-766-8

76 Stefan Ihrig
Wer sind die Moldawier?
Rumänismus versus Moldowanismus in Historiographie und Schulbüchern der Republik Moldova, 1991-2006
Mit einem Vorwort von Holm Sundhaussen
ISBN 978-3-89821-466-7

77 Galina Kozhevnikova in collaboration with Alexander Verkhovsky and Eugene Veklerov
Ultra-Nationalism and Hate Crimes in Contemporary Russia
The 2004-2006 Annual Reports of Moscow's SOVA Center
With a foreword by Stephen D. Shenfield
ISBN 978-3-89821-868-9

78 Florian Küchler
The Role of the European Union in Moldova's Transnistria Conflict
With a foreword by Christopher Hill
ISBN 978-3-89821-850-4

79 Bernd Rechel
The Long Way Back to Europe
Minority Protection in Bulgaria
With a foreword by Richard Crampton
ISBN 978-3-89821-863-4

80 Peter W. Rodgers
Nation, Region and History in Post-Communist Transitions
Identity Politics in Ukraine, 1991-2006
With a foreword by Vera Tolz
ISBN 978-3-89821-903-7

81 Stephanie Solywoda
The Life and Work of Semen L. Frank
A Study of Russian Religious Philosophy
With a foreword by Philip Walters
ISBN 978-3-89821-457-5

82 Vera Sokolova
Cultural Politics of Ethnicity
Discourses on Roma in Communist Czechoslovakia
ISBN 978-3-89821-864-1

83 Natalya Shevchik Ketenci
Kazakhstani Enterprises in Transition
The Role of Historical Regional Development in Kazakhstan's Post-Soviet Economic Transformation
ISBN 978-3-89821-831-3

84 Martin Malek, Anna Schor-Tschudnowskaja (Hrsg.)
Europa im Tschetschenienkrieg
Zwischen politischer Ohnmacht und Gleichgültigkeit
Mit einem Vorwort von Lipchan Basajewa
ISBN 978-3-89821-676-0

85 Stefan Meister
Das postsowjetische Universitätswesen zwischen nationalem und internationalem Wandel
Die Entwicklung der regionalen Hochschule in Russland als Gradmesser der Systemtransformation
Mit einem Vorwort von Joan DeBardeleben
ISBN 978-3-89821-891-7

86 Konstantin Sheiko in collaboration with Stephen Brown
Nationalist Imaginings of the Russian Past
Anatolii Fomenko and the Rise of Alternative History in Post-Communist Russia
With a foreword by Donald Ostrowski
ISBN 978-3-89821-915-0

87 Sabine Jenni
Wie stark ist das „Einige Russland"?
Zur Parteibindung der Eliten und zum Wahlerfolg der Machtpartei im Dezember 2007
Mit einem Vorwort von Klaus Armingeon
ISBN 978-3-89821-961-7

88 Thomas Borén
Meeting-Places of Transformation
Urban Identity, Spatial Representations and Local Politics in Post-Soviet St Petersburg
ISBN 978-3-89821-739-2

89 Aygul Ashirova
Stalinismus und Stalin-Kult in Zentralasien
Turkmenistan 1924-1953
Mit einem Vorwort von Leonid Luks
ISBN 978-3-89821-987-7

90 Leonid Luks
    Freiheit oder imperiale Größe?
    Essays zu einem russischen Dilemma
    ISBN 978-3-8382-0011-8

91 Christopher Gilley
    The 'Change of Signposts' in the
    Ukrainian Emigration
    A Contribution to the History of
    Sovietophilism in the 1920s
    With a foreword by Frank Golczewski
    ISBN 978-3-89821-965-5

92 Philipp Casula, Jeronim Perovic
    (Eds.)
    Identities and Politics
    During the Putin Presidency
    The Discursive Foundations of Russia's
    Stability
    With a foreword by Heiko Haumann
    ISBN 978-3-8382-0015-6

93 Marcel Viëtor
    Europa und die Frage
    nach seinen Grenzen im Osten
    Zur Konstruktion ‚europäischer Identität' in
    Geschichte und Gegenwart
    Mit einem Vorwort von Albrecht Lehmann
    ISBN 978-3-8382-0045-3

94 Ben Hellman, Andrei Rogachevskii
    Filming the Unfilmable
    Casper Wrede's 'One Day in the Life
    of Ivan Denisovich'
    Second, Revised and Expanded Edition
    ISBN 978-3-8382-0044-6

95 Eva Fuchslocher
    Vaterland, Sprache, Glaube
    Orthodoxie und Nationenbildung
    am Beispiel Georgiens
    Mit einem Vorwort von Christina von Braun
    ISBN 978-3-89821-884-9

96 Vladimir Kantor
    Das Westlertum und der Weg
    Russlands
    Zur Entwicklung der russischen Literatur und
    Philosophie
    Ediert von Dagmar Herrmann
    Mit einem Beitrag von Nikolaus Lobkowicz
    ISBN 978-3-8382-0102-3

97 Kamran Musayev
    Die postsowjetische Transformation
    im Baltikum und Südkaukasus
    Eine vergleichende Untersuchung der
    politischen Entwicklung Lettlands und
    Aserbaidschans 1985-2009
    Mit einem Vorwort von Leonid Luks
    Ediert von Sandro Henschel
    ISBN 978-3-8382-0103-0

98 Tatiana Zhurzhenko
    Borderlands into Bordered Lands
    Geopolitics of Identity in Post-Soviet Ukraine
    With a foreword by Dieter Segert
    ISBN 978-3-8382-0042-2

99 Кирилл Галушко, Лидия Смола
    (ред.)
    Пределы падения – варианты
    украинского будущего
    Аналитико-прогностические исследования
    ISBN 978-3-8382-0148-1

100 Michael Minkenberg (ed.)
    Historical Legacies and the Radical
    Right in Post-Cold War Central and
    Eastern Europe
    With an afterword by Sabrina P. Ramet
    ISBN 978-3-8382-0124-5

101 David-Emil Wickström
    Rocking St. Petersburg
    Transcultural Flows and Identity Politics in
    the St. Petersburg Popular Music Scene
    With a foreword by Yngvar B. Steinholt
    Second, Revised and Expanded Edition
    ISBN 978-3-8382-0100-9

102 Eva Zabka
    Eine neue „Zeit der Wirren"?
    Der spät- und postsowjetische Systemwandel
    1985-2000 im Spiegel russischer
    gesellschaftspolitischer Diskurse
    Mit einem Vorwort von Margareta Mommsen
    ISBN 978-3-8382-0161-0

103 Ulrike Ziemer
    Ethnic Belonging, Gender and
    Cultural Practices
    Youth Identitites in Contemporary Russia
    With a foreword by Anoop Nayak
    ISBN 978-3-8382-0152-8

104 Ksenia Chepikova
'Einiges Russland' - eine zweite
KPdSU?
Aspekte der Identitätskonstruktion einer
postsowjetischen „Partei der Macht"
Mit einem Vorwort von Torsten Oppelland
ISBN 978-3-8382-0311-9

105 Леонид Люкс
Западничество или евразийство?
Демократия или идеократия?
Сборник статей об исторических дилеммах
России
С предисловием Владимира Кантора
ISBN 978-3-8382-0211-2

106 Anna Dost
Das russische Verfassungsrecht auf dem
Weg zum Föderalismus und zurück
Zum Konflikt von Rechtsnormen und
-wirklichkeit in der Russländischen
Föderation von 1991 bis 2009
Mit einem Vorwort von Alexander Blankenagel
ISBN 978-3-8382-0292-1

107 Philipp Herzog
Sozialistische Völkerfreundschaft,
nationaler Widerstand oder harmloser
Zeitvertreib?
Zur politischen Funktion der Volkskunst
im sowjetischen Estland
Mit einem Vorwort von Andreas Kappeler
ISBN 978-3-8382-0216-7

108 Marlène Laruelle (ed.)
Russian Nationalism, Foreign Policy,
and Identity Debates in Putin's Russia
New Ideological Patterns after the Orange
Revolution
ISBN 978-3-8382-0325-6

109 Michail Logvinov
Russlands Kampf gegen den
internationalen Terrorismus
Eine kritische Bestandsaufnahme des
Bekämpfungsansatzes
Mit einem Geleitwort von
Hans-Henning Schröder
und einem Vorwort von Eckhard Jesse
ISBN 978-3-8382-0329-4

110 John B. Dunlop
The Moscow Bombings
of September 1999
Examinations of Russian Terrorist Attacks
at the Onset of Vladimir Putin's Rule
Second, Revised and Expanded Edition
ISBN 978-3-8382-0388-1

111 Андрей А. Ковалёв
Свидетельство из-за кулис
российской политики I
Можно ли делать добро из зла?
(Воспоминания и размышления о
последних советских и первых
постсоветских годах)
With a foreword by Peter Reddaway
ISBN 978-3-8382-0302-7

112 Андрей А. Ковалёв
Свидетельство из-за кулис
российской политики II
Угроза для себя и окружающих
(Наблюдения и предостережения
относительно происходящего после 2000 г.)
ISBN 978-3-8382-0303-4

113 Bernd Kappenberg
Zeichen setzen für Europa
Der Gebrauch europäischer lateinischer
Sonderzeichen in der deutschen Öffentlichkeit
Mit einem Vorwort von Peter Schlobinski
ISBN 978-3-89821-749-1

114 Ivo Mijnssen
The Quest for an Ideal Youth in
Putin's Russia I
Back to Our Future! History, Modernity, and
Patriotism according to Nashi, 2005-2013
With a foreword by Jeronim Perović
Second, Revised and Expanded Edition
ISBN 978-3-8382-0368-3

115 Jussi Lassila
The Quest for an Ideal Youth in
Putin's Russia II
The Search for Distinctive Conformism in the
Political Communication of Nashi, 2005-2009
With a foreword by Kirill Postoutenko
Second, Revised and Expanded Edition
ISBN 978-3-8382-0415-4

116 Valerio Trabandt
Neue Nachbarn, gute Nachbarschaft?
Die EU als internationaler Akteur am Beispiel
ihrer Demokratieförderung in Belarus und der
Ukraine 2004-2009
Mit einem Vorwort von Jutta Joachim
ISBN 978-3-8382-0417-6

117	Fabian Pfeiffer Estlands Außen- und Sicherheitspolitik I Der estnische Atlantizismus nach der wiedererlangten Unabhängigkeit 1991-2004 Mit einem Vorwort von Helmut Hubel ISBN 978-3-8382-0127-6	124	David R. Marples 'Our Glorious Past' Lukashenka's Belarus and the Great Patriotic War ISBN 978-3-8382-0574-8 (Paperback edition) ISBN 978-3-8382-0675-2 (Hardcover edition)
118	Jana Podßuweit Estlands Außen- und Sicherheitspolitik II Handlungsoptionen eines Kleinstaates im Rahmen seiner EU-Mitgliedschaft (2004-2008) Mit einem Vorwort von Helmut Hubel ISBN 978-3-8382-0440-6	125	Ulf Walther Russlands "neuer Adel" Die Macht des Geheimdienstes von Gorbatschow bis Putin Mit einem Vorwort von Hans-Georg Wieck ISBN 978-3-8382-0584-7
119	Karin Pointner Estlands Außen- und Sicherheitspolitik III Eine gedächtnispolitische Analyse estnischer Entwicklungskooperation 2006-2010 Mit einem Vorwort von Karin Liebhart ISBN 978-3-8382-0435-2	126	Simon Geissbühler (Hrsg.) Kiew – Revolution 3.0 Der Euromaidan 2013/14 und die Zukunftsperspektiven der Ukraine ISBN 978-3-8382-0581-6 (Paperback edition) ISBN 978-3-8382-0681-3 (Hardcover edition)
120	Ruslana Vovk Die Offenheit der ukrainischen Verfassung für das Völkerrecht und die europäische Integration Mit einem Vorwort von Alexander Blankenagel ISBN 978-3-8382-0481-9	127	Andrey Makarychev Russia and the EU in a Multipolar World Discourses, Identities, Norms With a foreword by Klaus Segbers ISBN 978-3-8382-0629-5
121	Mykhaylo Banakh Die Relevanz der Zivilgesellschaft bei den postkommunistischen Transformationsprozessen in mittel- und osteuropäischen Ländern Das Beispiel der spät- und postsowjetischen Ukraine 1986-2009 Mit einem Vorwort von Gerhard Simon ISBN 978-3-8382-0499-4	128	Roland Scharff Kasachstan als postsowjetischer Wohlfahrtsstaat Die Transformation des sozialen Schutzsystems Mit einem Vorwort von Joachim Ahrens ISBN 978-3-8382-0622-6
122	Michael Moser Language Policy and the Discourse on Languages in Ukraine under President Viktor Yanukovych (25 February 2010–28 October 2012) ISBN 978-3-8382-0497-0 (Paperback edition) ISBN 978-3-8382-0507-6 (Hardcover edition)	129	Katja Grupp Bild Lücke Deutschland Kaliningrader Studierende sprechen über Deutschland Mit einem Vorwort von Martin Schulz ISBN 978-3-8382-0552-6
123	Nicole Krome Russischer Netzwerkkapitalismus Restrukturierungsprozesse in der Russischen Föderation am Beispiel des Luftfahrtunternehmens "Aviastar" Mit einem Vorwort von Petra Stykow ISBN 978-3-8382-0534-2	130	Konstantin Sheiko, Stephen Brown History as Therapy Alternative History and Nationalist Imaginings in Russia, 1991-2014 ISBN 978-3-8382-0665-3

***ibidem*-Verlag**

Melchiorstr. 15

D-70439 Stuttgart

info@ibidem-verlag.de

www.ibidem-verlag.de
www.ibidem.eu
www.edition-noema.de
www.autorenbetreuung.de